PEARSON

ALWAYS LEARNING

W9-BZU-993

Preparing to Lead
Principles of Self-Leadership and Organizational Dynamics

Ninth Edition

Contributing Editors:
Danielle Litchford, LCDR, USN;
Patrick Bryant, LT. USN.

Cover Art: Courtesy of U.S. Naval Academy.

Pearson Learning Solutions, 330 Hudson Street, New York, New York 10013
A Pearson Education Company
www.pearsoned.com

Printed in the United States of America

1 2 3 4 5 6 7 8 9 10 V OZ N 18 17 16 15

000200010271980458

KG/KS

ISBN 10: 1-323-24591-X
ISBN 13: 978-1-323-24591-0

Copyright Acknowledgments

"Milgram's Electric Shock Machine," courtesy of Alexandra Milgram.

"Power, Influence, and Influence Tactics," by Richard L. Hughes, Robert C. Linnett and Gordon J. Curphy, reprinted from *Leadership: Enhancing the Lessons of Experience* (1999), by permission of McGrawHill Companies.

Excerpts from *Integrity*, edited by Stephen L. Carter, by permission of Perseus Books Group.

"The Greatest Threat Facing the Army Profession," by Dan Johnson, reprinted by permission from *Military Review* (2013).

"Foundations of Character," by permission of Via Institute of Character.

"Damn Exec," by Stuart Landersman, reprinted by permission from *Proceedings of the US Naval Institute* (1965).

Contents

Course
Introduction

"Never doubt that a small group of thoughtful, committed citizens can change the world. Indeed, it is the only thing that ever has."

Margaret Mead
US anthropologist (1901–1978)

Leaders change the world! When you strip away all of the "buzz words" and slogans that's what it comes down to. As leaders we are responsible for making the world a better place. No Lieutenant ever sat down with his Commanding Officer for his fitness report debrief and proudly pronounced, "Sir, I am a great leader! My unit is not any better than when I took over; not even a little. I can maintain the status quo better than anyone!"

John Kotter (1996) puts it this way, "Leadership defines what the future should look like, aligns people with that vision, and inspires them to make it happen despite the obstacles." (p. 25) He goes on to say, "…successful transformation is 70 to 90 percent leadership," and, "…this leadership often begins with just one or two people." (p. 26, 30)

You are going to become an officer in the Navy or Marine Corps. As such, you will define what the future will look like for yourself, the people you lead, your service, and the world around you, but will the future you define be as good as it should be? Will the person you become be a result of choice or circumstance? Will you be able to align your own actions with the future you desire? What about the actions of others? Will you be able to overcome obstacles? Will you be able to inspire others? Will you be able to lead yourself as well as others? In other words, will you be one of the few that change the world?

Becoming a world-changing leader does not happen overnight. It doesn't happen the instant you climb Herndon, put your Naval Academy ring on, or when you throw your cover up in the air at graduation. It is a process that takes place every day of your life. That process starts with self-knowledge. It continues with self-leadership and culminates in team leadership.

Self-knowledge is a lifelong pursuit that all leaders must undertake. It involves finding out our values and their priority, what type of personality we have, our strengths, and how our own perceptions may disguise reality. The better we know ourselves, the better we can control the will that drives our actions. The closer we can get to the core of who we are, the more our actions will originate from that core instead of originating from the opinions of others. It is only when we act from our core that we can effectively lead others towards something better.

Imagine if someone knew the cure for cancer, but chose not to tell anyone. What good are they? Any knowledge that is not used in some way to serve others is useless. Self-knowledge is no exception. You can know everything about who you are and how you work. However if you do not use that knowledge to better your life and the lives of those around you then what good are you? Knowledge has never changed the world; only applied knowledge changes things. If you want to be a world-changing leader then you have to know how to apply the knowledge you have.

When we choose to apply our self-knowledge we call that self-leadership. We apply the knowledge of our values by using them to govern the way we act. We apply the knowledge of our strengths by using them to define and accomplish goals. We apply the knowledge of our personality type by using it to find out how we best work with others to accomplish tasks. It is only when we apply the knowledge we have of ourselves, when we start practicing self-leadership, that we can truthfully say that we are living our own life instead of living the life others think we should. The last stanza of William Earnest Henley's poem Invictus states:

> *It matters not how strait the gate,*
> *How charged with punishments the scroll,*
> *I am the master of my fate:*
> *I am the captain of my soul.*

Are you the master of your fate? Are you leading yourself or being led by the wishes and expectations of others? Do you not only choose what you want to do with your life, but stick by those choices when it is hard to do so? It is only when we practice self-leadership that we can even hope to effectively lead others, *and* know what we are leading them towards.

A few years ago I saw a movie called Gladiator. At the beginning of the movie, the Roman general Maximus leads his army against the barbaric hoards in battle. In the middle of the chaos of war Maximus' men instantly obey his commands and are willing to sacrifice their lives for him. The battle scene is filled with fiery arrows and epic fight scenes that are incredibly exciting, but that is not what I liked best about it. What I liked best happened just before the battle began. Maximus walked among his troops, greeting many by name, checking to make sure they were prepared for the battle, and giving encouragement to those that seemed to need it. You see Maximus remembered something that a lot of modern leaders do not; that leading others is about *relationships* more than anything else.

Instant obedience and the willingness to sacrifice for a leader is not born on a battlefield, it is born and nurtured in the day-to-day relationships we have with those we lead. If you want to effectively lead others you must know yourself, you must practice self-leadership, and then you must understand, create, and maintain relationships between yourself and others as well as groups of people.

> *"True leaders have strong identification with the mission, projects, and job at hand. They are true believers full of enthusiasm coupled with honest concern for and with people and their families, and, to the extent possible, are familiar with their people's personal histories. Tell people what is to be done and why. Invite limited discussion. Identify the group as a team. Keep all informed. Be quick to publicly praise worthy performance, and do most of necessary personal criticism in private."*

CDR Lloyd Bucher
Former captain of U.S.S. Pueblo

Part
One

Self-Knowledge

Lesson

1 *On Building Leaders*

Develop a basic understanding of what we actually mean when we talk about leadership. Begin understanding how study and the classroom experience can benefit leader development.

READING 1

Reprinted from Johnson, W. B., & Harper, G. P. (2005). *Becoming a Leader the Annapolis Way: 12 Combat Lessons from the Navy's Leadership Laboratory.* The McGraw Hill Companies.

The scene is a crowded seminar room at the famed Wharton Business School at the University of Pennsylvania. The speaker, an esteemed professor of leadership and management at Wharton, is launching into a summer lecture to leaders from a range of organizations and businesses. To kick things off, the professor inquires of the audience: "I wonder whether most of you think leaders are born or whether they are made? Those who think leaders are born, raise your hands."

The vast majority of the audience members send their arms skyward. There are nods and smiles all around and emphatic murmurs of agreement as it becomes apparent that most in this group concur—excellent leadership is innate. Undeterred, the professor continues, "And does anyone feel that leaders are primarily made?"

In the front row of the hall, several white-sleeved arms shoot up. The crowd gawks in surprise, but these front-row occupants keep their hands aloft. Each arm belongs to a uniformed naval officer—a leadership instructor from the Naval Academy's Department of Leadership, Ethics, and Law. The group has come to glean the latest in leadership research and practice. They are accomplished junior officers who spend their days teaching midshipmen the mechanics of good leadership. Most of them are graduates of USNA themselves and all of them have seen midshipmen with apparently low aptitude for leading become outstanding leaders in the fleet. Their experiences at USNA and beyond have convinced them that, given the right mix of ability and aptitude, excellent leadership can be dramatically shaped and developed.

This true story from a recent Wharton seminar highlights an important assumption undergirding all that we do at USNA. The assumption goes something like this: Aptitude is important but it's not enough. Becoming an excellent leader requires hard work, intensive training, careful coaching, and deliberate feedback from seasoned leaders. Yes, certain traits seem to make leader-development easier for some, but traits alone will never make a leader.

The classic trait approach to leadership assumes that some people are simply natural born leaders. Unfortunately, massive research efforts in psychology and management have failed to elucidate these crucial personality characteristics—traits that reliably predict success in the leader role. Although personality features may make leadership somewhat more comfortable and effective, there are other important questions to ask about potential leaders than "What are they like?" For example, what do these people actually do in different situations? How do they spend their time? What are their priorities? How do they gain and use power? What are their interpersonal relationships like? How do various situations and contexts influence their leader behaviors? These are important variables and we have observed them at play in a vast number of naval leaders over the course of our careers.

Of course, we do not mean to ignore the importance of ability and aptitude when selecting leaders. Requiring one of the nation's most arduous collegiate application procedures, USNA enjoys the profound luxury of selecting only a small percentage of applicants from among a wide pool of remarkably bright and multitalented students. One cannot ignore the importance of choosing leaders who are intellectually bright, highly motivated, and imbued with positive personality traits. Still, these characteristics do not ensure excellent leadership. It takes more than capacity.

First, Forget What You've Been Told About Leaders

In this Lesson we debunk a few common leadership myths often propagated as common sense or "givens" whenever leadership is discussed. The worst of these myths include:

- Leaders are born, not made.
- Good leadership is all common sense.
- The only school that teaches leadership is the school of hard knocks.

Before becoming an effective leader in the military or anywhere else, you had better work at recognizing these statements as mythical and as antithetical to the hard work required to rise in the ranks of outstanding leaders. In the balance of this Lesson we dispatch each of these pernicious myths.

Leaders Are Made (Though Aptitude Sure Doesn't Hurt)

A particularly ridiculous yet maddeningly enduring leadership myth is that excellent leaders are simply born that way. Although most of us have heard this statement so many times that we tend to believe it on some level, it is actually quite a laughable idea. The statement that leaders are born implies that the world is full of leaders and non-leaders, that you either "have it" or don't in the leadership area. The fact is that each of us has a unique blend of emotional, intellectual, and behavioral talents and proclivities that place us somewhere on the continuum from poor to excellent leadership. And most important, one's location on the continuum is not static but fluid; leadership is responsive to a range of factors such as motivation, new learning, maturity, and experience. People often become more effective leaders. One alumnus shared with us an experience that we think illustrates this point very well. Robert Niewoehner, Class of '81 recalled

> Fall of my 3/c [second] year, I was a struggling member of the Lightweight Crew team. Because the team was not comprised of an even multiple of eight, several guys were left at the boat house every day to train by themselves. It seemed my number came up 2–3 times per week to stay behind. It was pretty discouraging, and I really wrestled with sticking it out.
>
> Thursday afternoons, after practice, the coach would pull four upperclassmen aside to pick boats for Friday's practice, an hour-long race from USNA around Holiday Island and back. This process was much like picking teams for sandlot baseball or soccer in elementary school. One Thursday after boats were picked, one second class took me aside and told me,
>
> "Rob, I think you're the most underrated member of the team. I specifically wanted you in my boat, and I want to see you make big puddles for me tomorrow." All the discouragement from the previous weeks was lifted by that one remark. He could certainly not have known the extent of my discouragement.
>
> I exhausted myself the next day on the end of that oar, determined not to disappoint his trust. I was staunchly his supporter when he was elected Team Captain the following year, for in my eyes he could do no wrong.
>
> His remark set the tone and the path for my entire Naval Academy experience.

I committed to crew and resolved that I was going to letter by graduation.

Though I finished second in my class, held five stripes, and finished a Master's in Electrical Engineering before graduation, I am far more proud of my "N" (varsity letter) for it came at a far greater price. Encouragement is a very powerful thing. Make a point to notice the quiet ones standing in the back, tentative about whether they can fit in or contribute. It may not take much to move them.

But what about personality? Don't people with specific personality traits make better leaders? The answer appears to be: Certain traits help, but they are not enough. Positive personality features assist excellent leadership but don't guarantee it (later in this Lesson we highlight some of the primary personality characteristics among those who lead well). For evidence that innate personality features do not alone predict leadership success, one only needs to consider the case of two famously successful World War II admirals.

We refer, of course, to Vice Admiral William F. "Bull" Halsey and Rear Admiral Raymond Spruance. Following the Japanese attack on Pearl Harbor and a series of Japanese naval victories, morale in the service was at low ebb. With the Japanese planning a bold attack on the U.S. naval base at Midway Island, America's ability to survive in the Pacific depended upon the success of an aircraft carrier task force led by the notoriously charismatic and outgoing VADM Halsey. A gung-ho leader who personified extroversion and was fond of large informal meetings, Halsey was interpersonally affable and prone to intuitive decision making. He was inspirational and popular among the enlisted ranks. Halsey was also a "brown shoe," a naval aviator, who was outgoing, bold, and sometimes maybe even a little too daring.

When Halsey became seriously ill shortly before the Midway battle, he was ordered hospitalized by Admiral Chester Nimitz and was quickly replaced by RADM Spruance. Now, Spruance was a "black shoe," a surface warfare officer. "Black shoes" traditionally have been quite different in their view of fleet operations when compared to their "brown shoe" brethren. "Black shoe" officers had long clung to the doctrine that battleships were the capital ships of the Navy and the carriers and naval aviators were only to be used to scout out the enemy for the battleships. The "black shoes" would then engage in the classic surface action in the tradition of the Battle of Jutland. "Black shoes" sailed at 30 knots, whereas "brown shoes" flew at 300 knots. Of course Pearl Harbor changed all of that.

Differences in the personality constellations between Halsey and Spruance were immediately noticeable. In fact, the two men appeared to be polar opposites on many dimensions of personality. In contrast to his predecessor, Spruance was quiet, reserved, and preferred reflection over constant interaction. More comfortable with small meetings and individual conversations, he was notorious for sifting through facts and analytical decision making. Officers in the carrier task force must have wondered how this introverted surface warfare officer could possibly succeed in replacing one of the most popular and admired naval aviators in history just before the most important battle of the war. Could Spruance possibly be as effective a leader? Sure enough, the wardroom had great difficulty adjusting to Spruance. Halsey had been outgoing; Spruance preferred quiet channels. Halsey paid minimal attention to detail; Spruance was compulsively focused on details and facts. Halsey was a free spirit; Spruance was deliberate and methodical.

In the end, Spruance led Carrier Task Force 16 to one of the greatest naval war victories of all time. It marked the crucial turning point in American resolve and morale in the Pacific theater. History shows that Spruance was a superb combat leader, as was his predecessor VADM Halsey.

It appears that nondescript introverts can lead as effectively as gregarious extroverts. This is a lesson learned over and over at USNA and in the Navy at large. Although certain personality traits may fit certain tasks and contexts better than others, personality will always be secondary to leader knowledge, skill, and attitude.

Excellent Leadership Requires More Than Common Sense

Related to the myth that leaders are born is the equally unsupportable notion that leadership is a matter of common sense. Translation: Anyone who is not a total flake can lead well because the keys to good leadership are self-evident. Again, we disagree. If leadership were common sense, it is unlikely that there would be so many problems with ineffective leadership in everyday life. Even the Navy suffers from its share of less than sterling leadership.

When USNA graduate CDR Michael Abrashoff, USN, became the commanding officer of the guided missile destroyer USS *Benfold,* he immediately set to work reading exit interviews from crewmembers who had recently departed the ship. He wondered why so many had been departing this ship and the Navy prematurely. What he found appalled him.

> I assumed that low pay would be the first reason, but in fact it was the fifth. The top reason was not being treated with respect or dignity; second was being prevented from making an impact on the organization; third, not being listened to; and fourth, not being rewarded with more responsibility.

Either Abrashoff's predecessor had no common sense or good leadership is more complex and demanding than most realize. As he set about listening to his sailors and seeking creative means to inspire and motivate them to turn the *Benfold* into a fighting community defined by high morale, Commander Abrashoff employed more than common sense. Aware of Gallup poll research showing that 65 percent of those who leave their companies are actually seeking to escape their direct managers, Abrashoff drew from science-based principles of reinforcement, organizational models of team building, and four years of intensive practice for leadership at the Naval Academy.

Commonsense leadership is rooted in the erroneous assumption that *if most people believe it, it must be right.* Of course, throughout history, the majority of military leaders have at times held to clearly false beliefs such as: "Unless your men fear you, they won't respect you," and "Good leaders know when to break some china!" Further, many forms of common sense are clearly incompatible. For example, if counseling a sailor about going to sea and leaving his girlfriend behind, which common sense advice would you give: "Absence makes the heart grow fonder," or "Out of sight, out of mind"?

It comes as no surprise that research in psychology and business consistently shows that people (including would-be leaders) frequently assume they know more than they actually do; we overestimate our understanding of how to lead. When students enter the Naval Academy, many are immediately thrust into leadership roles in their company, in their classes, and in the larger brigade of midshipmen.

The School of Hard Knocks is Not the Best Way to Learn Leadership

A final myth bearing on leadership training holds that the best way to train a naval leader is to send him or her directly to sea where leadership will be inculcated in the raw and unforgiving school of hard knocks.

Academic preparation accelerates learning in the fleet. Midshipmen learn models of leadership and behavioral principles for motivating and influencing others and then apply them in the context of pervasive feedback—both around the yard and during summer assignments with the Navy and Marine Corps.

John McCain recently recounted his first class cruise and some of the lessons he learned:

> I boarded the USS *Hunt* to begin my first class cruise to Rio de Janeiro in June 1957. The *Hunt* was an old destroyer. It had seen better days. It seemed to me a barely floating rust bucket that should have been scrapped years before, unfit even for mothballing. I spent most of the cruise on the bridge, where the skipper would order me to take the conn. There is a real mental challenge to running a ship of that size, and I had little practical experience for the job. But I truly enjoyed it. I made more than a few mistakes, and every time I screwed up, the skipper would explode, letting loose an impressive blast of profane derision. "Dammit, McCain, you useless bastard. Give up the conn right now. Get the hell off my bridge. I mean it, goddammit; I won't have a worthless S.O.B. at the helm of my ship. You've really screwed up this time McCain. Get the hell out of here." As I began to skulk off the bridge, he would call me back. "Hold on a second, come on back here, Mister. Get over here and take the conn." And then he would begin, more calmly, to explain what I had done wrong and how the task was done properly. We would go along pleasantly until I committed my next unpardonable error, when he would unleash another string of salty oaths in despair over my unfitness for service, only to beckon me back for a last chance to prove myself worthy of his fine ship. One beautiful afternoon, the flagship of the Destroyer Division to which the *Hunt* was attached, flying the ensign of the commanding Admiral, approached us for the purpose of replenishing the *Hunt*'s depleted stores. The skipper gave me the conn, and without a trace of apprehension, made me bring her alongside the Admiral's flagship. He told me to bring her up slowly, but offered no rebuke when I ordered, "All engines ahead two-thirds." At precisely the right moment I ordered, "All engines back full." A few moments later, again well timed, I ordered, "All engines ahead one-third." Thrillingly and to my great relief, the *Hunt* slipped into place so gracefully that any observer would have thought the skipper himself, master shiphandler that he was, had the conn. The skipper was proud of me, and I was much indebted to him. He had given me his trust, and I had had the good fortune to avoid letting him down. After the two ships were tied up, he sent a message to the Admiral. "Midshipman McCain had the conn." The impressed Admiral sent a message to the Superintendent of the Naval Academy informing him of my accomplishment.

Deliberate training and education equip new officers for the range of leadership challenges they will certainly encounter in the fleet. The school of hard knocks has proven inadequate as a leadership laboratory. More than 230 years of American naval experience has taught us this lesson: If you want great leaders, prepare them to lead. And never assume that hard knocks alone produce leadership skills.

If leadership is more than personality, common sense, and experience born of hard knocks then what do leaders need to learn? Our answer is lots. But here is a summary of some key things leaders learn to do—not just as students, but also as a way of life.

- Manage time effectively.
- Make commitments to tasks and organizations and be faithful.
- Recognize that following well is a prerequisite to outstanding leadership.
- Actively seek out opportunities for leadership.
- Observe and critically evaluate one's own leadership performance. Reflect on outcomes and explore alternatives for use in future situations.
- Understand that character matters; leadership requires virtue.
- Correctly diagnose leadership situations and select the most appropriate leader style for the situation.
- Constantly and tenaciously work at increasing both technical and interpersonal expertise and competence.
- Become inoculated to stress and capable of maintaining emotional equanimity during difficult situations; maintain focus without disturbance.
- Develop interpersonal skills and communication savvy; heighten emotional intelligence.
- Empower and praise always.
- Be an intentional model; lead by example.
- Take care of your people first.

READING 2

"Thinking and Learning about Leadership" Cronin. *Presidential Studies Quarterly* 14 (Winter 1984) 22–24, 33–34. From "The Leader's Companion" Wren. The Free Press

Thomas Cronin is a former White House Fellow and White House aide. In 1986, he won the American Political Science Association's Charles E. Merriam Award for significant contributions to the art of government. He is widely published, and currently serves as President of Whitman College.

Leadership is one of the most widely talked about subjects and at the same time one of the most elusive and puzzling. Americans often yearn for great, transcending leadership for their communities, companies, the military, unions, universities, sports teams, and for the nation. However, we have an almost love-hate ambivalence about power wielders. And we especially dislike anyone who tries to boss us around. Yes, we admire the Washingtons and Churchills, but Hitler and Al Capone were leaders too—and that points up a fundamental problem. Leadership can be exercised in the service of noble, liberating, enriching ends, but it can also serve to manipulate, mislead and repress.

"One of the most universal cravings of our time," writes James MacGregor Burns, "is a hunger for compelling and creative leadership." But exactly what is creative leadership? *A Wall Street Journal* cartoon had two men talking about leadership. Finally, one turned to the other in exasperation and said: "Yes, we need leadership, but we also need someone to tell us what to do." That is to say, leadership for most people most of the time is a rather hazy, distant and even confusing abstraction. Hence, thinking about or defining leadership is a kind of intellectual leadership challenge in itself.

What follows are some thoughts about leadership and education for leadership. These thoughts and ideas are highly personal and hardly scientific. As I shall suggest below, almost anything that can be said about leadership can be contradicted with counter examples. Moreover, the whole subject is riddled with paradoxes. My ideas here are the product of my studies of political leadership and my own participation in politics from the town meeting level to the White House staff. Some of my ideas come from helping to advise universities and foundations and the Houston-based American Leadership Forum on how best to go about encouraging leadership development. Finally, my thoughts have also been influenced in a variety of ways by numerous conversations with five especially insightful writers on leadership—Warren Bennis, James MacGregor Burns, David Campbell, Harlan Cleveland and John W. Gardner.

Teaching Leadership

Can we teach people to become leaders? Can we teach leadership? People are divided on these questions. It was once widely held that "leaders are born and not made," but that view is less widely held today. We also used to hear about "natural leaders" but nowadays most leaders have learned their leadership ability rather than inherited it. Still there is much mystery to the whole matter. In any event, many people think colleges and universities should steer clear of the whole subject. What follows is a set of reasons why our institutions of higher learning generally are "bashful about teaching leadership." These reasons may overstate the case, but they are the objections that serious people often raise.

First, many people still believe that leaders are born and not made. Or that leadership is somehow almost accidental or at least that most leaders emerge from circumstances and normally do not create them. In any event, it is usually added, most people, most of the time, are not now and never will be leaders.

Second, American cultural values hold that leadership is an elitist and thus anti-American phenomenon. Plato and Machiavelli and other grand theorists might urge upon their contemporaries the need for selecting out and training a select few for top leadership roles. But this runs against the American grain. We like to think that anyone can become a top leader here. Hence, no special training should be given to some special select few.

Third is the complaint that leadership training would more than likely be pre-occupied with skills, techniques, and the means of getting things done. But leadership for what? A focus on means divorced from ends makes people—especially intellectuals—ill at ease. They hardly want to be in the business of training future Joe McCarthys or Hitlers or Idi Amins.

Fourth, leadership study strikes many as an explicitly vocational topic. It's a practical and applied matter—better learned in summer jobs, in internships or on the playing fields. You learn it on the job. You learn it from gaining experience, from making mistakes and learning from these. And you should learn it from mentors.

Fifth, leadership often involves an element of manipulation or deviousness, if not outright ruthlessness. Some consider it as virtually the same as learning about jungle-fighting or acquiring "the killer instinct." It's just not "clean" enough a subject matter for many people to embrace. Plus, "leaders" like Stalin and Hitler gave "leadership" a bad name. If they were leaders, then spare us of their clones or imitators.

Sixth, leadership in the most robust sense of the term is such an ecumenical and intellectually all-encompassing subject that it frightens not only the timid but even the most well educated of persons. To teach leadership is an act of arrogance. That is, it is to suggest one understands far more than even a well educated person can understand—history, ethics, philosophy, classics, politics, biography, psychology, management, sociology, law, etc. . . . and [is] steeped deeply as well in the "real world."

Seventh, colleges and universities are increasingly organized in highly specialized divisions and departments all geared to train specialists. While the mission of the college may be to educate "the educated person" and society's future leaders, in fact the incentive system is geared to training specialists. Society today rewards the expert or the super specialist—the data processors, the pilots, the financial whiz, the heart surgeon, the special team punt returners, and so on. Leaders, however, have to learn to become generalists and usually have to do so well after they have left our colleges, graduate schools and professional schools.

Eighth, leadership strikes many people (and with some justification) as an elusive, hazy and almost mysterious commodity. Now you see it, now you don't. So much of leadership is intangible, you can't possibly define all the parts. A person may be an outstanding leader here, but fail there. Trait theory has been thoroughly debunked. In fact, leadership is highly situational and contextual. A special chemistry develops between leaders and followers and it is usually context specific. Followers often do more to determine the leadership they will get than can any teacher. Hence, why not teach people to be substantively bright and well-read and let things just take their natural course.

Ninth, virtually anything that can be said about leadership can be denied or disproven. Leadership studies, to the extent they exist, are unscientific. Countless paradoxes and contradictions litter every manuscript on leadership. Thus, we yearn for leadership, but yearn equally to be free and left alone. We admire risk-taking, entrepreneurial leadership, but we roundly criticize excessive risk-taking as bull-headedness or plain stupid. We want leaders who are highly self-confident and who are perhaps incurably optimistic—yet we also dislike hubris and often yearn for at least a little self-doubt (e.g., Creon in Antigone). Leaders have to be almost single-minded in their drive and commitment but too much of that makes a person rigid, driven and unacceptable. We want leaders to be good listeners and represent their constituents, yet in the words of Walter Lippmann, effective leadership often consists of giving the people not what they want but what they will learn to want. How in the world, then, can you be rigorous and precise in teaching leadership?

Tenth, leadership at its best comes close to creativity. And how do you teach creativity? We are increasingly made aware of the fact that much of creative thinking calls upon unconscious thinking, dreaming and even fantasy. Some fascinating work is being done on intuition and the nonrational—but it is hardly a topic with which traditional disciplines in traditional colleges are comfortable. . . .

Learning About Leadership

Permit me to return again to the question of whether leadership can be learned, and possibly taught. My own belief is that students cannot usually be taught to be leaders. But students, and anyone else for that matter, can profitably be exposed to leadership, discussions of leadership skills and styles, and leadership strategies and theories. Individuals can learn in their own minds the strengths as well as limitations of leadership. People can learn about the paradoxes and contradictions and ironies of leadership, which, however puzzling, are central to appreciating the diversity and the dilemmas of problem-solving and getting organizations and nations to function.

Learning about leadership means recognizing bad leadership as well as good. Learning about leadership means understanding the critical linkage of ends and means. Learning about leadership also involves the study of the special chemistry that develops between leaders and followers, not only the chemistry that existed between Americans and Lincoln, but also between Mao and the Chinese peasants, Lenin and the Bolsheviks, between Martin Luther King, Jr., and civil rights activists, between Jean Monnet and those who dreamed of a European Economic Community.

Students can learn to discern and define situations and contexts within which leadership has flourished. Students can learn about the fallibility of the trait theory. Students can learn about the contextual problems of leadership, of why and when leadership is sometimes transferable, and sometimes not. Students can learn about the crucial role that advisors and supporters play in the leadership equation. Students can also learn about countless problem-solving strategies and theories, and participate in role playing exercises that sharpen their own skills in such undertakings.

Students of leadership can learn widely from reading biographies about both the best and the worst leaders. Plutarch's Lives would be a good place to start. Much can be learned from mentors and from intern-participant observing. Much can also be learned about leadership by getting away from one's own culture and examining how leaders in other circumstances go about the task of motivating and mobilizing others. Countless learning opportunities exist that can sharpen a student's skills as a speaker, debater, negotiator, problem clarifier and planner. Such skills should not be minimized. Nor should anyone underestimate the importance of history, economics, logic, and a series of related substantive fields that help provide the breadth and the perspective indispensible to societal leadership.

Above all, students of leadership can make an appointment with themselves and begin to appreciate their own strengths and deficiencies. Personal mastery is important. So too the ability to use one's intuition, and to enrich one's creative impulses. John Gardner suggests, "It's what you learn after you know it all that really counts." Would-be leaders learn to manage their time more wisely. Would-be leaders learn that self-pity and resentment are like toxic substances. Would-be leaders learn the old truth that most people are not for or against you but rather preoccupied with themselves. Would-be leaders learn to break out of their comfortable imprisonments; they learn to cast aside dull routines and habits that enslave most of us. Would-be leaders learn how to become truly sharing and caring people—in their families, their professions and in their communities. And would-be leaders constantly learn too that they have more to give than they have ever given, no matter how much they have given.

Let me conclude by paraphrasing from John Adams:

> We must study politics [and leadership] and war [and peace] that our sons [and daughters] have the liberty to study mathematics and philosophy, geography, natural history and naval architecture, navigation, commerce, and agriculture, in order to give their children a right to study painting, poetry, music, architecture, statuary, tapestry, and porcelain.

READING 3

"Ch. 11 - Authentic Leadership" Northouse. *Leadership Theory and Practice 6 ed*. Sage Publications Inc. Thousand Oaks, CA

Description

Authentic leadership represents one of the newest areas of leadership research. It focuses on whether leadership is genuine and "real." As the title of this approach implies, authentic leadership is about the *authenticity* of leaders and their leadership. Unlike many of the theories that we have discussed in this book, authentic leadership is still in the formative phase of development. As a result, authentic leadership needs to be considered more tentatively: It is likely to change as new research about the theory is published.

In recent times, upheavals in society have energized a tremendous demand for authentic leadership. The destruction on 9/11, corporate scandals at companies like WorldCom and Enron, and massive failures in the banking industry have all created fear and uncertainty. People feel apprehensive and insecure about what is going on around them, and, as a result, they long for bona fide leadership they can trust and for leaders who are honest and good. People's demands for trustworthy leadership make the study of authentic leadership timely and worthwhile.

In addition to the public's interest, authentic leadership has been intriguing to researchers: It was identified earlier in transformational leadership research but never fully articulated (Bass, 1990; Bass & Steidlmeier, 1999; Burns, 1978; Howell & Avolio, 1993). Furthermore, practitioners had developed approaches to authentic leadership that were not evidence based, and so needed further clarification and testing. In attempts to more fully explore authentic leadership, researchers set out to identify the parameters of authentic leadership and more clearly conceptualize it, efforts that continue today.

Authentic Leadership Defined

On the surface, authentic leadership appears easy to define. In actuality, it is a complex process that is difficult to characterize. Among leadership scholars, there is no single accepted definition of authentic leadership. Instead, there are multiple definitions, each written from a different view-point and with a different emphasis (Chan, 2005).

One of those viewpoints is the *intrapersonal* perspective, which focuses closely on the leader and what goes on within the leader. It incorporates the leader's self-knowledge, self-regulation, and self-concept. In Shamir and Eilam's (2005) description of the intrapersonal approach, they suggest that authentic leaders exhibit genuine leadership, lead from conviction, and are originals, not copies. This perspective emphasizes a leader's life experiences and the meaning he or she attaches to those experiences as being critical to the development of the authentic leader.

A second way of defining authentic leadership is as an *interpersonal* process. This perspective outlines authentic leadership as relational, created by leaders and followers together (Eagly, 2005). It results not from the leader's efforts alone, but also from the response of followers. It is a reciprocal process because leaders affect followers and followers affect leaders.

Finally, authentic leadership can be defined from a *developmental* perspective, which is exemplified in the work of Avolio and his associates (Avolio & Gardner, 2005; Gardner, Avolio, & Walumbwa, 2005; Walumbwa, Avolio, Gardner, Wernsing, & Peterson, 2008). This perspective, which underpins the approaches to authentic leadership discussed in the following section, views authentic leadership as something that can be nurtured in a leader, rather than as a fixed trait. Authentic leadership develops in people over a lifetime and can be triggered by major life events, such as a severe illness or a new career.

Taking a developmental approach, Walumbwa et al. (2008) conceptualized authentic leadership as a pattern of leader behavior that develops from and is grounded in the leader's positive psychological qualities and strong ethics. They suggest that authentic leadership is composed of four distinct but related components: self-awareness, internalized moral perspective, balanced processing, and relational transparency (Avolio, Walumbwa, & Weber, 2009). Over a lifetime, authentic leaders learn and develop each of these four types of behavior.

In summary, the Authentic Action Wheel is a visual diagnostic tool to help leaders frame problems. Leaders, with their followers, locate the problem on the wheel and then strategically respond to the major issues of concern. The Terry approach encourages individuals to see things differently and more clearly. In essence, this approach urges leaders to be authentic or "true" to themselves, their organization, and their world, and to base their actions on what is really going on in the situation.

Bill George's Authentic Leadership Approach.   Although the Terry Authentic Action Wheel focuses on problem areas, the authentic leadership approach developed by George (2003; George & Sims, 2007) focuses on the characteristics of authentic leaders. George describes, in a practical way, the essential qualities of authentic leadership and how individuals can develop these qualities if they want to become authentic leaders.

Based on his experience as a corporate executive and through interviews with a diverse sample of 125 successful leaders, George found that authentic leaders have a genuine desire to serve others, they know themselves, and they feel free to lead from their core values. Specifically, authentic leaders demonstrate five basic characteristics: (1) They understand their purpose, (2) they have strong values about the right thing to do, (3) they establish trusting relationships with others, (4) they demonstrate self-discipline and act on their values, and (5) they are passionate about their mission (i.e., act from their heart).

In his interviews, George found that authentic leaders have a real sense of *purpose*. They know what they are about and where they are going. In addition to knowing their purpose, authentic leaders are inspired and intrinsically motivated about their goals. They are *passionate* individuals who have a deep-seated interest in what they are doing and truly care about their work.

A good example of an authentic leader who exhibited passion about his goals was Terry Fox, a cancer survivor, whose leg was amputated after it was overcome by bone cancer. Using a special leg prosthesis, Terry Fox attempted to run across Canada, from the Atlantic to the Pacific, to raise awareness and money for cancer research. Although Terry died before he finished his run, his courage and passion affected the lives of millions of people. He also accomplished his goals to increase cancer awareness and to raise money for cancer research. Today, the Terry Fox

Foundation is going strong and has raised more than $400 million (Canadian) for cancer research (http://www.terryfoxrun.org). Of the dimensions and characteristics, Terry Fox clearly demonstrated purpose and passion in his leadership.

Authentic leaders understand their own *values* and *behave* toward others based on these values. Stated another way, George suggests that authentic leaders know their "True North." They have a clear idea of who they are, where they are going, and what the right thing is to do. When tested in difficult situations, authentic leaders do not compromise their values, but rather use those situations to strengthen their values.

An example of a leader with a strong set of values is Nobel Peace Prize Laureate Nelson Mandela. Mandela is a deeply moral man with a strong conscience. While fighting to abolish apartheid in South Africa, he was unyielding in his pursuit of justice and equality for all. When he was in prison and offered early release in exchange for denouncing his viewpoint, he chose to remain incarcerated rather than compromise his position. Nelson Mandela knew who he was at his core. He knew his values, and his leadership reflected those values.

A third characteristic of authentic leadership in the George approach is strong *relationships*. Authentic leaders have the capacity to open themselves up and establish a *connection* with others. They are willing to share their own story with others and listen to others' stories. Through mutual disclosure, leaders and subordinates develop a sense of trust and closeness.

George argued that people today want to have access to their leaders and they want their leaders to be open with them. In a sense, people are asking leaders to soften the boundary around their leadership role and to be more transparent. People want to have a trusting relationship with their leaders. In exchange, people are willing to give leaders greater loyalty and commitment.

As we discussed in Lesson 10 (leader–member exchange theory), effective leader-follower relationships are marked by high-quality communication in which leaders and followers demonstrate a high degree of mutual trust, respect, and obligation toward each other. Leaders and followers are tied together in productive ways that go beyond the stereotypical leader–subordinate relationship. This results in strong leader–member relationships, greater understanding, and higher productivity.

Self-discipline is another dimension of authentic leadership, and is the quality that helps leaders to reach their goals. Self-discipline gives leaders focus and determination. When leaders establish objectives and standards of excellence, self-discipline helps them to reach these goals and to keep everyone accountable. Furthermore, self-discipline gives authentic leaders the energy to carry out their work in accordance with their values.

Like long-distance runners, authentic leaders with self-discipline are able to stay focused on their goals. They are able to listen to their inner compass and can discipline themselves to move forward, even in challenging circumstances. In stressful times, self-discipline allows authentic leaders to remain cool, calm, and *consistent*. Because disciplined leaders are predictable in their behavior, other people know what to expect and find it easier to communicate with them. When the leader is self-directed and "on course," it gives other people a sense of security.

Last, the George approach identifies *compassion* and *heart* as important aspects of authentic leadership. Compassion refers to being sensitive to the plight of others, opening one's self to others, and being willing to help them. George (2003, p. 40) argued that as leaders develop compassion, they learn to be authentic. Leaders can develop compassion by getting to know others' life stories, doing community service projects, being involved with other racial or ethnic groups, or traveling to developing countries (George, 2003). These activities increase the leader's sensitivity to other cultures, backgrounds, and living situations.

In summary, George's authentic leadership approach highlights five important features of authentic leaders. Collectively, these features provide a practical picture of what people need to do to become authentic in their leadership. Authentic leadership is a lifelong developmental process, which is formed and informed by each individual's life story.

Theoretical Approach

Although still in its initial stages of development, a theory of authentic leadership is emerging in social science literature. In this section, we identify the basic components of authentic leadership and describe how these components are related to one another.

Background to the Theoretical Approach.   Although people's interest in "authenticity" is probably timeless, research on authentic leadership is very recent, with the first article appearing in 2003. The primary catalyst for this research was a leadership summit at the University of Nebraska. This summit was sponsored by the Gallup Leadership Institute, and focused on the nature of authentic leadership and its development. From the summit, two sets of publications emerged: (1) a special issue of *Leadership Quarterly* in Summer 2005, and (2) *Monographs in Leadership and Management*, titled "Authentic Leadership Theory and Process: Origins, Effects and Development," also published in 2005. Prior to the summit, Luthans and Avolio (2003) published an article on authentic leadership development and positive organizational scholarship. The article also helped to ignite this area of research.

Interest in authentic leadership increased during a time in which there was a great deal of societal upheaval and instability in the United States.

Lesson

2 *Perception and Bias*

Gain a basic awareness of our thinking process, and how it leads to the development of innate biases that we may be unaware. Begin understanding how blind spots/stereotypes/prejudice can hinder the leadership relationship.

- **Reading:** Social Perception and Cognition   20

READING

Ch. 4 Social Perception and Cognition "Social Psychology" 7th ed. Delamater & Myers

Introduction

It is 10 p.m., and the admitting physician at the psychiatric hospital is interviewing a respectable-looking man who has asked for treatment. "You see," the patient says, "I keep hearing voices." After taking a full history, the physician diagnoses the man with schizophrenia and assigns him to an inpatient unit. The physician is well-trained and makes the diagnosis with apparent ease. Yet to diagnose correctly someone's mental condition is a difficult problem in social perception. The differences between paranoia, schizophrenia, depression, and normality are not always easy to discern.

A classic study conducted by Rosenhan (1973) demonstrates this problem. Eight pseudo-patients who were actually research investigators gained entry into mental hospitals by claiming to hear voices. During the intake interviews, the pseudo-patients gave true accounts of their backgrounds, life experiences, and present (quite ordinary) psychological condition. They falsified only their names and their complaint of hearing voices. Once in the psychiatric unit, the pseudo-patients stopped simulating symptoms of schizophrenia. They reported that the voices had stopped, talked normally with other patients, and made observations in their notebooks. Although some other patients suspected that the investigators were not really ill, the staff continued to believe they were. Even upon discharge, the pseudo-patients were still diagnosed with schizophrenia, although now it was "schizophrenia in remission."

A man voluntarily checking into a psychiatric hospital may pose a confusing problem for the hospital staff. Is he really "mentally ill" and in need of hospitalization, or is he "healthy"? Is he no longer able to function in the outside world? Or is he merely faking and trying to get a break from his work or his family?

To try to answer these questions, the admitting physician gathers information about the person and classifies it as indicating illness or health. Then the doctor combines these facts to form a general diagnosis (paranoia, schizophrenia, or depression) and determines what treatment the person needs. While performing these actions, the doctor is engaging in **social perception**. Broadly defined, *social perception* refers to constructing an understanding of the social world from the data we get through our senses. More narrowly defined, *social perception* refers to the processes by which we form impressions of other people's traits and personalities.

In making her diagnosis, the physician not only forms an impression about the traits and characteristics of the new patient, she also tries to understand the causes of that person's behavior. She tries, for instance, to figure out whether the patient acts as he does because of some internal dispositions or because of external pressures from the environment. Social psychologists term this process **attribution**. In attribution, we observe others' behavior and then infer backward to causes—intentions, abilities, traits, motives, and situational pressures—that explain why people act as they do.

Social perception and attribution are not passive activities. We do not just register the stimuli that impinge on our senses. Rather, our expectations and cognitive structures influence what we notice and how we interpret it. The intake physician at the psychiatric hospital, for example, does not expect to encounter researchers pretending to be mentally ill. Instead, she expects to meet people who are mentally ill. Even before the interaction begins, the doctor has categorized the patient as mentally ill, and thus she focuses on information relevant to that condition and interprets the information based on the expectation that the patient is a real patient.

Most of the time, the impressions we form of others are sufficiently accurate to permit smooth interaction. After all, few people who are admitted to psychiatric hospitals are researchers faking mental illness. Yet social perception and attribution can be unreliable. Even highly trained observers can misperceive, misjudge, and reach the wrong conclusions.

In February 1999, police officers in New York City were attempting to track down a serial rapist. Sketches of the rapist had been circulated to the police, and so they had some idea what the rapist looked like. Four White officers patrolling the Bronx encountered Amadou Diallo, a Black man, and thought that he resembled the sketches of the rapist. As Diallo was entering his apartment building, the police officers ordered him to stop. Diallo stopped and began to reach for his wallet to produce his identification. The police officers interpreted this action quite differently, however, and, believing he was reaching for a gun, opened fire. They fired a total of 41 shots, and Diallo died immediately. Diallo was not the rapist and had no criminal record—the officers' snap judgments were wrong.

The image of a Black man in a bad neighborhood, reaching into his pocket as he was being stopped by the police, provided too many dangerous cues and the officers reacted immediately. Many have wondered if the police officers would have been slower to act if Diallo had been White. Did race help activate a dangerous image in the police officers' minds and encourage them to respond aggressively? Studies conducted in laboratory settings confirm this type of dynamic. In one study, subjects were asked to act as police officers and decide whether to shoot at suspected criminals. The suspected criminals were either holding a gun (in which case the officer should shoot) or were holding a neutral object such as a cell phone (in which case the officer should not shoot). The results showed that the subjects were more likely to mistakenly shoot a suspect holding a cell phone if the suspect was Black. Similarly, they were also more likely to mistakenly hold back from shooting a suspect holding a gun if the suspect was White (Plant, Peruche, & Butz, 2005).

This lesson focuses on these processes of social perception and attribution and addresses the following questions:

1. How do we make sense of the flood of information that surrounds us? How do we categorize that information and use it in social situations?
2. Why do we rely so much on notions about personality and group stereotypes? What problem does this practice solve, and what difficulties does it create?
3. How do we form impressions of others? That is, how do we integrate the information into a coherent, overall impression?
4. How do we ascertain the causes of other people's behavior and interpret the origins of actions we observe? For instance, when we judge someone's behavior, how do we know whether to attribute the behavior to that person's internal dispositions or to the external situation affecting that person?
5. What sorts of errors do we commonly make in judging the behavior of others, and why do we make such errors?

Schemas

The human mind is a sophisticated system for processing information. One of our most basic mental processes is **categorization**—our tendency to perceive stimuli as members of groups or classes rather than as isolated, unique entities. For instance, at the theater, we see a well-groomed woman on stage wearing a short dress and dancing on her toes; rather than viewing her as a novel entity, we immediately categorize her as a "ballerina."

How do we go about assigning people or things to categories? For instance, how do we know the woman should be categorized as a ballerina and not as an "actress" or a "cheerleader"? To categorize some person, we usually compare that person to our prototype of the category. A **prototype** is an abstraction that represents the "typical" or quintessential instance of a class or group—as least to us. Others may have different prototypes for the same category. Usually, prototypes are specified in terms of a set of attributes. For example, the prototype of a "cultured person" may be someone who is knowledgeable about literature, classical music, fine food, and foreign cultures, and who indulges these tastes by regularly attending concerts, eating at fine restaurants, and traveling worldwide.

Categorizing people, objects, situations, events, and even the self becomes complicated because the categories we use are not isolated from one another. Rather, they link together and form a structure. For instance, we may think of a person (Jonathan) not only as having various attributes (tall, wealthy) but also as bearing certain relations to other persons or entities (friend of Caroline, stronger than Bill, owner of a Honda). These other persons or entities will themselves have attributes (Caroline: thin, athletic, brunette; William: short, fat, mustachioed; Honda: blue, four-door, new). They also have relations with still other persons and entities (Caroline: cousin of William, wife of George; William: friend of George, owner of a Buick). In this way, we build a cognitive structure consisting of persons, attributes, and relations.

Social psychologists use the term **schema** to denote a well-organized structure of cognitions about some social entity such as a person, group, role, or event. Schemas usually include information about an entity's attributes and about its relations with other entities. To illustrate, suppose that Chandra, who is somewhat cynical about politics, has a schema about the role of "member of Congress." In Chandra's schema, the member of Congress will claim to insist that he or she serves the needs of his constituents, but will actually vote for the special interests of those who contributed most to his campaign; will run TV advertisements containing half-truths at election time; will spend more time in Washington, D.C., than in his home district; will put avoiding scandal above ethics; will vote for large pay raises and retirement benefits for himself; and above all, will never do anything to lessen his own power.

Someone else, of course, may hold a less cynical view of politics than Chandra and have a different schema about the role of "member of Congress." But, like Chandra's, this schema will likely incorporate such elements as the congressional representative's typical activities, relations, motives, and tactics. Whatever their exact content, schemas enable us to organize and remember facts, to make inferences that go beyond the facts immediately available, and to assess new information (Fiske & Linville, 1980; Wilcox & Williams, 1990).

Types of Schemas

There are several distinct types of schemas, including person schemas, self-schemas, group schemas, role schemas, and event schemas (Eckes, 1995; Taylor & Crocker, 1981).

Person schemas are cognitive structures that describe the personalities of others. Person schemas can apply either to specific individuals (such as Barack Obama, Brittany Spears, your father) or to types of individuals (such as introvert, bipolar, sociopath). Person schemas organize our conceptions of others' personalities and enable us to develop expectations about others' behavior.

Self-schemas are structures that organize our conception of our own characteristics (Catrambone & Markus, 1987; Markus, 1977). For instance, if you conceive of yourself as independent (as opposed to dependent), you may see yourself as individualistic, unconventional, and assertive. Then, if you behave in a manner consistent with your self-schema, you may refuse to accept money from your parents, refuse to ask others for help with school-work, take a part-time job, or dye your hair an unusual color.

Group schemas, also called **stereotypes**, are schemas regarding the members of a particular social group or social category (Hamilton, 1981). Stereotypes indicate the attributes and behaviors considered typical of members of that group or social category. American culture uses a wide variety of stereotypes about different races (Blacks, Hispanics, Asians), religious groups (Protestants, Catholics, Jews), and ethnic groups (Germans, Irish, Poles, Greeks, Italians).

Role schemas indicate which attributes and behaviors are typical of persons occupying a particular role in a group. Chandra's conception of the role of a Congressional representative illustrates a role schema. Role schemas exist for most occupational roles—nurses, cab drivers, store managers, and the like—but they also exist for other kinds of roles in groups: group leader, captain of a sports team. Role schemas are often used to understand and to predict the behaviors of people who occupy roles.

Event schemas (also called *scripts*) are schemas regarding important, recurring social events (Abelson, 1981; Hue & Erickson, 1991; Schank & Abelson, 1977). In our society, these events include weddings, funerals, graduation ceremonies, job interviews, cocktail parties, and first dates. An event schema specifies the activities that constitute the event, the predetermined order or sequence for these activities, and the persons (or role occupants) participating in the event. Scripts can be revealed by asking people to describe what typically happens during an event. In one study, researchers asked male and female college students to describe the typical sequence of activities on a first date (Rose & Frieze, 1993). There was substantial agreement between male and female respondents, as shown in Table 2.1. Several activities were mentioned by more than half of the participants, including grooming and dressing, picking up the date, and taking the date home. A number of activities were important in both male and female scripts: worrying about appearance, leaving, confirming plans, eating, and going home. Reflecting the impact of gender roles, both men and women agreed that the man would take the initiative in picking up the date, taking the date home, and kissing her goodnight. Notice that irrelevant activities were not mentioned, such as taking a driver's license test or going to the dentist; these are not appropriate for a first date. Note also that the script specifies a sequence or expected order for the various activities—the man will not kiss the woman goodnight before they eat dinner.

Schematic Processing

Why Do We Use Schemas? Although schemas may produce reasonably accurate judgments much of the time, they do not always work. Wouldn't it be better for us to rely less on schemas and so perhaps be able to avoid the kind of tragic mistake the police made with Amadou Diallo? Perhaps, but we come to rely on schemas because they give us a way to efficiently organize, understand, and react to the complex world around us. It is simply impossible to process all the information present in each interaction. We have to find a way to focus on what is most important in defining the situation and the persons involved so that we can respond appropriately. Schemas help us do this in several ways: (1) they influence our capacity to recall information by making certain kinds of facts more salient and easier to remember; (2) they help us process information faster; (3) they guide our inferences and judgments about people and objects; (4) they allow us to reduce ambiguity by providing a way to interpret ambiguous elements in the situation. Once we have applied a schema to the situation, our decisions about how to interact in it become much more straightforward (Mayer, Rapp, & Williams, 1993).

TABLE 2.1 Core Actions of the First Date Script

SCRIPT FOR WOMAN	SCRIPT FOR MAN
GROOM AND DRESS*	
BE NERVOUS	
Worry about Appearance	WORRY ABOUT APPEARANCE
PICK UP DATE (BY MAN)	PICK UP DATE MEET PARENTS/ROOMMATES
Leave	Leave
Confirm plans	Confirm plans
Get to know and evaluate date	Get to know and evaluate date
TALK, JOKE, LAUGH	TALK, JOKE, LAUGH
GO TO MOVIES, SHOW, PARTY	
Eat	EAT
Take date home (by man)	TAKE DATE HOME
Kiss goodnight (by man)	Kiss goodnight
Go home	Go home

*Capital letters indicate the action was mentioned by 50% or more of the participants; lowercase letters indicate the action was mentioned by fewer than 50% of the participants.
SOURCE: Rose and Frieze, 1993.

Schematic Memory. Human memory is largely reconstructive. That is, we do not usually remember all the precise details of what transpired in a given situation—we are not a video camera instantly recording all the images and sounds. Instead, we typically remember some of what happened—enough to identify the appropriate schema and then rely on that schema to fill in other details. Schemas organize information in memory and, therefore, affect what we remember and what we forget (Hess & Slaughter, 1990; Sherman, Judd, & Park, 1989). When trying to recall something, people often remember better those facts that are consistent with their schemas. For instance, one study (Cohen, 1981) investigated the impact of an occupational role schema on recall. Participants viewed a videotape of a woman celebrating her birthday by having dinner with her husband at home. Half the participants were told the woman was a librarian; the other half were told she was a waitress.

Some characteristics of the woman were consistent with the schema of a librarian: She wore glasses, had spent the day reading, had previously traveled in Europe, and liked classical music. Other characteristics of the woman, however, were consistent with the schema of a waitress: She drank beer, had a bowling ball in the room, ate chocolate birthday cake, and flirted with her husband. Later, when participants tried to recall details of the videotape, they recalled most accurately those facts consistent with the woman's occupational label. That is, participants who thought she was a librarian remembered facts consistent with the librarian schema, whereas those who thought she was a waitress remembered facts consistent with the waitress schema.

What about memory for material inconsistent with schemas? Several studies have tested the recall of three types of information: material consistent with schemas, material contradictory to schemas, and material irrelevant to schemas. The results show that people recall both schema-consistent and schema-contradictory material better than schema-irrelevant material (Cano, Hopkins, & Islam, 1991; Higgins & Bargh, 1987). People recall schema-contradictory material better when the schema itself is concrete (for example, spends money wisely, often tells lies, brags about her accomplishments) rather than abstract (for example, practical, dishonest, egotistical).

Schematic Inference.   Schemas affect the inferences we make about persons and other social entities (Fiske & Taylor, 1991). That is, they supply missing facts when gaps exist in our knowledge. If we know certain facts about a person but are ignorant about others, we fill in the gaps by inserting suppositions consistent with our schema for that person. For example, knowing your roommate is a nonsmoker, you can infer he will not want to spend time with your new friend who smokes. Of course, the use of schemas can lead to erroneous inferences. If the schema is incomplete or does not correctly mirror reality, some mistakes are likely. For instance, the police officers who confronted Amadou Diallo applied a schema that was incorrect. Their schema for "a Black man who puts his hand in his pocket as he is being confronted by the police" includes the element that the suspect would have a gun in his pocket. From this, they inferred that he would try to shoot at them, and they reacted according to that erroneous inference.

Schemas—especially well-developed schemas—can help us infer new facts. For instance, if a physician diagnoses a patient as having chicken pox, he can make inferences about how the patient contracted the disease, which symptoms might be present, what side effects or complications might arise, and what treatment will be effective. For another person who has no schema regarding this disease, these inferences would be virtually impossible.

Schematic Judgment.   Schemas can influence our judgments or feelings about persons and other entities. For one thing, the schemas themselves may be organized in terms of evaluative dimensions; this is especially true of person schemas. For another thing, the level of complexity of our schemas affects our evaluations of other persons. Greater schematic complexity leads to less extreme judgments. That is, the greater the complexity of our schemas about groups of people, the less extreme are our evaluations of persons in those groups. This is called the *complexity–extremity effect.*

For instance, in one study (Linville & Jones, 1980), White college students evaluated a person applying for admission to law school. Depending on treatment, the applicant was either. White or Black and had an academic record that was either strong or weak. The results showed an interaction effect between academic record and race. Participants rated a weak Black applicant more negatively than a weak Black applicant more negatively than a weak White applicant, but they rated a strong Black applicant more positively than a strong White applicant. Judgments about Black applicants were more extreme—in both directions—than those about White applicants because the participants' schema for their own in-group (White) was more complex than their schema for the out-group (Black). Further research (Linville, 1982) shows that the complexity–extremity effect also holds for other attributes, such as age. College students have less complex schemas for older persons than for persons their own age, so they are more extreme in judgments of older persons.

Drawbacks of Schematic Processing. Although schemas provide certain advantages, they also entail some corresponding disadvantages. First, people are overly accepting of information that fits consistently with a schema. In fact, some research suggests that perceivers show a confirmatory bias when collecting new information relevant to schemas (Higgins & Bargh, 1987; Synder & Swann, 1978). That is, when gathering information, perceivers tend to ask questions that will obtain information supportive of the schemas rather than questions that will obtain information contradictory to the schemas.

Second, when faced with missing information, people fill in gaps in knowledge by adding elements that are consistent with their schemas. Sometimes these added elements turn out to be erroneous or factually incorrect. When this happens, it will, of course, create inaccurate interpretations or inferences about people, groups, or events.

Third, because people are often reluctant to discard or revise their schemas, they occasionally apply schemas to persons or events even when the schemas do not fit the facts very well. Forced misapplication of a schema may lead to incorrect characterization and inferences, and this in turn can produce inappropriate or inflexible responses toward other persons, groups, or events.

Person Schemas and Group Stereotypes

Person Schemas

As noted earlier, person schemas are cognitive structures that describe the personalities of other individuals. There are several distinct types of person schemas. Some person schemas are very specific and pertain to particular people. For example, Caroline married George 3 years ago, and she knew him for 4 years before that. By this time, she has an elaborate schema regarding George, and she can usually predict how he will react to new situations, opportunities, or problems. Similarly, we often have individual schemas for public figures (for instance, Oprah Winfrey—talk show host, actor, advocate for women, Black, extremely wealthy) or for famous historical personages (for instance, Abraham Lincoln—political leader during the Civil War, honest, determined, opposed to slavery, committed to holding the Union together).

Other person schemas are very abstract and focus on the relations among personality traits. A schema of this type is an implicit personality theory—a set of unstated assumptions about which personality traits are correlated with one another (Anderson & Sedikides, 1991; Grant & Holmes, 1981; Sternberg, 1985). These theories often include beliefs about the behaviors that are associated with various personality traits (Skowronski & Carlston, 1989). They are considered implicit because in everyday life we usually do not subject our person schemas to close examination, nor are we explicitly aware of their contents.

Implicit Personality Theories and Mental Maps.   As do all schemas, implicit personality theories enable us to make inferences that go beyond the available information. Instead of withholding judgment, we use them to flesh out our impressions of a person about whom we have little information. For instance, if we learn someone has a warm personality, we might infer she is also likely to be sociable, popular, good-natured, and so on. If we hear that somebody else is pessimistic, we may infer he is humorless, irritable, and unpopular, even though we lack evidence that he actually has these traits.

We can depict an implicit personality theory as a mental map indicating the way traits are related to one another. Based on judgments made by college students, this figure shows how various personality traits stand in relation to one another (Rosenberg, Nelson, & Vivekananthan, 1968). Traits thought to be similar are located close together within our mental map, meaning that we expect people who have one trait to have the other. Traits thought to be dissimilar are located far apart, meaning we believe they rarely occur together in one person.

If your mental map resembles the one portrayed, you think that people who are wasteful are also likely to be unintelligent and irresponsible (see the lower left part of the map). Similarly, you think that people who are persistent are also likely to be determined and skillful (the upper right part of the map).

As portrayed in some mental maps, personality traits fall along two distinct evaluative dimensions—a social dimension and an intellectual dimension. These dimensions are represented by the lines. For instance, the traits "warm" and "cold" differ mainly on the social dimension, whereas "frivolous" and "industrious" differ on the intellectual dimension (Rosenberg & Sedlak, 1972). Some traits (such as "important") are good on both the social and the intellectual dimensions; other traits (such as "unreliable") are bad on both. Traits usually tend to be either good on both dimensions or bad on both dimensions, which explains a common bias in impression formation. We tend to judge persons who have several good traits as generally good and persons who have several bad traits as generally bad. And, if we have several bad characteristics associated with an important social marker, such as race, these bad characteristics can be unthinkingly attributed to a person of a particular race. This process of applying stereotypes has been demonstrated in a number of studies that also show how Whites place characteristics that are stereotypically Black with negative characteristics and characteristics that are stereotypically White with positive characteristics (Wittenbrink, Judd, & Park, 2001). Once we have a global impression of someone as, say, generally good, we assume that other positive traits (located nearby in the mental map) also apply. This tendency for our general or overall liking for a person to influence our subsequent assessment of more specific traits of that person is called the **halo effect** (Lachman & Bass, 1985; Thorndike, 1920). The halo effect produces bias in impression formation; it can lead to inaccuracy in our ratings of others' traits and performances (Cooper, 1981; Fisicaro, 1988).

Group Stereotypes

- "The Irish are hot-headed, drunken, and belligerent."
- "Blacks are lazy and unreliable, and aren't good at anything except singing, dancing, and sports."
- "Feminists are left-wing, militant, man-hating radicals."
- "Jocks may be strong, but they're stupid and arrogant."
- "Southerners are rednecked, speech-slurring, barefooted bigots."
- "Republicans are heartless, racist, elitist reactionaries."
- "Lawyers are shrewd, contentious, overpriced troublemakers."

An unfortunate reality in our society is that we have all heard remarks like these—categorical, extreme, inaccurate characterizations. Each of these is an example of a group schema or stereotype. A stereotype is a set of characteristics attributed to all members of some specified group or social category (McCauley, Stitt, & Segal, 1980; Taylor, 1981). Just like other types of schemas, stereotypes simplify the complex social world. Rather than treating each member of a group individually, stereotypes encourage us to think about and treat all feminists, Southerners, or lawyers the same way. By helping us to quickly place people into categories, stereotypes let us form impressions of people and predict their behavior with only minimal information: the groups to which they belong.

Stereotypes, however, involve overgeneralization. They lead us to think that all members of a particular group or social category have certain attributes. Although stereotypes might contain a kernel of truth—some members of the stereotyped group may have some of the imputed characteristics—it is almost never the case that all members have those characteristics. For this reason, stereotypes often lead to inaccurate inferences. Consider, for instance, all the persons you know of Irish descent. Perhaps one of them does—as the stereotype suggests—have a quick temper, and maybe another once got into a fistfight. It is certainly false, however, that all your Irish acquaintances spend most of their time fighting, arguing, drinking, and eating potatoes. Moreover, the Irish people you know probably do not get into angry fights any more often than people who are not Irish.

Although stereotypes are overgeneralizations, we still constantly use them and are often unaware of their impact on our judgments of others (Hepburn & Locksley, 1983). And, although there is nothing inherent in stereotypes that requires them to be negative, many stereotypes do contain negative elements. Of course, some stereotypes are positive ("Asians excel at math"; "Graduate students are hardworking"), but many others disparage or diminish the group stereotyped. Stereotypes can have many negative effects, especially when they are used to limit access to important social roles—for example, when an individual applies for a job or for admission to college. Stereotypes can also have less direct effects on members of stereotyped groups through a process called **stereotype threat** (Steele, 1997). When a member of a group believes that there is a real threat of being judged based on group stereotypes, the result can be poorer performance. Box 2.1 explains how stereotype threat reduces the performance of some students on academic tasks and standardized tests.

Common Stereotypes. As the foregoing examples suggest, in American society, some widely known stereotypes pertain to ethnic, racial, and gender groups. Ethnic (national) stereotypes held by Americans might include, for example, the view that

Box 2.1 Research Update: Stereotype Threat

When people act on their stereotypes, they can produce many negative effects for those who are the subjects of their stereotypes. Members of racial groups may be denied jobs or promotions because the schema the employer holds of their racial group include laziness. Other groups may be denied admissions to selective colleges because admissions officers believe people from that group are lazy or irresponsible. As damaging as these direct uses of stereotypes can be, researchers have recently discovered a second, less direct negative effect of stereotypes called stereotype threat (Steele, 1997, 1999).

Stereotype threat occurs when a member of a group suspects that he or she will be judged based on a common stereotype that is held of that group. For example, one stereotype of women is that they are less proficient at mathematics than men. If a woman enters a situation where her mathematical ability is being judged and she believes that the judgment will be negatively affected by the stereotype about women's mathematical ability, her performance on the exam may deteriorate (Spencer, Steele, & Quinn, 1999). To test for this kind of effect, Steele and Aronson (1995) gave Stanford University students a very difficult test using questions from the Graduate Record Examination in literature. The difficulty of the test provided a stereotype threat for Black students because poor performance would confirm a stereotype that they were not as able as White students. Even though the White and Black students were matched on ability, the Black students scored much lower than the White students. However, when researchers told the students that the test was part of a study to understand how people solved problems and that it did not measure ability, the stereotype threat was removed and the Black and White students did equally well.

Why does performance deteriorate when stereotype threat is present? Isn't it possible that the desire to disprove the stereotype might cause students to try harder and thereby cause them to do even better than they normally would? In a follow-up study, students took the exam on a computer, so that the researchers could time how long the students took with each question. The results showed that under conditions of stereotype threat, Black students were exerting extra effort and were overthinking the questions. They reread questions, changed their answers, and generally became less efficient at taking the test (Steele, 1999). This result also made sense of Steele's finding that stereotype threat affected academically strong students more than academically weak students—for those students who saw academics as an important part of their self-concept, the threat was much more meaningful than for those who cared less about academics (Steele, 1997).

In real life, it may be possible to reduce stereotype threat and to even the playing field. One way of doing this is to convince students who may be experiencing stereotype threat that the test being used is not biased. This is not easy to do given current deeply held beliefs about the unfairness of testing and the pervasiveness of racial stereotypes. However, Cohen, Steele, and Ross (1999) found that they could reduce stereotype threat by informing students that the evaluations of their performance would use very high standards and that they believed the students could perform up to those standards. Such an approach lets the student know that assessment is based on standards rather than stereotypes and that students are not viewed stereotypically. Stereotypes may not have disappeared over time, but they have changed form (Dovidio & Gaertner, 1996).

Germans are industrious and technically minded; Italians, passionate; Irish, quick-tempered; and Americans, materialistic (Karlins, Coffman, & Walters, 1969). Investigators have studied ethnic, racial, and gender stereotypes for many years, and the results show that the content of stereotypes changes over time (Diekman, Eagly, Mladinic, & Ferreira, 2005). For instance, few of us now believe—as many once did—that the typical Native American is a drunk, the typical African American is superstitious, or the typical Chinese American is conservative and inscrutable. Stereotypes may not have disappeared over time, but they have changed form (Dovidio & Gaertner, 1996).

Just as stereotypes about ethnic and racial groups are commonly held in our society, so also are stereotypes about gender groups. Usually, our first judgment when meeting people involves classifying them as male or female. This classification is likely to activate an elaborate stereotype. This stereotype depicts male persons as more independent, dominant, competent, rational, competitive, assertive, and stable in handling crises. It characterizes female persons as more emotional, sensitive, expressive, gentle, helpful, and patient (Ashmore, 1981; Martin, 1987; Minnigerode & Lee, 1978). Research on the nature of these stereotypes of male and female persons is discussed in Box 2.2. Within gender, stereotypes are linked to titles. For instance, women labeled "Ms." are seen as more achieving, more masculine, and less likable than women labeled "Mrs." (Dion & Schuller, 1991). In addition to using ethnic, racial, and gender stereotypes, people also stereotype groups defined by occupation, age, political ideology, mental illness, hobbies, school attended, and so on (Milburn, 1987; Miller, 1982).

Box 2.2 Gender Schemas and Stereotypes

One of the most consistent research findings on stereotypes is that many people believe men and women have different personality traits. What are the traits believed to be typical of each sex? Where do these sex stereotypes come from?

Studies of sex stereotyping have established a number of characteristics that people associate differentially with men and women. In the accompanying chart, 20 characteristics are listed that studies have found to be consistently associated with men or women. To see how aware you are of these stereotypes, fill out the chart by indicating which of the traits listed are more typical of men and which are more typical of men and which are more typical of women. Also indicate if you consider each trait as a desirable or an undesirable characteristic.

	MOST TYPICAL OF		DESIRABLE	
TRAIT	MEN	WOMEN	YES	NO
Independent	——	——	——	——
Aggressive	——	——	——	——
Ambitious	——	——	——	——
Strong	——	——	——	——
Blunt	——	——	——	——
Passive	——	——	——	——
Emotional	——	——	——	——
Easily influenced	——	——	——	——
Talkative	——	——	——	——
Tactful	——	——	——	——
Excitable in minor crises	——	——	——	——
Aware of others' feelings	——	——	——	——
Submissive	——	——	——	——
Strong need for security	——	——	——	——
Feelings easily hurt	——	——	——	——
Self-confident	——	——	——	——
Adventurous	——	——	——	——
Acts as a leader	——	——	——	——
Makes decisions easily	——	——	——	——
Likes math and science	——	——	——	——

Broverman and colleagues (1972) found that both men and women agreed on the sex stereotypes and on the desirability of each trait. The first five traits listed in the chart were seen as more typical of men, whereas the next five were seen as more typical of women. That is, men were seen as more independent, aggressive, ambitious, strong, and blunt; women were seen as more passive, emotional, easily influenced, talkative, and tactful. In general, men were perceived as stronger and more confident than women, and women as weaker and more expressive than men. Subsequent studies have found that these stereotypes have persisted over time (Bergen & Williams, 1991; Deaux & Lewis, 1983).

Broverman and others (1972) also found that most traits stereotyped as masculine were evaluated as desirable, whereas most traits stereotyped as feminine were evaluated as undesirable. In other words, traits associated with men were usually considered to be better than those associated with women. Did your evaluations of trait desirability favor the male stereotyped traits? If not, you may fit in with a trend among educated respondents toward valuing some traditionally feminine traits (say, emotional) more positively and some traditionally masculine traits (say, ambitious) more negatively (Der-Karabetian & Smith, 1977; Lottes & Kuriloff, 1994; Pleck, 1976). This trend means that even if sex stereotypes persist, women may be evaluated less negatively than before.

Origins of Stereotypes. How do various stereotypes originate? Some theorists suggest that stereotypes arise out of direct experience with some members of the stereotyped group (Campbell, 1967). We may once have known Italians who were passionate, Blacks who were musical, or Japanese who were polite. We then build a stereotype by generalizing—that is, we infer that all members of a group share the attribute we know to be characteristic of some particular members.

Other theorists (Eagly & Steffen, 1984) suggest that stereotypes derive in part from a biased distribution of group members into social roles. Roles have associated characteristics, and eventually those characteristics are attached to the persons occupying the roles. If a social group is concentrated in roles with negative characteristics, an unflattering stereotype of that group may emerge that ascribe the negative characteristics of the job to members of the group.

Stereotyping may also be a natural outcome of social perception. When people have to process and remember a lot of information about many others, they store this information in terms of group categories rather than in terms of individuals (Taylor, Fiske, Etcoff, & Ruderman, 1978). In trying to remember what went on in a classroom discussion, you may recall that several women spoke and a Black person expressed a strong opinion, although you cannot remember exactly which women spoke or who the Black person was. Because people remember behavior by group category rather than by individual, they attach the behavior to the groups (Rothbart, Fulero, Jensen, Howard, & Birrell, 1978). Remembering that women spoke and a Black person expressed a strong opinion, you might infer that in general, women are talkative and Blacks are opinionated. You would not form these stereotypes if you recalled these attributes as belonging to individuals.

Errors Caused by Stereotypes. Because stereotypes are overgeneralizations, they foster various errors in social perception and judgment. First, stereotypes lead us to assume that all members of a group are alike and possess certain traits. Yet individual members of a group obviously differ in many respects. One person wearing a hard hat may shoulder you into the stairwell on a crowded bus; another may offer you his seat. Second, stereotypes lead us to assume that all the members of one group differ from all the members of other groups. Stereotypes of football players and ballet dancers may suggest, for instance, that these groups have nothing in common. But both groups contain individuals who are patient, neurotic, hardworking, intelligent, and so on. In fact, there are ballet dancers who also play football.

Although stereotypes can produce inaccurate inferences and judgments in simple situations, they are especially likely to do so in complex situations. When the judgment to be made is multifaceted and involves a lot of complex data, reliance on stereotypes can prove particularly misleading. If an observer uses a stereotype as a central theme around which to organize information relevant to a decision, he or she may neglect information that is inconsistent with the stereotype (Bodenhausen & Lichtenstein, 1987). Research also indicates that people of higher status have a tendency to use stereotypes more than people of lower status. This seems to occur because people of higher status have more people competing for their attention and thus have more incentive to use shortcuts, and because they can afford to make more mistakes because of their power (Goodwin, Gubin, Fiskc, & Yzerbyt, 2000). This dynamic occurs even when subjects are randomly assigned to higher and lower status roles (Richeson & Ambady, 2003).

Although stereotypes involve overstatement and overgeneralization, they resist change even in the face of concrete evidence that contradicts them. This occurs because people tend to accept information that confirms their stereotypes and to ignore or explain away information that disconfirms them (Lord, Lepper, & Mackie, 1984; Snyder, 1981; Weber & Crocker, 1983). Suppose, for example, that Stan stereotypes gay men as effeminate, nonathletic, and artistic. If he stumbles into a gay bar, he is especially likely to notice the men in the crowd who fit this description, thereby confirming his stereotype. But how does he construe any rough-looking, athletic men who are there? It is possible that these individuals might challenge his stereotype, but reconstructing schemas is a lot of work, and Stan is more likely to find a way around this challenge. He might scrutinize those who don't fit his stereotype for hidden signs of effeminacy; he might underestimate their number or consider them the exceptions that prove the rule—or even assume they are straight. Through cognitive strategies like these, people explain away contradictory information and preserve their stereotypes.

Lesson

3 *Critical Thinking*

Begin to grasp the foundations of critical thinking, and how it forces us to become aware of, and better manage our innate biases, while promoting the creative thinking and decision-making processes that are critical to leaders, especially in the military.

READING

"What It Means to Think Critically" Brookfield. *Developing Critical Thinkers: challenging Adults to Explore Alternative Ways to Thinking and Acting* (San Francisco Jossey-Bass, 1987) p. 3–14. From "The Leader's Companion" Wren. The Free Press

The need to develop critical thinkers is currently something of a cause-celebre. The New York Times reports that "the public schools have discovered the importance of critical thinking, and many of them are trying to teach children how to do it" (Hechinger, 1987, p. 27). Educational journals regularly advertise conferences on critical thinking, and three recent major reports on American education, Involvement in Learning (National Institute of Education, 1984), A Nation at Risk (National Commission on Excellence in Education, 1983), and Higher Education and the American Resurgence (Newman, 1985), all call for the development of critical thinkers as a national priority for both civic and economic reasons. Civically, a critically informed populace is seen as more likely to participate in forms of democratic political activity. Economically, a critically active and creative work force is seen as the key to American economic resurgence in the face of crippling foreign trade competition. Johnston (1986, p. 4) observes that "it is generally agreed that nothing is more important to the nation's ability to meet the competitive challenge of the future than what Samuel Ehrenhalt (1983, p. 43) of the Department of' Labor has termed a 'flexible, adaptable labor force.' That the message contained in these reports is having some practical effect is evident from case studies of education for critical thinking (Young, 1980; Gamson and Associates, 1984; Stice, 1987), from special issues being devoted to this topic in such journals as Phi Delia Kappan and National Forum in 1985, from a flow of grant monies for projects to research applications of critical thinking, and from a recent upsurge in conferences on critical thinking. There have been attempts to propose a new concept described as critical literacy (Kretovics, 1985) and to outline the foundations of a critical pedagogy (Greene, 1986; Livingstone, 1987) that would foster this capacity. As Sternberg (1985, p. 194) observes, "It would be difficult to read anything at all in the contemporary literature of education without becoming aware of this new interest in teaching critical thinking."

But critical thinking is an activity that can be observed in settings and domains very far removed from the school or college classroom. Indeed, there is no clear evidence that any of the skills of critical thinking learned in schools and colleges have much transferability to the contexts of adult life. Sternberg (1985) points out the lack of correspondence between what is required for critical thinking in adulthood and what is taught in school programs intended to develop critical thinking. He writes that "the problems of thinking in the real world do not correspond well with the problems of the large majority of programs that teach critical thinking. We are preparing students to deal with problems that are in many respects unlike those that they will face as adults" (p. 194). In adulthood, we are thinking critically whenever we question why we, or our partners, behave in certain ways within relationships. Critical thinking is evident whenever employees question the appropriateness of a certain technique, mode of production, or organizational form. Managers who are ready to jettison outmoded organizational norms or unwieldy organizational hierarchies, and who are prepared to open up organizational lines of communication in order to democratize the workplace and introduce participatory forms of management, are critical thinkers. Citizens who ask "awkward" questions regarding the activities of local, regional, and national government offices, who call for political leaders to account for their actions, and who are ready to challenge the legitimacy of existing policies and political structures are critical thinkers. Television viewers who are skeptical of the accuracy of media depictions of what are portrayed as "typical" families, or of the neutrality and objectivity of television's reporting of political events, are critical thinkers.

Recognizing Critical Thinking

What characteristics do we look for in critical thinkers? How can we recognize when critical thinking is happening? What are the chief capacities we are trying to encourage when we help people to become critical thinkers? What activities and processes are taking place when people are thinking critically? These questions, and others, are addressed in nine critical thinking "themes."

1. *Critical thinking is a productive and positive activity.* Critical thinkers are actively engaged with life. They see themselves as creating and re-creating aspects of their personal, workplace, and political lives. They appreciate creativity, they are innovators, and they exude a sense that life is full of possibilities. Critical thinkers see the future as open and malleable, not as closed and fixed. They are self-confident about their potential for changing aspects of their worlds, both as individuals and through collective action. Critical thinkers are sometimes portrayed as cynical people who often condemn the efforts of others without contributing anything themselves. Those who hold this view see being critical as somehow antisocial; it is seen as a belittling activity engaged in only by those with false assumptions of superiority. In fact, the opposite is true. When we think critically we become aware of the diversity of values, behaviors, social structures, and artistic forms in the world. Through realizing this diversity, our commitments to our own values, actions, and social structures are informed by a sense of humility; we gain an awareness that others in the world have the same sense of certainty we do—but about ideas, value and actions that are completely contrary to our own.

2. *Critical thinking is a process, not an outcome.* Being critical thinkers entails a continual questioning of assumptions. People can never be in a state of complete critical development. If we ever felt that we had reached a state of fully developed or realized critical awareness, we would be contradicting one of the central tenets of critical thinking—namely, that we are skeptical of any claims to universal truth or total certainty. By its nature, critical thinking can never be finished in some final, static manner.

3. *Manifestations of critical thinking vary according to the contexts in which it occurs.* The indicators that reveal whether or not people are thinking critically vary enormously. For some people, the process appears to be almost wholly internal; very few external features of their lives appear to change. With these individuals, we can look for evidence of the critical process in their

writing or talking. With others, critical thinking will manifest itself directly and vividly in their external actions. People who renegotiate aspects of their intimate relationships, managers who deliberately depart from their habitual ways of coming to decisions or solving problems, workers who reshape their workplace according to nonhierarchical organizational norms after establishing a worker cooperative, or citizens campaigning for a nuclear freeze after observing the effects of a radiation leak in their community are all example of how critical thinking can prompt dramatic action.

4. *Critical thinking is triggered by positive as well as negative events.* A theme common to many discussions of critical thinking is that this activity usually results from people having experienced traumas or tragedies in their lives. These events, so the argument goes, cause people to question their previously trusted assumptions about how the world works; and this questioning prompts a careful scrutiny of what were previously unquestioned ways of thinking and living. This often happens. It is also true, however, that critical thinking is triggered by a joyful, pleasing, or fulfilling event – a "peak" experience such as falling in love, being unexpectedly successful in some new workplace role, or finding that others place great store by abilities or accomplishments that we exhibit almost without being aware of them. In such circumstances we being to reinterpret our past actions and ideas from a new vantage point. We begin to wonder if our old assumptions about our roles, personalities, and abilities were completely accurate. We begin to be aware of and to explore new possibilities with our intimates, at our workplace, and in our political involvements.

5. *Critical thinking is emotive as well as rational.* Critical thinking is sometimes regarded as a kind of pure, ascetic cognitive activity above and beyond the realm of feeling and emotions. In fact, emotions are central to the critical thinking process. As we try to think critically and help others to do so, we cannot help but become aware of the importance of emotions to this activity. Asking critical questions about our previously accepted values, ideas, and behaviors is anxiety-producing. We may well feel fearful of the consequences that might arise from contemplating alternatives to our current ways of thinking and living; resistance, resentment, and confusion are evident at various stages in the critical thinking process. But we also feel joy, release, relief, and exhilaration as we break through to new ways of looking at our personal, work, and political worlds. As we abandon assumptions that had been inhibiting our development, we experience a sense of liberation. As we realize that we have the power to change aspects of our lives, we are changed with excitement. As we realize these changes, we feel a pleasing sense of self-confidence. Critical thinkers and helpers ignore these emotions at their peril.

Components of Critical Thinking

1. *Identifying and challenging assumptions is central to critical thinking.* Trying to identify the assumptions that underlie the ideas, beliefs, values, and actions that we (and others) take for granted is central to critical thinking. Once these assumptions are identified critical thinkers examine their accuracy and validity. They ask awkward questions concerning whether the taken-for-granted,

common-sense ideas about how we are supposed to organize our workplaces, act in our intimate relationships, become politically involved, and view television fit the realities of our lives. They are open to jettisoning old assumptions when these are clearly inappropriate (for example, "Workers are there to work, not to think"; "Decisions made by executive directors, parents, and presidents are infallible and inviolable"; "Women should be kept barefoot and pregnant") and to search for new assumptions that fit more closely their experiences of the world.

2. *Challenging the importance of context is crucial to critical thinking.* When we are aware of how hidden and uncritically assimilated assumptions are important to shaping our habitual perceptions, understandings, and interpretations of the world, and to influencing the behaviors that result from these interpretations, we become aware of how context influences thoughts and actions. Critical thinkers are aware that practices, structures, and actions are never context-free. What we regard as appropriate ways of organizing the workplace, of behaving toward our intimates, of acting politically, and of viewing television reflect the culture and time in which we live. In realizing this, critical thinkers are contextually aware.

3. *Critical thinkers try to imagine and explore alternatives.* Central to critical thinking is the capacity to imagine and explore alternatives to existing ways of thinking and living. Realizing that so many ideas and actions spring from assumptions that might be inappropriate for their lives, critical thinkers are continually exploring new ways of thinking about aspects of their lives. Being aware of how context shapes what they consider normal and natural ways of thinking and living, critical thinkers realize that in other contexts entirely different norms of organizing the workplace, behaving politically, interpreting media, and living in relationships are considered ordinary. These contexts are scrutinized for assumptions that might be adopted and integrated into their own lives

4. *Imagining and exploring alternatives leads to reflective skepticism.* When we realize that alternatives to supposedly fixed belief systems, habitual behaviors, and entrenched social structures always exist, we become skeptical of claims to universal truth or to ultimate explanations. In short, we exhibit what might be called reflective skepticism. People who are reflectively skeptical do not take things as read. Simply because a practice or structure has existed for a long time does not mean that it is the most appropriate for all time, or even for this moment. Just because an idea is accepted by everyone else does not mean that we have to believe in its innate truth without first checking its correspondence with reality as we experience it. Just because a chief executive officer, executive director, prime minister, president, religious leader, or parent says something is right or good does not make it so. Critical thinkers become immediately suspicious of those who say they have the answers to all of life's problems. They are wary of the management consultant who argues that "if only you will buy my training package and follow these steps to executive development, your executives will double the company's output in the next fiscal quarter." They distrust the educator who purports to have a curriculum or model of teaching appropriate for all learners or subjects. They scrutinize carefully the therapist or counselor who argues that he or she has discovered the key to resolving difficulties within intimate relationships.

How Others Contribute to Critical Thinking

On a very personal level, practically all adults function in some way as critical thinkers. At some time or another, most people decide that some aspect of their lives is unsatisfactory, and decide of their own volition to change this. Such self changes are often (though not always) connected to externally imposed crises. Being fired or suffering crippling mental or physical disability is not something we choose to happen. When an intimate relationship dissolves, or a loved one dies, several reactions are possible. We may be thrown into an apathetic resignation to these changed circumstances, or we may deny this disappearance of a previously stable element in our life. We may well fluctuate between periods of acceptance of, and flight from, these changes. Energy alternates with apathy as we first scramble to deny or forget the changes forced upon us, and then become aware of their overwhelming reality. The rollercoaster turbulence of these changes is tiring and debilitating, and we describe ourselves as exhausted, burned out, or finished.

As people try to make sense of these externally imposed changes, they are frequently at teachable moments as far as the process of becoming critical thinkers is concerned. As people begin to look critically at their past values, common-sense ideas, and habitual behaviors, they begin the precarious business of contemplating new self perspectives, and actions. Skilled helpers can support these first tentative stages in critical thought by listening empathetically to people's "travelers' tales" of their journeys into unexplored personal and political territories. Helpers act as sounding boards, providing reactions to people's experiences, pleasures, and anxieties. They help to make connections between apparently disparate occurrences and assist people in reflecting on the reasons for their actions and reactions. They encourage people to identify the assumptions under lying their behaviors, choices, and decisions. They help clients, learners, friends, and colleagues to recognize aspects of their situations that are of their own making and hence open to being changed by an act of will. They encourage skepticism of anyone claiming to have "the answer." They help people to realize that while actions are shaped by context, context can be altered to be more congruent with people's desires.

When helpers and educators work in these ways, they are encouraging critical thinking. Critical thinking is complex and frequently perplexing, since it requires the suspension of belief and the jettisoning of assumptions previously accepted without question. As people strive for clarity in self-understanding, and as they try to change aspects of' their lives, the opportunity to discuss these activities is enormously helpful. By providing an opportunity for reflection and analysis, educators and other helpers, such as counselors, therapists, trainers, and friends, are crucial. They are sympathizers, empathizers, reactors, devil's advocates, initiators, and prompters. They help people to articulate and understand the assumptions underlying their actions. In short, they assist people to become critical thinkers.

Concepts of Critical Thinking

Phrases such as critical thinking, critical analysis, critical awareness, critical consciousness, and critical rejection are exhortatory, heady, and often conveniently vague. We can justify almost any action with a learner, client, friend, or colleague by claiming that it assists the process of critical thinking. Haranguing a friend who feels satisfied with life, forcing a learner to view things the way we do, and requiring that lovers reevaluate their relationship or that colleagues change their work patterns may all be claimed (inaccurately) as examples of facilitating critical thinking. Central to developing critical thinkers must be some minimal level of consent on the part of those involved. Trying to force people to analyze critically the assumptions under which they have been thinking and living is likely to serve no function other than intimidating them to the point where resistance builds up against this process. We can, however, try to awaken, prompt, nurture, and encourage this process without making people feel threatened or patronized. These are the skills of critical helpers.

As a concept, critical thinking has been interpreted in a variety of ways. It has been equated with the development of logical reasoning abilities (Hallet, 1984; Ruggiero, 1975), with the application of reflective judgment (Kitchener, 1986), with assumption hunting (Scriven, 1976), and with the creation, use, and testing of meaning (Hullfish and Smith, 1961). Ennis (1962) lists twelve aspects of critical thinking, which include analytical and argumentative capacities such as recognizing ambiguity in reasoning, identifying contradictions in arguments, and ascertaining the empirical soundness of generalized conclusions. D'Angelo (1971) specifies ten attitudes that are necessary conditions for being critical, including curiosity, flexibility, skepticism, and honesty. As the central component of critical thinking, O'Neill (2985) proposes the ability to distinguish bias from reason and fact from opinion. To Halpern (1984), critical thought is a rational and purposeful attempt to use thought in moving toward a future goal.

Critical thinking is generally conceptualized as an intellectual ability suitable for development by those involved in higher education (Drake, 1976; Young, 1980; Meyers, 1986; Stice, 1987). Empirical studies of the development of critical thinking capacities focus on young adults (Kitchener, 1986; King, Kitchener, and Wood, 1985) or college students (Perry, 1970, 1981). While this setting for critical thinking is undoubtedly crucial, it is but one of the many settings in which critical thinking is practiced, particularly in adult life. The concepts of critical thinking, analysis, and reflection need to be taken out of the classroom and placed firmly in the contexts of adults' lives—in their relationships, at their workplaces, in their political involvements, and in their reactions to mass media of communication. Critical thinking is not seen as a wholly rational, mechanical activity. Emotive aspects—feelings, emotional responses, intuitions, sensing—are central to critical thinking in adult life. In particular, the ability to imagine alternatives to one's current ways of thinking and living is one that often entails a deliberate break with rational modes of thought in order to prompt forward leaps in creativity.

One alternative interpretation of the concept of critical thinking is that of *emancipatory learning*. The idea of emancipatory learning is derived from the work of Habermas (1979), who distinguished this as one of the three domains of learning (technical and communicative learning being the other two). As interpreted by adult educators (Collins, 1985; Hart, 1985; Apps, 1985), emancipatory learning is evident in learners becoming aware of the forces that have brought them to their current situations and taking action to change some aspect of these situations. To Apps (1985, P. 151), "emancipatory learning is that which frees people from personal, institutional, or environmental forces that prevent them from seeing new directions, from gaining control of their lives, their society and their world."

A second concept closely related to that of critical thinking is *dialectical thinking*. Dialectical thinking is viewed as a particular form of critical thinking that focuses on the understanding and resolution of contradictions. Morgan (1986, p. 266) writes that "dialectical analysis (thus) shows us that the management of organization, of society, and of personal life ultimately involves the management of contradiction."

As proposed by Riegel (1973) and Basseches (1984), dialectical thinking is thinking in which elements of relativistic thought (for example, "Morality can be understood only in the context of the culture concerned") are fused with elements of universalistic thought (for example, "Moral conduct is recognizable in any society by certain innate features"). Dialectical thinkers engage in a continual process of making judgments about aspects of their lives, identifying the general rules implicit in these judgments, modifying the original judgments in light of the appropriateness of these general rules, and so on. To Deshler (1985, p. 6), "dialectical thinking is thinking which looks for, recognizes, and welcomes contradictions as a stimulus to development." Change is regarded as the fundamental reality, forms and structures are perceived as temporary, relationships are held to involve developmental transformations, and openness is welcomed. Hence, we are involved in a constant process of trying to create order in the world—to discover what elements are missing from our existing ordering and to create new orderings that include these. Daloz (1986, p. 141) echoes this idea in his belief that dialectical thinking "presumes change rather than a static notion of 'reality.' As each assertion is derived from the one before, truth is always emergent, never fixed; relative, not absolute."

Being a critical thinker involves more than cognitive activities such as logical reasoning or scrutinizing arguments for assertions unsupported by empirical evidence. Thinking critically involves our recognizing the assumptions underlying our beliefs and behaviors. It means we can give justifications for our ideas and actions. Most important, perhaps, it means we try to judge the rationality of these justifications. We can do this by comparing them to a range of varying interpretations and perspectives. We can think through, project, and anticipate the consequences of those actions that are based on these justifications. And we can test the accuracy and rationality of these justifications against some kind of objective analysis of the "real" world as we understand it.

Critical thinking, then, involves a reflective dimension. The idea of *reflective learning* is a third concept closely related to that of critical thinking. Boyd and Fales (1983, p. 100) define reflective learning as "the process of internally examining and exploring an issue of concern, triggered by an experience, which creates and clarifies meaning in terms of self, and which results in a changed conceptual perspective." Boud, Keogh, and Walker (1985, p. 3) view reflection as "a generic term for those intellectual and affective activities in which individuals engage to explore their experiences in order to lead to new understandings and appreciation." To Schlossberg (1981, p. 5), the outcome of these activities is "a change in assumptions about oneself and the world" requiring "a corresponding change in one's behavior and relationship."

Conclusion

Critical thinking is a lived activity, not an abstract academic pastime. It is something we all do, though its frequency, and the credibility we grant it, vary from person to person. Our lives are sufficiently complex and perplexing that it would be difficult to escape entirely from feeling that at times the world is not working the way we thought it was supposed to, or that there must be other ways of living. Critical thinking is at the heart of what it means to be a developed person living in a democratic society. The ability to think critically is crucial to understanding our personal relationships, envisioning alternative and more productive ways of organizing the workplace, and becoming politically literate.

Lesson

4 *Talents and Strengths*

Start to gain insight into the aptitudes we bring to the table as individuals, how they can be refined, and how they can be augmented by others with different aptitudes

READING 1

Reprinted from Clifton, D. O., Anderson, E., & Schreiner, L. A. (2006). *StrengthsQuest: Discover and Develop Your Strengths in Academics, Career, and Beyond*. New York, NY: Gallup Press.

At the 1996 Olympic Games in Atlanta, Kerri Strug was a gymnast on the United States women's gold-medal team. Her performance on the vault, as she nursed an injured ankle, remains one of the most memorable in Olympic history.

With 32,000 people in the Georgia Dome and millions watching her on television, Kerri fell on her first attempt at her most difficult twisting vault, severely spraining her left ankle. With less than a minute between vaults, and in great pain, she again attempted the vault, further injuring her ankle — but this time successfully landing on both feet. So she stood erect on one foot, raising both hands to salute the judges, then collapsed to her knees.

The crowd went wild. Kerri's vault earned a 9.712, and the U.S. women won the gold medal.

During that same year, Kerri was a freshman at UCLA. One of her classes required a research paper similar to a mini-doctoral dissertation. Students had to formulate their own research question and develop a questionnaire that was consistent with their research question. Then, the students would administer the questionnaire, collect and analyze the data, draw conclusions, and write a report that described the process. The written report was to be 35-40 pages long.

Taking the Clifton StrengthsFinder assessment was one of the class requirements. When Kerri took it, she scored extremely high in the Focus theme. But doesn't that make sense? Who else but a person with tremendous Focus talents could concentrate on completing her most difficult vault on an injured ankle in front of 32,000 screaming fans while Olympic gold hung in the balance? Who else could block out all of those distractions and then land on one foot without falling?

While Kerri certainly had other talents that enabled her to succeed, her Focus talents played a critical role. Without them, she might never have enjoyed such stunning Olympic success.

But there's more to the story. Toward the end of the fall term, as research papers were coming due, Kerri turned her paper in three days early, before any of the other 300-plus UCLA students in the class. She did this while traveling nearly every weekend on a national tour with fellow Olympic medalists. Even more remarkable was the way that Kerri could go out on an arena floor, do a routine, and then go underneath the stands and work on the paper. She would then go back out on the floor and do another routine and return to do more homework.

You see, Kerri also applied her Focus talents to succeed in academics.

Kerri is a remarkable young woman. But the excellence she achieved wasn't due simply to the fact that she naturally possessed talents. She recognized her Focus talents and built on them by adding skills and knowledge to create strength — the ability to produce consistent, near-perfect performance. She obviously did so at the Olympics — even while in severe pain and under tremendous pressure — but she was also able to apply her Focus in academics, where she achieved despite rigorous assignments and the myriad pressures of her athletic career.

Kerri has presented each of us with more than a shared pride in her Olympic success. We can learn from her. You, too, have talents. And in those talents you have the ability to meet challenges and achieve just as surely as Kerri did.

The Basics of Strengths

Talent: The Beginning of Strength

What is a strength? That's a good question, but strength begins with talent, so let's start there. A talent is a naturally recurring pattern of thought, feeling, or behavior that can be productively applied. A great number of talents naturally exist within you, and each of them is very specific. They are among the most real and most authentic aspects of your personhood. Your specific set of talents is a major part of what makes you a unique person, and that uniqueness holds great value for you and those around you. And your talents work in various combinations each time you do something very well, in your own unique way.

There is a direct connection between your talents and your achievements. Your talents empower you. They make it possible for you to move to higher levels of excellence and fulfill your potential. This is why it is so important for you to know, understand, and value your talents.

A talent represents a capacity to *do* something. In fact, when you are able to do something very well, you can be sure that at least one of your talents is involved. Just think about all the things you do very well. You'll realize that you have many talents!

And talents help you do something well not just once; they help you do it well over and over again. Because talents are naturally recurring patterns, they are "automatic," almost like breathing, so they repeatedly help you achieve.

That's not all, either. Each of your many talents can enable you to do more than one thing very well. We're not saying that each of your talents enables you to do *everything* very well, but know that each of them can be applied to multiple areas of achievement.

The great value in your talents is not merely that they help you achieve, but that they help you achieve at levels of *excellence*. Your greatest talents are inextricably linked to your top achievements and to what you do best. Your talents make you exceptional. Therefore, coming to know, understand, and value your talents is directly linked to achieving in classes, careers, and throughout your life.

Talent Versus Other Concepts of Ability

The concept of talent is more specific in terms of the quality it describes and the things that various types of talent help a person to do very well. Traditional concepts and measures of ability (for example, I.Q. and aptitude testing) are more global and are not designed to explain what a person can specifically do.

The concept of talent also goes beyond the limits of traditional concepts of academic abilities (for example, in the areas of reading, math, and composition) in that it also addresses the qualities that help a person achieve in all aspects of life.

The 34 Themes of Talent Measured by the Clifton StrengthsFinder

What is a theme? Essentially, it's is a group of similar talents.

Kerri Strug once again provides a good illustration. Kerri used a wide variety of talents in the Focus theme to achieve in athletics and academics. Among them was her talent for focusing on the precise steps required to perform complicated gymnastic maneuvers, and, during the intense pressure of the Olympics, her talent for blocking out the distraction of intense pain to produce a gold-medal performance.

Kerri used other types of talents, too. Her talents in the Adaptability theme enabled her to achieve excellence in athletics and academics at the same time. Her talent to balance two extremely high priorities, easily moving from one to the other, was crucial to her success in each area.

As a result of studying top achievers for more than three decades,

Gallup was able to identify more than 400 themes of talent. The 34 most prevalent themes are measured by StrengthsFinder.

Back to Your Question: What Is a Strength?

Now, let's go to the definition of a strength: A strength is the ability to provide consistent, near-perfect performance in a given activity.

As you read earlier, the concept of strengths begins with talent. Each person naturally has a group of talents. Talents are like "diamonds in the rough," whereas strengths are like diamonds that show brilliance after they have been carefully cut and polished.

Your greatest areas of talent, your most likely sources of potential strengths, are identified by StrengthsFinder.

Just as finished diamonds start as diamonds in the rough, strengths begin with talents. And just as rough diamonds are naturally found in the earth, talents are naturally found within you. But while diamonds are refined with blades and polishing wheels, strengths are produced when talents are refined with *knowledge* and *skill*.

Unlike talent, which must naturally exist within you, skills and knowledge can be acquired. Skills are the basic ability to perform the specific steps of an activity. Knowledge consists of facts and lessons learned.

Many of the skills and much of the knowledge that are combined with talent to create a strength come through experience, and sometimes a great deal of it. Skills and knowledge are also developed in a "book learning" sense, such as in the academic arenas of high school, college, technical school, and training classes.

When you have supplemented your greatest talents with knowledge and skill to the point at which you can provide consistent, near-perfect performance in a given activity, you have a strength. And in applying and even further refining your strengths, you move closer and closer to fulfilling your natural potential as an individual.

Each person has a unique and profound set and combination of talents that are developed and used to different degrees. This combination of talents makes each person like no other.

While each person defines success for himself or herself, achievement and excellence result from fully developing and applying strengths. Some roles require several strengths, all working together, to produce excellence.

You probably already have some strengths, and you certainly will have plenty of opportunity to develop more strengths throughout your lifetime.

What Do Strengths Produce?

As you develop strengths by building on your greatest talents, achievements will naturally follow. But there is also a great sense of personal satisfaction that results from knowing that you are becoming more and more of whom you have the potential to be. In a sense, the development and application of strengths generate a feeling that you are fulfilling your personal destiny. This can produce enormous satisfaction and enhance the quality of your life.

While the experiences of individual people differ tremendously, most report that it is a rewarding experience to be fully living in tune with their natural talents by building and using strengths. Almost everyone says increased confidence and optimism as they become aware of, affirm, and celebrate their talents. Many describe the experience as "coming alive," or even feeling joy as they develop and apply strengths. Reports about the exact inner experiences may differ, but nearly everyone who develops and uses strengths reports a sense of positive and pleasant psychological rewards.

Our initial goal is for you to become more aware of your talents and your potential strengths. We hope you are filled with appreciation for your particular talents, for the positive differences they have already made in your life, and for the excellence strengths can produce in your future achievements, relationships, and other life experiences.

Findings From Gallup's Study of the Best

Here is what Gallup knows about top achievers: *They fully recognize their talents and build on them to develop strengths.* In contrast, underachieves, the merely average, and even above-average achievers often fail to recognize their powerful talents and develop strengths. But the best achievers are certain to do so.

Top achievers apply their greatest talents in roles that best suit them. Clearly, to achieve, one must apply his or her abilities, and many do so to some level of success. But the best apply their most naturally powerful talents and do so in roles that are best suited to those talents. The ability to achieve with excellence in one area is not proof of the ability to perform equally well in another area. A proper "fit" between an individuals talents and the task at hand is essential.

Top achievers invent ways to apply their greatest talents to their achievement tasks. Every role, position, and career entails a group of tasks that must be completed, and quite often the person who performs them must consciously seek, even invent, ways to apply his or her talents to that end — even when one's role is well suited to his or her talents.

Your Strengths Quest Begins With You

As described earlier, the seeds of your personal greatness — your talents — are already in you. Therefore, your strengths quest — your quest to achieve excellence and become all you can be through your own natural talents — is really a quest to discover, develop, and apply who you truly are. Your strengths quest begins as you look within yourself as an individual to recognize your own natural talents.

Your quest will then continue as you build on your talents to develop strengths — abilities to provide consistent, near-perfect performances in specific activities.

As you do this, your self-identity and personal values should become clearer, and as a result, you will likely become more confident, optimistic, and focused. As you achieve through your greatest talents, you will likely aspire to higher goals.

Your strengths quest is a lifelong adventure. Each of the three aspects — discovery, development, and application — will continue throughout your life. This exciting and fulfilling process should bring you a lifetime of great satisfaction and joy.

· · ·

You have taken the Clifton StrengthsFinder, received your Signature Themes report, and discussed your Signature Themes with three people who know you very well. Now, it's time for you to affirm the Signature Themes indicated by your StrengthsFinder responses.

Affirming a Signature Theme simply means that you *agree* that it is one of your dominant areas of talent. It also means being able to see how your talent in that theme enables you to do certain things very well. Affirming your Signature Themes may seem easy, but many people experience some difficulty in doing so. Listed below are some of those difficulties and the reasons for them.

Difficulties in Affirming Our Signature Themes

1. *Many people are blind to their own greatest talents, and often to the greatest talents of others.* Some of our talents are called upon so frequently that we take them for granted. We don't consider them special, and we don't even perceive them as talents. Consequently, our Signature Themes may not seem important, valuable, or even special to us.
2. *Our talents sometimes threaten others. Rather than admit their insecurity, some people criticize us for having talents they wish they had.* As a result, we might mistakenly come to think that our Signature Themes hold weaknesses rather than talents.
3. *In some cases, we end up in positions or roles that simply don't fit our dominant talents.* Or, those talents may conflict with the roles and expectations of the positions we are in. This can make us feel like there is something wrong with us. But the problem may only be a mismatch between our dominant talents and the expectations of a role we are in.
4. *The fear of becoming proud and arrogant may interfere with seeing and affirming our Signature Themes.* In reality, pride and arrogance often stem from feelings of inadequacy. Affirming our dominant areas of talent usually results in humble gratitude for having been blessed with them.
5. *Some people have difficulty affirming their Signature Themes because they don't see how the talents in them will help them achieve their goals.* If that is the case, they will benefit from a better understanding of their talents. Talents are always valuable, and they can often be applied toward achievement in less obvious, or even surprising, ways.

Questions You Might Be Asking

If a Particular Theme Is Not Among Your Signature Themes, Is It Necessarily an Area of Weakness?

No. The Clifton StrengthsFinder *does not* simultaneously measure weakness and talent. StrengthsFinder measures talent, and that's all it does. So, if a particular theme is not among your Signature Themes, it simply means that at least five other themes are more dominant in you. For example, your Responsibility theme might not be among your Signature Themes. That doesn't mean you are irresponsible. It just means that your overall talents in at least five other themes are more dominant than those in your Responsibility theme.

By focusing on your Signature Themes, you will concentrate your attention on where you have the greatest potential for achieving excellence and personal fulfillment. Focusing on any other area may serve as nothing more than a distraction.

What If You Believe You Have Dominant Talent in a Theme That Was Not Identified as a Signature Theme?

Our response is simple and direct: Claim it! Affirm and celebrate your talents in that theme, then build on them to fully develop and apply strengths. Just remember that we limited your Signature Themes to five because focusing on your *most* dominant areas of talent will provide the greatest opportunities for achievement.

Is Having Talent Always a Positive Experience?

Talent is always positive in the sense that it enables a person to do certain things very well. Your talents always hold potential for positive results in terms of achievements, success, personal fulfillment, and a better quality of life.

At the same time, talents place demands on the people who have them. And from that standpoint, talents can present a bit of a challenge.

Some people honestly say that they wish that their talents weren't so powerful in certain themes because they make their lives more demanding. They simply may experience more pressure because other people place higher expectations on them to achieve.

READING 2

"What Makes a Great Leadership Team," by Tom Rath and Barry Conchie, reprinted by permission from *Gallup Business Journal* (2009).

"What Makes a Great Leadership Team?" Rath & Conchie. Gallup Management Journal

Over the years, Gallup has studied thousands of executive teams. In most cases, our leadership consultants conduct an in-depth interview with a team's formal leader (usually the CEO) and also conduct interviews with each member of the leadership team. This enables us to compare the strengths of each person sitting around the table so that we can start thinking about each one's individual development and succession planning–and perhaps most importantly, how the team looks as a whole.

As we worked with these leadership teams, we began to see that while each member had his or her own unique strengths, the most cohesive and successful teams possessed broader groupings of strengths. So we went back and initiated our most thorough review of this research to date. From this dataset, four distinct domains of leadership strength emerged: Executing, Influencing, Relationship Building, and Strategic Thinking.

While these categories appear to be general, especially when compared to the specific talent themes within the StrengthsFinder assessment, it struck us that these broader categories of strengths could be useful for thinking about how leaders can contribute to a team. A more detailed language may work best for individual development, but these broad domains offer a more practical lens for looking at the composition of a team.

We found that it serves a team well to have a representation of strengths in each of these four domains. Instead of one dominant leader who tries to do everything or individuals who all have similar strengths, contributions from all four domains lead to a strong and cohesive team. *Although individuals need not be well-rounded, teams should be.*

TABLE 4.1 The Four Domains of Leadership Strength

EXECUTING	INFLUENCING	RELATIONSHIP BUILDING	STRATEGIC THINKING
Achiever	Activator	Adaptability	Analytical
Arranger	Command	Developer	Context
Belief	Communication	Connectedness	Futuristic
Consistency	Competition	Empathy	Ideation
Deliberative	Maximizer	Harmony	Input
Discipline	Self-Assurance	Includer	Intellection
Focus	Significance	Individualization	Learner
Responsibility	Woo	Positivity	Strategic
Restorative		Relator	

This doesn't mean that each person on a team must have strengths exclusively in a single category. In most cases, each team member will possess some strength in multiple domains. A tool like Gallup's StrengthsFinder assessment can be useful in determining how all team members can maximize their contribution to the group's collective goals.

According to our latest research, the 34 StrengthsFinder themes naturally cluster into these four domains of leadership strength based on a statistical factor analysis and a clinical evaluation by Gallup's top scientists. As you think about how you can contribute to a team and who you need to surround yourself with, this may be a good starting point. (See graphic "The Four Domains of Leadership Strength" to see how the 34 StrengthsFinder themes sort into the four domains of leadership strength.)

Explaining the Four Domains

Leaders with dominant strength in the **Executing** domain know how to make things happen. When you need someone to implement a solution, these are the people who will work tirelessly to get it done. Leaders with a strength to execute have the ability to "catch" an idea and make it a reality.

For example, one leader may excel at establishing a quality process using themes such as Deliberative or Discipline, while the next leader will use her Achiever theme to work tirelessly toward a goal. Or a leader with strong Arranger may determine the optimal configuration of people needed to complete a task.

Those who lead by **Influencing** help their team reach a much broader audience. People with strength in this domain are always selling the team's ideas inside and outside the organization. When you need someone to take charge, speak up, and make sure your group is heard, look to someone with the strength to influence.

For example, a leader with a lot of Command or Self-Assurance may use few words, but her confidence will continue to project authority and win followers. In contrast, a leader using Communication or Woo might get people involved by helping individuals feel comfortable and connected to the issue at hand.

Those who lead through **Relationship Building** are the essential glue that holds a team together. Without these strengths on a team, in many cases, the group is simply a composite of individuals. In contrast, leaders with exceptional Relationship Building strength have the unique ability to create groups and organizations that are much greater than the sum of their parts.

Within this domain, a leader with Positivity and Harmony may work hard to minimize distractions and to keep the team's collective energy high. On the other hand, a leader with Individualization might use a more targeted approach to getting people involved. Or a leader with strong Relator or Developer may be a great mentor and guide as he pushes others toward bigger and better achievements.

Leaders with great **Strategic Thinking** strengths are the ones who keep us all focused on what *could be*. They are constantly absorbing and analyzing information and helping the team make better decisions. People with strength in this domain continually stretch our thinking for the future.

Within this domain, a leader using Context or Strategic might explain how past events influenced present circumstances or navigate the best route for future possibilities. Someone with strong Ideation or Input may see countless opportunities for growth based on all of the information she reviews. Or a leader drawing from his Analytical theme might help the team drill into the details of cause and effect.

In recent years, we have studied leaders who built great schools, created major nonprofit organizations, led big businesses, and transformed entire nations. But we have yet to find two leaders who have the exact same sequence of strengths. While two leaders may have identical expectations, the way they reach their goals is always dependent on the unique arrangement of their strengths.

READING 3

"Leadership: Do Traits Matter?" Kirkpatrick & Locke. *Academy of Management* Executive 5 (1991): 48-60. From "The Leader's Companion" Wren. The Free Press

Shelley A. Kirkpatrick received her Ph.D. in organizational behavior from the University of Maryland and has taught at Carnegie Mellon University and American University. She co-authored (with Edwin A. Locke, among others) the book *The Essence of Leadership*. Currently she is associated with Pelavin Research Institute. Edwin Locke is chairman of the Department of Management and Organizations at the University of Maryland's College of Business and Management. He has written over 140 books, chapters, and articles including (with Gary P. Latham) *A Theory of Goal Setting and Task Performance*.

Few issues have a more controversial history than leadership traits and characteristics. In the 19th and early 20th centuries, "great man" leadership theories were highly popular. These theories asserted that leadership qualities were inherited, especially by people from the upper class. Great men were born not made (in those days, virtually all business leaders were men). Today, great man theories are a popular foil for so-called superior models. To make the new models plausible, the "great men" are endowed with negative as well as positive traits. In a recent issue of the *Harvard Business Review,* for example, Slater and Bennis write,

> The passing years have . . . given the coup de grace to another force that has retarded democratization—the 'great man' who with brilliance and farsightedness could preside with dictatorial powers as the head of a growing organization.

Such great men, argue Slater and Bennis, become "outmoded" and dead hands on "the flexibility and growth of the organization." Under the new democratic model, they argue, "the individual *is* of relatively little significance."

Early in the 20th century, the great man theories evolved into trait theories. ("Trait" is used broadly here to refer to people's general characteristics, including capacities, motives, or patterns of behavior.) Trait theories did not make assumptions about whether leadership traits were inherited or acquired. They simply asserted that leaders' characteristics are different from non-leaders. Traits such as height, weight, and physique are heavily dependent on heredity, whereas others such as knowledge of the industry are dependent on experience and learning.

The trait view was brought into question during the mid-century when a prominent theorist, Ralph Stogdill, after a thorough review of the literature concluded that "A person does not become a leader by virtue of the possession of some combination of traits." Stogdill believed this because the research showed that no traits were universally associated with effective leadership and that situational factors were also influential. For example, military leaders do not have traits identical to those of business leaders.

Since Stogdill's early review, trait theory has made a comeback, though in altered form. Recent research, using a variety of methods, has made it clear that successful leaders are not like other people. The evidence indicates that there are certain core traits which significantly contribute to business leaders' success.

Traits alone, however, are not sufficient for successful business leadership—they are only a precondition. Leaders who possess the requisite traits must take certain actions to be successful (e.g. formulating a vision, role modeling, setting goals). Possessing the appropriate traits only makes it more likely that such actions will be taken and be successful. After summarizing the core leadership traits, we will discuss these important actions and the managerial implications.

The Evidence: Traits Do Matter

The evidence shows that traits do matter. Six traits on which leaders differ from nonleaders include: drive, the desire to lead, honesty/integrity, self-confidence, cognitive ability, and knowledge of the business.

Drive

The first trait is labeled "drive" which is not to be confused with physical need deprivation. We use the term to refer to a constellation of traits and motives reflecting a high effort level. Five aspects of drive include achievement motivation, ambition, energy, tenacity, and initiative.

Achievement. Leaders have a relatively high desire for achievement. The need for achievement is an important motive among effective leaders and even more important among successful entrepreneurs. High achievers obtain satisfaction from successfully completing challenging tasks, attaining standards of excellence, and developing better ways of doing things. To work their way up to the top of the organization, leaders must have a desire to complete challenging assignments and projects. This also allows the leader to gain technical expertise, both through education and work experience, and to initiate and follow through with organizational changes. . . .

Ambition. Leaders are very ambitious about their work and careers and have a desire to get ahead. To advance, leaders actively take steps to demonstrate their drive and determination. Ambition impels leaders to set hard, challenging goals for themselves and their organizations. Walt Disney, founder of Walt Disney Productions, had a "dogged determination to succeed" and C.E. Woolman of Delta Air Lines had "inexhaustible ambition."

Effective leaders are more ambitious than nonleaders. In their 20-year study, psychologists Ann Howard and Douglas Bray found that among a sample of managers at AT&T, ambition, specifically the desire for advancement, was the strongest predictor of success twenty years later. . . .

Energy. To sustain a high achievement drive and get ahead, leaders must have a lot of energy. Working long, intense work weeks (and many weekends) for many years, requires an individual to have physical, mental, and emotional vitality. Leaders are more likely than nonleaders to have a high level of energy and stamina and to be generally active, lively, and often restless. Leaders have been characterized as "electric, vigorous, active, full of life" as well as possessing the "physical vitality to maintain a steadily productive work pace." . . . The need for energy is even greater today than in the past, because more companies are expecting all employees, including executives, to spend more time on the road visiting the organization's other locations, customers, and suppliers.

Tenacity. Leaders are better at overcoming obstacles than nonleaders. They have the "capacity to work with distant objects in view" and have a "degree of strength of will or perseverance." Leaders must be tirelessly persistent in their activities and follow through with their programs. Most organizational change programs take several months to establish and can take many years before the benefits are seen. Leaders must have the drive to stick with these programs, and persistence is needed to ensure that changes are institutionalized. . . . It is not just the direction of action that counts, but sticking to the direction chosen. Effective leaders must keep pushing themselves and others toward the goal. . . .

Persistence, of course, must be used intelligently. Dogged pursuit of an inappropriate strategy can ruin an organization. It is important to persist in the right things. But what are the right things? In today's business climate, they may include the following: satisfying the customer, growth, cost control, innovation, fast response time, and quality. Or, in Tom Peters' terms, a constant striving to improve just about everything.

Initiative. Effective leaders are proactive. They make choices and take action that leads to change instead of just reacting to events or waiting for things to happen; that is, they show a high level of initiative. . . .

Instead of sitting "idly by or [waiting] for fate to smile upon them," leaders need to "challenge the process."

Leaders are achievement-oriented, ambitious, energetic, tenacious, and proactive. These same qualities, however, may result in a manager who tries to accomplish everything alone, thereby failing to develop subordinate commitment and responsibility. Effective leaders must not only be full of drive and ambition, they must *want to lead others*.

Leadership Motivation

Studies show that leaders have a strong desire to lead. Leadership motivation involves the desire to influence and lead others and is often equated with the need for power. People with high leadership motivation think a lot about influencing other people, winning an argument, or being the greater authority. They prefer to be in a leadership rather than subordinate role. The willingness to assume responsibility, which seems to coincide with leadership motivation, is frequently found in leaders.

Sears psychologist Jon Bentz describes successful Sears executives as those who have a "powerful competitive drive for a position of . . . authority . . . [and] the need to be recognized as men of influence." . . .

Psychologist Warren Bennis and colleague Burt Nanus state that power is a leader's currency, or the primary means through which the leader gets things done in the organization. A leader must want to gain the power to exercise influence over others. Also, power is an "expandable pie," not a fixed sum; effective leaders give power to others as a means of increasing their own power. Effective leaders do not see power as something that is competed for but rather as something that can be created and distributed to followers without detracting from their own power. . . .

Successful leaders must be willing to exercise power over subordinates, tell them what to do and make appropriate use of positive and negative sanctions. Previous studies have shown inconsistent results regarding dominance as a leadership trait. According to Harvard psychologist David McClelland, this may be because there are two different types of dominance: a personalized power motive or power lust, and a socialized power motive, or the desire to lead.

Personalized Power Motive. Although a need for power is desirable, the leader's effectiveness depends on what is behind it. A leader with a personalized power motive seeks power as an end in itself. These individuals have little self-control, are often impulsive, and focus on collecting symbols of personal prestige. Acquiring power solely for the sake of dominating others may be based on profound self-doubt. The personalized power motive is concerned with domination of others and leads to dependent, submissive followers.

Socialized Power Motive. In contrast, a leader with a socialized power motive uses power as a means to achieve desired goals, or a vision. Its use is expressed as the ability to develop networks and coalitions, gain cooperation from others, resolve conflicts in a constructive manner, and use role modeling to influence others.

Individuals with a socialized power motive are more emotionally mature than those with a personalized power motive. They exercise power more for the benefit of the whole organization and are less likely to use it for manipulation. These leaders are also less defensive, more willing to take advice from experts, and have a longer-range view. They use their power to build up their organization and make it successful. The socialized power motive takes account of followers' needs and results in empowered, independent followers.

Honesty and Integrity

Honesty and integrity are virtues in all individuals, but have special significance for leaders. Without these qualities, leadership is undermined. Integrity is the correspondence between word and deed and honesty refers to being truthful or non-deceitful. The two form the foundation of a trusting relationship between leader and followers.

In his comprehensive review of leadership, psychologist Bernard Bass found that student leaders were rated as more trustworthy and reliable in carrying out responsibilities than followers. Similarly, British organizational psychologists Charles Cox and Cary Cooper's "high flying" (successful) managers preferred to have an open style of management, where they truthfully informed workers about happenings in the company. Morgan McCall and Michael Lombardo of the Center for Creative Leadership found that managers who reached the top were more likely to follow the following formula: "I will do exactly what I say I will do when I say I will do it. If I change my mind, I will tell you well in advance so you will not be harmed by my actions."

Successful leaders are open with their followers, but also discreet and do not violate confidences or carelessly divulge potentially harmful information. One subordinate in a study by Harvard's John Gabarro made the following remark about his new president: "He was so consistent in what he said and did, it was easy to trust him." Another subordinate remarked about an unsuccessful leader, "How can I rely on him if I can't count on him consistently?"

Professors James Kouzes, Barry Posner, and W.H. Schmidt asked 1500 managers "What values do you look for and admire in your superiors?" Integrity (being truthful and trustworthy, and having character and conviction) was the most frequently mentioned characteristic. Kouzes and Posner conclude:

"Honesty is absolutely essential to leadership. After all, if we are willing to follow someone whether it be into battle or into the boardroom, we first want to assure ourselves that the person is worthy of our trust. We want to know that he or she is being truthful, ethical, and principled. We want to be fully confident in the integrity of our leaders."

Effective leaders are credible, with excellent reputations, and high levels of integrity. The following description (from Gabarro's study) by one subordinate of his boss exemplifies the concept of integrity: "By integrity, I don't mean whether he'll rob a bank, or steal from the till. You don't work with people like that. It's whether you sense a person has some basic principles and is willing to stand by them."

Bennis and Nanus warn that today credibility is at a premium, especially since people are better informed, more cautious, and wary of authority and power. Leaders can gain trust by being predictable, consistent, and persistent and by making competent decisions. An honest leader may even be able to overcome lack of expertise, as a subordinate in Gabarro's study illustrates in the following description of his superior: "I don't like a lot of the things he does, but he's basically honest. He's genuine article and you'll forgive a lot of things because of that. That goes a long way in how much I trust him."

Self-Confidence

There are many reasons why a leader needs self-confidence. Being a leader is a very difficult job. A great deal of information must be gathered and processed. A constant series of problems must be solved and decisions made: Followers have to be convinced to pursue specific courses of action. Setbacks have to be overcome. Competing interests have to be satisfied. Risks have to be taken in the face of uncertainty. A person riddled with self-doubt would never be able to take the necessary actions nor command the respect of others.

Self-confidence plays an important role in decision-making and in gaining others' trust. Obviously, if the leader is not sure of what decision to make, or expresses a high degree of doubt, then the followers are less likely to trust the leader and be committed to the vision.

Not only is the leader's self-confidence important, but so is others' perception of him. Often, leaders engage in impression management to bolster their image of competence; by projecting self-confidence they arouse followers' self-confidence. Self-confident leaders are also more likely to be assertive and decisive, which gains others' confidence in the decision. This is crucial for effective implementation of the decision. Even when the decision turns out to be a poor one, the self-confident leader admits the mistake and uses it as a learning opportunity, often building trust in the process. . . .

Emotional Stability. Self confidence helps effective leaders remain even-tempered. They do get excited, such as when delivering an emotionally charged pep talk, but generally do not become angry or enraged. . . .

Emotional stability is especially important when resolving interpersonal conflicts and when representing the organization. A top executive who impulsively flies off the handle will not foster as much trust and teamwork as an executive who retains emotional control. . . .

Researchers at the Center for Creative Leadership found that leaders are more likely to "derail" if they lack emotional stability and composure. Leaders who derail are less able to handle pressure and more prone to moodiness, angry outbursts, and inconsistent behavior, which undermines their interpersonal relationships with subordinates, peers, and superiors. In contrast, they found the successful leaders to be calm, confident, and predictable during crisis.

Psychologically hardy, self-confident individuals consider stressful events interesting, as opportunities for development, and believe that they can influence the outcome. K. Labich in *Fortune* magazine argued that "By demonstrating grace under pressure, the best leaders inspire those around them to stay calm and act intelligently."

Cognitive Ability

Leaders must gather, integrate, and interpret enormous amounts of information. These demands are greater than ever today because of rapid technological change. Thus, it is not surprising that leaders need to be intelligent enough to formulate suitable strategies, solve problems, and make correct decisions.

Leaders have often been characterized as being intelligent, but not necessarily brilliant and as being conceptually skilled. Kotter states that a "keen mind" (i.e., strong analytical ability, good judgement, and the capacity to think strategically and multidimensionally) is necessary for effective leadership, and that leadership effectiveness requires ">above average intelligence," rather than genius.

An individual's intelligence and the perception of his or her intelligence are two highly related factors. Professors Lord, DeVader, and Alliger concluded that intelligence is a key characteristic in predicting leadership perceptions." Howard and Bray found that cognitive ability predicted managerial success twenty years later in their AT&T study. Effective managers have been shown to display greater ability to reason both inductively and deductively than ineffective managers.

Intelligence may be a trait that followers look for in a leader. If someone is going to lead, followers want that person to be more capable in *some* respects than they are. Therefore, the follower's perception of cognitive ability in a leader is a source of authority in the leadership relationship.

Knowledge of the Business

Effective leaders have a high degree of knowledge about the company, industry, and technical matters. For example, Jack Welch, president of GE, has a PhD in engineering; George Hatsopolous of Thermo Electron Corporation, in the years preceding the OPEC boycott, had both the business knowledge of the impending need for energy-efficient appliances and the technical knowledge of thermodynamics to create more efficient gas furnaces. Technical expertise enables the leader to understand the concerns of subordinates regarding technical issues. Harvard Professor John Kotter argues that expertise is more important than formal education.

Effective leaders gather extensive information about the company and the industry. Most of the successful general managers studied by Harvard's Kotter spent their careers in the same industry, while less successful managers lacked industry-specific experiences. Although cognitive ability is needed to gain a through understanding of the business, formal education is not a requirement. Only forty percent of the business leaders studied by Bennis and Nanus had business degrees. In-depth knowledge of the organization and industry allows effective leaders to make well-informed decisions and to understand the implications of those decisions.

Other Traits

Charisma, creativity/originality, and flexibility are three traits with less clear-cut evidence of their importance to leadership. Effective leaders may have charisma; however, this traits may only be important for political leaders. Effective leaders also may be more creative than nonleaders, but there is no consistent research demonstrating this. Flexibility or adaptiveness may be important traits for a leader in today's turbulent environment. Leaders must be able to make decisions and solve problems quickly and initiate and foster change.

There may be other important traits needed for effective leadership; however, we believe that the first six that we discussed are the core traits.

The Rest of the Story

A complete theory of leadership involves more than specifying leader traits. Traits only endow people with the potential for leadership. . . .

It is clear that leadership is a very demanding activity and that leaders who have the requisite traits–drive, desire to lead, self-confidence, honesty (and integrity), cognitive ability, and industry knowledge–have a considerable advantage over those who lack these traits. Without drive, for example, it is unlikely that an individual would be able to gain the expertise required to lead an organization effectively, let alone implement and work toward long-term goals. Without the desire to lead, individuals are not motivated to persuade others to work toward a common goal; such an individual would avoid or be indifferent to leadership tasks. Self-confidence is needed to withstand setbacks, persevere through hard times, and lead others in new directions. Confidence gives effective leaders the ability to make hard decisions and to stand by them. A leader's honesty and integrity form the foundation on which the leader gains followers' trust and confidence; without honesty and integrity, the leader would not be able to attract and retain followers. At least a moderate degree of cognitive ability is needed to gain and understand technical issues as well as the nature of the industry. Cognitive ability permits leaders to accurately analyze situations and make effective decisions. Finally, knowledge of the business is needed to develop suitable strategic visions and business plans.

Management Implications

Individuals can be *selected* either from outside the organization or from with-in non- or lower-managerial ranks based on their possession of traits that are less change-able or trainable. Cognitive ability (not to be confused with knowledge) is probably the least trainable of the six traits. Drive is fairly constant over time although it can change; it is observable in employees assuming they are given enough autonomy and responsibility to show what they can do. The desire to lead is more difficult to judge in new hires who may have had little opportunity for leadership early in life. It can be observed at lower levels of management and by observing people in assessment center exercises.

Two other traits can be developed through experience and *training*. Knowledge of the industry and technical knowledge come from formal training, job experience and a mentally active approach toward new opportunities for learning. Planned job rotation can facilitate such growth. Self-confidence is both general and task specific. People differ in their general confidence in mastering life's challenges but task-specific self-confidence comes from mastering the various skills that leadership requires as well as the technical and strategic challenges of the industry. Such confidence parallels the individual's growth in knowledge.

Honesty does not require skill building; it is a virtue one achieves or rejects by choice. Organizations should look with extreme skepticism at any employee who behaves dishonestly or lacks integrity, and should certainly not reward dishonesty in any form, especially not with a promotion. The key role models for honest behavior are those at the top. On this issue, organizations get what they model, not what they preach.

Conclusions

Regardless of whether leaders are born or made or some combination of both, it is unequivocally clear that *leaders are not like other people.* Leaders do not have to be great men or women by being intellectual geniuses or omniscient prophets to succeed but they do need to have the "right stuff" and this stuff is not equally present in all people. Leadership is a demanding, unrelenting job with enormous pressures and grave responsibilities. It would be a profound disservice to leaders to suggest that they are ordinary people who happened to be in the right place at the right time. Maybe the place matters, but it takes a special kind of person to master the challenges of opportunity. Let us not only give credit, but also use the knowledge we have to select and train our future leaders effectively. We believe that in the realm of leadership (and in every other realm), the individual *does* matter.

Lesson

5

Personality Types

Gain an understanding of the building blocks of one's personality as introduced using the MBTI personality assessment. Begin understanding how different personalities can lead to conflict, but also how they are critical to growing an effective and efficient leadership team.

READING

"Introduction to Type: A Guide to Understanding Your Results on the MBTI Instrument" 6th ed. Myers CPP Inc.

What Are Preferences?

Try this exercise to get a sense of what Jung and Myers meant by *preferences*.

> First, sign your name below as you usually do.
>
> [   ]

> Now, sign your name again, but this time use your other hand.
>
> [   ]

What was it like writing your name the first time, with your preferred hand? How does this compare to the second time?

Most people who try this immediately notice some major differences:

PREFERRED HAND	NONPREFERRED HAND
Feels natural	Feels unnatural
Don't have to think about it	Have to concentrate
Seems effortless, easy	Seems awkward, clumsy
Looks neat, legible, adult	Looks childlike

This exercise demonstrates the idea of preferences in the MBTI assessment. You can use either one of your hands when you have to, and you use both of them regularly. But when writing, you favor one of your hands over the other, and it feels natural and competent. Writing with your other hand takes effort and feels awkward. You can develop skill in writing with your opposite, nonpreferred hand, but imagine how hard it would be if you had to write with it all day.

Similarly, you're naturally inclined to favor one of the two opposites in each of the four preference pairs. You use both opposites at different times, but not both at once and not with the same confidence. When you use your preferences, you are generally at your best and feel most competent, natural, and energetic.

Your Myers-Briggs personality type represents your natural preferences in the four aspects of personality described, which account for the natural differences between people. There is no right or wrong to these preferences. Each identifies normal and valuable human behaviors.

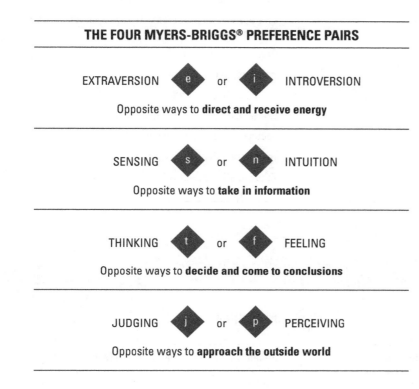

THE FOUR MYERS-BRIGGS® PREFERENCE PAIRS

EXTRAVERSION **e** or **i** INTROVERSION

Opposite ways to **direct and receive energy**

SENSING **s** or **n** INTUITION

Opposite ways to **take in information**

THINKING **t** or **f** FEELING

Opposite ways to **decide and come to conclusions**

JUDGING **j** or **p** PERCEIVING

Opposite ways to **approach the outside world**

As you use your preferences in these four areas, you develop what Jung and Myers defined as a personality type—an underlying personality pattern that comes from the dynamic interaction of your four preferences, environmental influences, and your own choices. People tend to develop behaviors, skills, and attitudes associated with their type, and individuals with types different from yours will likely be opposite to you in many ways. Each type represents a valuable and reasonable way to be.

Each has its own potential strengths, as well as its likely blind spots.

What are your Preferences?

In the following tables, highlight the element in each preference pair that best describes your natural way of doing things—the way you are outside of any roles you might play in life, when you are just being yourself.

EXTRAVERSION

 INTROVERSION

People who prefer Extraversion like to focus on the outside world. They direct their energy and attention outward and are energized by interacting with people and taking action.

Characteristics associated with people who prefer Extraversion:

Drawn to the outside world

Prefer to communicate by talking

Work out ideas by talking them through

Learn best through doing or discussing

Have broad interests

Tend to be sociable and expressive

Readily take initiative in work and relationships

People who prefer Introversion like to focus on their own inner world. They direct their energy and attention inward and are energized by reflecting on their own and others' ideas, memories, and experiences.

Characteristics associated with people who prefer Introversion:

Drawn to their inner world

Prefer to communicate in writing

Work out ideas by reflecting on them

Learn best by reflection, mental "practice"

Focus in depth on a few interests

Tend to be private and contained

Take initiative selectively—when the situation or issue is very important to them

 SENSING

 INTUITION

People who prefer Sensing like to take in information that is real and tangible—what they perceive using the five senses. They pay close attention to what is going on around them and are especially attuned to practical realities.

Characteristics associated with people who prefer Sensing:

Oriented to present realities

Factual and concrete

Focus on what is real and actual

Observe and remember specifics

Build carefully and thoroughly toward conclusions

Understand ideas and theories through practical applications

Trust experience

People who prefer Intuition like to take in information by seeing the big picture, focusing on the relationships and connections between facts. They look for patterns and are especially attuned to seeing new possibilities.

Characteristics associated with people who prefer Intuition:

Oriented to future possibilities

Imaginative and verbally creative

Focus on the patterns and meanings in data

Remember specifics when they relate to a pattern

Move quickly to conclusions, follow hunches

Want to clarify ideas and theories before putting them into practice

Trust inspiration

THE T–F PREFERENCE PAIR | How do you decide and come to conclusions?

THINKING

 FEELING

People who prefer Thinking like to decide things by looking at the logical consequences of their choice or action. They want to mentally remove themselves from the situation so they can examine the pros and cons objectively. They enjoy analyzing what's wrong with something so they can solve the problem. Their goal is to find a standard or principle that will apply in all similar situations.

Characteristics associated with people who prefer Thinking:

Analytical

Use cause-and-effect reasoning

Solve problems with logic

Strive for an objective standard of truth

Reasonable

Can be "tough-minded"

Fair—want everyone treated equally

People who prefer Feeling like to decide things by considering what's important to them and to others involved. They mentally insert themselves into the situation to identify with everyone so they can make decisions that honor people. They enjoy appreciating and supporting others, and look for qualities to praise. Their goal is to create harmony and treat each person as a unique individual.

Characteristics associated with people who prefer Feeling:

Empathetic

Guided by personal and social values

Assess impacts of decisions on people

Strive for understanding, harmony, and positive interactions

Compassionate

May appear "tenderhearted"

Fair—want everyone treated as an individual

 JUDGING

 PERCEIVING

People who prefer Judging like to live in a planned, orderly way. They want to make decisions, come to closure, and move on. Their lives tend to be structured and organized, and they like to have things settled. Sticking to a plan and schedule is very important to them, and they enjoy getting things done.

Characteristics associated with people who prefer Judging:

Scheduled

Organize their lives

Systematic

Methodical

Make short- and long-term plans

Like to have things decided

Try to avoid last-minute stress

People who prefer Perceiving like to live in a flexible, spontaneous way, and want to experience and understand life rather than control it. Detailed plans and final decisions feel confining to them; they prefer to stay open to new information and last-minute options. They enjoy being resourceful in adapting to the opportunities and demands of the moment.

Characteristics associated with people who prefer Perceiving:

Spontaneous

Flexible

Casual

Open-ended

Adapt, change course

Like things loose and open to change

Find last-minute pressures energizing

What is your Type?

The first step in figuring out which Myers-Briggs type fits you best is to put together the preferences you chose as you were listening to an explanation of type or reading the preceding section in this booklet.

The MBTI assessment uses letters to represent the preferences, so you can estimate your type by combining the letters next to the preferences you highlighted. For example, suppose you highlighted the letters I, S, T, and J.

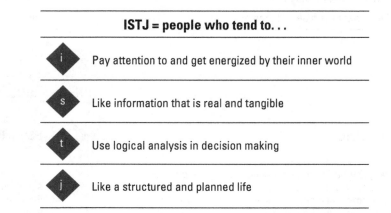

ISTJ = people who tend to...

i — Pay attention to and get energized by their inner world

s — Like information that is real and tangible

t — Use logical analysis in decision making

j — Like a structured and planned life

A person with opposite preferences on all four preference pairs would have highlighted the letters E, N, F, and P.

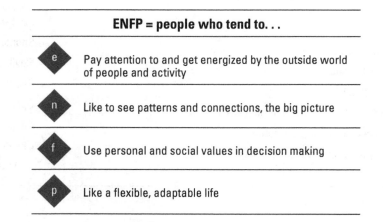

ENFP = people who tend to...

e — Pay attention to and get energized by the outside world of people and activity

n — Like to see patterns and connections, the big picture

f — Use personal and social values in decision making

p — Like a flexible, adaptable life

There are 16 possible combinations of the MBTI preferences, leading to 16 different personality types.

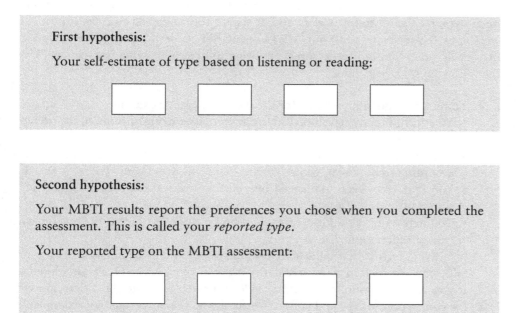

First hypothesis:

Your self-estimate of type based on listening or reading:

☐ ☐ ☐ ☐

Second hypothesis:

Your MBTI results report the preferences you chose when you completed the assessment. This is called your *reported type*.

Your reported type on the MBTI assessment:

☐ ☐ ☐ ☐

Your MBTI report may also show a number next to each letter. This number refers to your preference clarity. It indicates how clearly or consistently you chose the preference shown over its opposite when you responded to the MBTI questions. The numbers do not indicate how well developed the preferences are or how well you use them.

Verifying your Type

The MBTI assessment is one of the most reliable and valid personality tools available, but no assessment is perfect. Because of this, it is important that you verify your "bestfit" type—the four-letter combination that best describes your natural way of doing things. Your self-estimate and your reported type are considered hypotheses at this point—best guesses about your personality type—and they may or may not agree. Although most people agree with their MBTI results, it is not unusual for people's self-estimated and reported types to differ on one or more of the preferences.

The 16 full-page type descriptions presented later in this booklet are the basic resource for verifying your type.

- "At Their Best" summarizes qualities that most people of that type feel are characteristic of them.
- "Characteristics of . . ." and "How Others May See Them" describe how the type functions based on the Jung-Myers theory.
- "Potential Areas for Growth" highlights some developmental issues and characteristic reactions to stress.

If your self-estimate and your MBTI results are identical, turn to the full-page description of that type. Of course, no description can completely capture anyone—individuals are a lot more complex than their type! However, if the description makes you feel comfortably understood, it is probably your best-fit type. If not, . . .

If your self-estimate and your MBTI results differ, or if your type description doesn't fit, you will need to do some exploring to determine your best-fit type. Use the following steps as a guide.

1. Think about possible reasons for the discrepancy. For example:
   - You may not have developed a clear preference on one or more of the preference pairs.
   - You may have answered the MBTI questions or estimated your preferences according to how you would like to be or think you should be.
   - You may have been influenced by your current job requirements or living situation.
   - You may be under a lot of stress and find it difficult to identify your typical way of functioning.

   Identifying factors that influenced your answers to the MBTI questions or your self-estimate may lead you to a tentative decision about which type is your best fit.
2. If you are still unsure or want to explore further, read the short descriptions for your reported type and your self-estimate on the next page. For example, if both hypotheses indicated E, N, and P, but they differed on the T–F preference pair, read the brief descriptions for ENFP and ENTP.
3. Choose the type that seems most like you and read its two-page description, highlighting parts that seem to fit you and noting parts that don't. To double-check, you can do the same for the other type you are exploring.
4. Turn to the "Applying Type" section of this booklet to read about effects of type at work, in careers, in relationships, and on the way people learn.
5. If you are a participant in a Myers-Briggs training, observe type exercises related to the preference pair you are questioning. Note if one of the preferences "pulls" you. Or, you may become more sure because one of the preferences seems to push you away—makes you feel uncomfortable.
6. Continue to explore by reading additional type information and descriptions in the many other resources that are available.

If you're still not sure, that's okay. Determining your best-fit type can be a process of self-discovery. Narrow down your type as much as you can, observe yourself for a few days, and then revisit the type descriptions.

Characteristics Frequently Associated with each Type

ISTJ

Quiet, serious, succeed by being thorough and dependable. Practical, matter-of-fact, realistic, and responsible. Decide logically what should be done and work toward it steadily, regardless of distractions. Take pleasure in making everything orderly and organized—their work, their home, their life. Value traditions and loyalty.

ISFJ

Quiet, friendly, responsible, and conscientious. Committed and steady in meeting their obligations. Thorough, painstaking, and accurate. Loyal, considerate, notice and remember specifics about people who are important to them, concerned with how others feel. Strive to create an orderly and harmonious environment at work and at home.

INFJ

Seek meaning and connection in ideas, relationships, and material possessions. Want to understand what motivates people and are insightful about others. Conscientious and committed to their firm values. Develop a clear vision about how best to serve the common good. Organized and decisive in implementing their vision.

INTJ

Have original minds and great drive for implementing their ideas and achieving their goals. Quickly see patterns in external events and develop long-range explanatory perspectives. When committed, organize a job and carry it through. Skeptical and independent, have high standards of competence and performance— for themselves and others.

ISTP

Tolerant and flexible, quiet observers until a problem appears, then act quickly to find workable solutions. Analyze what makes things work and readily get through large amounts of data to isolate the core of practical problems. Interested in cause and effect, organize facts using logical principles, value efficiency.

ISFP

Quiet, friendly, sensitive, and kind. Enjoy the present moment, what's going on around them. Like to have their own space and to work within their own time frame. Loyal and committed to their values and to people who are important to them. Dislike disagreements and conflicts, don't force their opinions or values on others.

INFP

Idealistic, loyal to their values and to people who are important to them. Want to live a life that is congruent with their values. Curious, quick to see possibilities, can be catalysts for implementing ideas. Seek to understand people and to help them fulfill their potential. Adaptable, flexible, and accepting unless a value is threatened.

INTP

Seek to develop logical explanations for everything that interests them. Theoretical and abstract, interested more in ideas than in social interaction. Quiet, contained, flexible, and adaptable. Have unusual ability to focus in depth to solve problems in their area of interest. Skeptical, sometimes critical, always analytical.

ESTP

Flexible and tolerant, take a pragmatic approach focused on immediate results. Bored by theories and conceptual explanations; want to act energetically to solve the problem. Focus on the here and now, spontaneous, enjoy each moment that they can be active with others. Enjoy material comforts and style. Learn best through doing.

ESFP

Outgoing, friendly, and accepting. Exuberant lovers of life, people, and material comforts. Enjoy working with others to make things happen. Bring common sense and a realistic approach to their work, and make work fun. Flexible and spontaneous, adapt readily to new people and environments. Learn best by trying a new skill with other people.

ENFP

Warmly enthusiastic and imaginative. See life as full of possibilities. Make connections between events and information very quickly, and confidently proceed based on the patterns they see. Want a lot of affirmation from others, and readily give appreciation and support. Spontaneous and flexible, often rely on their ability to improvise and their verbal fluency.

ENTP

Quick, ingenious, stimulating, alert, and outspoken. Resourceful in solving new and challenging problems. Adept at generating conceptual possibilities and then analyzing them strategically. Good at reading other people. Bored by routine, will seldom do the same thing the same way, apt to turn to one new interest after another.

ESTJ

Practical, realistic, matter-of-fact. Decisive, quickly move to implement decisions. Organize projects and people to get things done, focus on getting results in the most efficient way possible. Take care of routine details. Have a clear set of logical standards, systematically follow them and want others to also. Forceful in implementing their plans.

ESFJ

Warmhearted, conscientious, and cooperative. Want harmony in their environment, work with determination to establish it. Like to work with others to complete tasks accurately and on time. Loyal, follow through even in small matters. Notice what others need in their day-to-day lives and try to provide it. Want to be appreciated for who they are and what they contribute.

ENFJ

Warm, empathetic, responsive, and responsible. Highly attuned to the emotions, needs, and motivations of others. Find potential in everyone, want to help others fulfill their potential. May act as catalysts for individual and group growth. Loyal, responsive to praise and criticism. Sociable, facilitate others in a group, and provide inspiring leadership.

ENTJ

Frank, decisive, assume leadership readily. Quickly see illogical and inefficient procedures and policies, develop and implement comprehensive systems to solve organizational problems. Enjoy long-term planning and goal setting. Usually well informed, well read, enjoy expanding their knowledge and passing it on to others. Forceful in presenting their ideas.

At their Best

ISTJs have a strong sense of responsibility and great loyalty to their organizations, families, and relationships. They work steadily to fulfill their commitments as promised and on time. They will go to almost any effort to complete something they see as necessary but will resist doing anything that doesn't make sense to them.

ISTJs generally prefer to work alone and be accountable for the results. However, they are comfortable working as part of a team when that is necessary to do the job right, when roles are clearly defined, and when everyone fulfills assigned responsibilities. Competence and responsibility are extremely important to ISTJs, who expect others to be as dutiful and trustworthy as they require themselves to be.

Characteristics of ISTJs

ISTJs have a profound respect for facts. They use their Sensing primarily internally, where they have a storehouse of information upon which they draw to help them understand the present. Thus, they are likely to be

- Practical, sensible, and realistic
- Systematic

ISTJs use Thinking in decision making, taking an objective, logical, and tough-minded approach. Their focus is on the task or system as a whole rather than on individuals. Thus, ISTJs tend to be

- Logical and analytical
- Detached and reasonable

ISTJs are clear and steadfast in their opinions because they have arrived at them by carefully and thoroughly applying logical criteria based on their experience and knowledge. They believe standard procedures exist because they work. They will support change only when facts demonstrate that it will bring about better results.

How Others May See Them

ISTJs are sociable when they are comfortable in the roles they are playing However, they generally don't share their wealth of rich observations and memories except with close friends. Others see their standards and opinions, their desire for structure and schedules, but they may not see their individual, sometimes humorous, private reactions.

Although it can be hard for ISTJs to see the sense in needs that are very different from theirs, once they are convinced that something matters to a person they care about, that need becomes a fact. Then they will go to great lengths to meet the need, even while continuing to think it doesn't make sense.

Others usually see ISTJs as

- Calm, reserved, and serious
- Consistent and orderly
- Valuing traditions

Potential Areas for Growth

Sometimes life circumstances have not supported ISTJs in the development and expression of their favorite processes, Sensing and Thinking.

- If they have not developed their Sensing, ISTJs may rush into premature decisions and actions without considering new information.
- If they have not developed their Thinking, they may not have reliable ways of dealing with the outside world and instead may focus solely on their memories and internal data.

If ISTJs don't find a place where they can use their gifts and be appreciated for their contributions, they usually feel frustrated and may

- Become rigid about time, schedules, and procedures
- Be critical and judgmental
- Find it difficult to delegate—to trust anyone else to do the job right

It is natural for ISTJs to give less attention to their less favored processes, Intuition and Feeling. If they neglect them too much, however, they may

- Not see the wider ramifications of current, expedient decisions
- Concentrate on logic so much that they don't consider impacts on people
- Fail to respond appropriately to others' needs for connection and intimacy

When greatly stressed, ISTJs may be unable to use their customary calm, reasonable judgment and get caught up in imagining negative possibilities for themselves and others in both the immediate and distant future.

At their Best

ISFJs are dependable and considerate, committed to the people and groups they are associated with, and faithful in carrying out their responsibilities. They work steadily to complete jobs fully and on time. They will go to great lengths to do something they see as necessary but dislike doing anything that doesn't make sense to them.

ISFJs focus on what people need and want, and they establish orderly procedures to ensure that those needs and wants are met. They take roles and responsibilities seriously and want others to do the same. Family is extremely important to ISFJs, who fulfill their roles conscientiously and expect other family members to do likewise.

Characteristics of ISFJs

ISFJs have a realistic and practical respect for facts. They use their Sensing primarily internally, where they have a large storehouse of information. They can clearly remember details about things that have personal meaning for them, such as tones of voice and facial expressions. Thus, ISFJs are likely to be

- Practical and realistic
- Concrete and specific

ISFJs use Feeling to make decisions based on their personal values and concern for others. They value harmony and cooperation and work to create them. Thus, they are likely to be

- Cooperative and thoughtful
- Kind and sensitive

Their opinions are firm because their decisions are based on careful application of their clear values and their wealth of stored information. ISFJs respect established procedures and authority, believing that these have persisted because they work well. Therefore, they will support change only when new data show it will be of practical benefit to people.

How Others May See Them

ISFJs are unassuming and quiet in their interactions, often putting the needs of others—especially family members—ahead of their own. They are uncomfortable with confrontation and will try hard to accommodate others, though their respect for traditions and people's feelings can lead them to challenge actions they perceive as hurtful or insensitive. People see their values, their desire for structure and closure, their kindness. What others may not see is their wealth of rich, accurate internal Sensing impressions and memories.

Others usually see ISFJs as

- Quiet, serious, and conscientious
- Considerate, good caretakers
- Honoring commitments, preserving traditions

Potential Areas for Growth

Sometimes life circumstances have not supported ISFJs in the development and expression of their favorite processes, Sensing and Feeling.

- If they have not developed their Sensing, ISFJs may rush into value judgments or taking care of others without considering the practical realities.
- If they have not developed their Feeling, they may not have reliable ways of dealing with the outside world and instead may focus solely on their impressions and memories.

If ISFJs don't find a place where they can use their gifts and be appreciated for their contributions, they usually feel frustrated and may

- Become rigid in supporting hierarchy, authority, and procedures
- Feel unappreciated and resentful—complain a lot
- Be overly focused on immediate impacts of decisions

It is natural for ISFJs to give less attention to their less favored processes, Intuition and Thinking. If they neglect them too much, however, they may

- Not see the wider ramifications of current decisions or procedures
- Find it difficult to assert their needs
- Be uncomfortable applying impersonal criteria to decisions, even when necessary

When greatly stressed, ISFJs can get caught up in imagining negative possibilities. They may then express these without their usual consideration for the impact on people around them.

At their Best

ENFPs see life as a creative adventure full of exciting possibilities. Unusually perceptive about people and the world, they are insightful about the present and future. ENFPs experience a wide range of feelings and intense emotions. They need affirmation from others and readily give appreciation and support.

ENFPs are good at understanding how people and groups work and are persuasive and compelling in pursuing what is important to them. They are adaptable, making the best of any situation. Their energy and enthusiasm encourage others to make the best of things, too.

Characteristics of ENFPs

ENFPs are innovators, initiating projects and putting a lot of energy into getting them going. Using Intuition primarily externally, they are stimulated by new people, ideas, and experiences. They readily find meaning and significance in things and see connections that others don't. They are likely to be

- Curious, creative, and imaginative
- Energetic, enthusiastic, and spontaneous

ENFPs value harmony and goodwill. They like to please people and will adapt to their needs and wishes when possible. ENFPs primarily use Feeling internally, making decisions by applying their personal values while keeping others' needs in mind. They are likely to be

- Warm, friendly, and caring
- Cooperative and supportive

ENFPs have exceptional insight into possibilities for others and the energy and motivation to help bring them to fruition. They feel confident moving ahead based on their insights, and their enthusiasm tends to bring others along with them.

How Others may See Them

ENFPs are usually lively, gregarious, and sociable, with a large circle of friends. They are interested in almost everything and have a zest for life that draws others to them. At the same time, they value depth and authenticity in their close relationships and will go to great lengths to create and support open and honest communication.

ENFPs hate routine, schedules, and structure and usually manage to avoid them. They are normally verbally fluent, even in extemporaneous situations; however, when talking about their deepest values, they may suddenly become awkward and express their opinions with uncharacteristic intensity.

Others usually see ENFPs as

- Personable, perceptive, and persuasive
- Enthusiastic, spontaneous, and versatile
- Giving and seeking affirmation

Potential Areas for Growth

Sometimes life circumstances have not supported ENFPs in the development and expression of their favorite processes, Intuition and Feeling.

- If they have not developed their Intuition, ENFPs may fail to take in enough information, mistrust their own insights, be uncertain, and accept others' perceptions too quickly.
- If they have not developed their Feeling, they may go from enthusiasm to enthusiasm, never committing the energy needed to actualize their insights, or they may make overly personal decisions.

If ENFPs don't find a place where they can use their gifts and be appreciated for their contributions, they usually feel frustrated and may

- Become scattered, have trouble focusing, be easily distracted
- Fail to follow through on decisions
- Become rebellious, excessively nonconforming
- Ignore deadlines and procedures

It is natural for ENFPs to pay less attention to their less favored processes, Sensing and Thinking. If they neglect them too much, however, they may

- Not take care of the details and routine required for implementing their inspirations
- Overextend themselves—have trouble saying no to interesting possibilities and people
- Fail to apply reason and logic to assess their inspirations and decisions

When greatly stressed, ENFPs may get overwhelmed by detail and lose their normal sense of perspective and options. Then they tend to focus on an unimportant or distorted detail, fixating on it to the point that it becomes the central fact of their universe.

At their Best

ENTPs constantly scan their environment for opportunities and possibilities. They see patterns and connections not obvious to others and at times seem able to see into the future. They are adept at generating conceptual possibilities and then analyzing them strategically.

ENTPs are good at understanding how systems work and are enterprising and resourceful in maneuvering within them to achieve their goals.

Characteristics of ENTPs

ENTPs are enthusiastic innovators. Their world is full of possibilities, interesting concepts, and exciting challenges. They are stimulated by difficulties, quickly devising creative responses and plunging into activity, trusting their ability to improvise. They use their Intuition primarily externally and enjoy exercising their ingenuity in the world. ENTPs are likely to be

- Creative, imaginative, and clever
- Theoretical, conceptual, and curious

ENTPs use their Thinking primarily internally to analyze situations and their own ideas and to plan. They admire competence, intelligence, precision, and efficiency. ENTPs are usually

- Analytical, logical, rational, and objective
- Assertive and questioning

ENTPs are enterprising, resourceful, active, and energetic. They respond to challenging problems by creating complex and global solutions. They are usually adept at "reading" other people, seeing how to motivate them, and assuming leadership. They can do almost anything that captures their interest.

How Others May See Them

ENTPs are spontaneous and adaptable. They find schedules and standard operating procedures confining and work around them whenever possible. They are remarkably insightful about the attitudes of others, and their enthusiasm and energy can mobilize people to support their vision.

Their conversational style is seen by many as challenging and stimulating because they love to debate ideas. They are fluent conversationalists, are mentally quick, and enjoy verbal sparring. When they express their underlying Thinking principles, however, they may speak with an intensity and abruptness that seem to challenge others.

Others usually see ENTPs as

- Independent, autonomous, and creative
- Lively, enthusiastic, and energetic
- Assertive and outspoken

Potential Areas for Growth

Sometimes life circumstances have not supported ENTPs in the development and expression of their favorite processes, Intuition and Thinking.

- If they have not developed their Intuition, ENTPs may not take in enough relevant information, resulting in "insights" unrelated to current reality.
- If they have not developed their Thinking, they may not have reliable ways to evaluate their insights and make plans to carry them through. Then they will go from enthusiasm to enthusiasm with little actually accomplished.

If ENTPs don't find a place where they can use their gifts and be appreciated for their contributions, they usually feel frustrated and may

- Behave in a brash, rude, and abrasive manner
- Criticize others, especially those they deem inefficient or incompetent
- Become rebellious and combative
- Become scattered—unable to focus

It is natural for ENTPs to give less attention to their less favored processes, Sensing and Feeling. If they neglect them too much, however, they may

- Not take care of the details and routine required to implement their insights
- Not fully appreciate the impact on others of their ideas and plans
- Be excessively and inappropriately "challenging and stimulating"

When greatly stressed, ENTPs can get overwhelmed by details and lose their ability to generate possibilities. Then they will focus on a minor or distorted detail, treating it as extremely important.

At their Best

ESTJs like to organize projects, procedures, and people and then act to get things done. They live by a set of clear standards and beliefs, make a systematic effort to follow these, and expect the same of others. They value competence, efficiency, and results and display them in their work and play.

ESTJs enjoy interacting and working with others, as long as the others are responsible about meeting deadlines and completing assigned tasks. They work best in situations where clear, known problems can be solved with proven techniques.

Characteristics of ESTJs

ESTJs take an objective approach to problem solving and are tough when the situation requires it. They use their Thinking primarily externally to organize their life and work, and they have little patience with confusion, inefficiency, or lack of follow-through. ESTJs are likely to be

- Logical, analytical, and objectively critical
- Decisive, clear, and assertive

ESTJs focus on the present—what is real and actual. They apply and adapt relevant past experience to deal with problems, and they prefer jobs where results are immediate, visible, and tangible. ESTJs are likely to be

- Practical, realistic, and matter-of-fact
- Systematic and pragmatic

ESTJs are usually excellent administrators because they understand systems and logistics. They can project the steps needed to accomplish a task, foresee potential problems, assign responsibilities, and marshal resources. They deal with all aspects of a situation, leaving no unresolved issues or unfinished business, and get things done on time. When they see that something is not working, they will plan and act to correct it. Otherwise, they prefer proven procedures and systems. Their orientation is toward tasks, action, and the bottom line.

How Others may See Them

Because ESTJs naturally devise systems, procedures, and schedules, others rely on them to take charge and get results. Others may find ESTJs overpowering at times because they are so certain about how things should be. Because they are clear and straightforward in their communication, people seldom have to wonder where they stand.

ESTJs can be quite gregarious and generally enjoy interacting with people, especially around tasks, games, traditions, and family activities. They take relationship roles seriously and fulfill them responsibly.

Others usually see ESTJs as

- Conscientious and dependable
- Decisive, outspoken, and self-confident

Potential Areas for Growth

Sometimes life circumstances have not supported ESTJs in the development and expression of their favorite processes, Thinking and Sensing.

- If they have not developed their Thinking, ESTJs may not have a reliable way of evaluating information and thus may make inconsistent or overly harsh decisions.
- If they have not developed their Sensing, they may make decisions too quickly, before they have taken in enough information. Then their decisions will reflect their previously formed judgments or biases.

If ESTJs don't find a place where they can use their gifts and be appreciated for their contributions, they usually feel frustrated and may

- Become rigid and dogmatic
- Be intrusive, "know-it-all" experts, overpowering others and refusing to listen
- Get picky about details and be impatient with those who don't follow procedures exactly

It is natural for ESTJs to give less attention to their less favored processes, Feeling and Intuition. If they neglect them too much, however, they may

- Apply logic even when emotions and impacts on people need primary consideration
- Fail to respond to others' needs for intimate connection and processing of feelings
- Not always see the wider ramifications of a seemingly simple, direct action

When greatly stressed, ESTJs may feel alone and unappreciated and be unable to communicate their feelings of distress and despair.

At Their Best

ESFJs like to organize people and situations and then work with others to complete tasks accurately and on time. They are conscientious and loyal, following through even in small matters, and they want others to be the same. They value security and stability.

Sociable and outgoing, ESFJs enjoy celebrations and traditions and bring personal caring to their workplace and home. They want to be appreciated for who they are and for what they give to others.

Characteristics of ESFJs

ESFJs use their Feeling primarily externally and radiate warmth and energy. They are encouraged by approval and hurt by indifference or unkindness. Conflict-filled or tense situations make them uncomfortable, and they work to ensure that these don't occur. ESFJs are likely to be

- Warm, sympathetic, and helpful
- Personable, cooperative, and tactful

ESFJs focus on the present and base their decisions on experience and facts. Though they enjoy variety, they adapt well to routine and don't like work that demands mastery of abstract ideas or impersonal analysis. They enjoy their possessions and take good care of them. ESFJs are likely to be

- Practical, realistic, and down-to-earth
- Decisive, thorough, and consistent

ESFJs are sensitive to the needs of each individual in their environment and good at providing practical caring. Much of their pleasure and satisfaction comes from the comfort and pleasure of others.

How Others May See Them

ESFJs are energized by interaction with others and genuinely interested in others' lives and concerns. They feel most comfortable in structured situations and enjoy creating order, structure, and schedules. They prefer to do things the traditional and accepted way.

For the sake of harmony, ESFJs will agree with others when they can. However, they also have strong values, which they express clearly and confidently when they think it is appropriate.

ESFJs value family and social ties. They enjoy belonging and are good at celebrations and traditions.

Others usually see ESFJs as

- Sociable, outgoing, enthusiastic, and energetic
- Organized and orderly
- Committed to preserving traditions

Potential Areas for Growth

Sometimes life circumstances have not supported ESFJs in the development and expression of their favorite processes, Feeling and Sensing.

- If they have not developed their Feeling, ESFJs may be tentative and uncertain, accepting the thoughts and opinions of others too quickly.
- If they have not developed their Sensing, they may not take in much information before making decisions and thus may jump to conclusions before fully understanding a situation. They may then impose their decisions on everyone around them.

If ESFJs don't find a place where they can use their gifts and be appreciated for their contributions, they usually feel frustrated and may

- Doubt themselves and focus their attention entirely on satisfying the needs of others
- Worry and feel guilty
- Become controlling in their push for harmony—"we will all get along"
- Become overly sensitive, imagining slights where none was intended

It is natural for ESFJs to give less attention to their less favored processes, Thinking and Intuition. If they neglect them too much, however, they may

- Find it difficult to acknowledge and deal with negative realities and problems that can't be ignored, especially when people or things they care about are involved
- Support those in charge or the standard procedures too uncritically
- Fail to see wider possibilities or alternative ways of doing things

When greatly stressed, ESFJs may find themselves uncharacteristically critical of themselves and others. Their negative thoughts and opinions then trouble them greatly.

At Their Best

ENFJs are highly attuned to others, using empathy to quickly understand emotional needs, motivations, and concerns. Their focus is on supporting others and encouraging their growth.

ENFJs are friendly persuaders who can build consensus among people whose interests and motives are quite diverse. They often act as catalysts, including everyone and drawing out the best in others. They can be inspiring leaders as well as loyal followers.

Characteristics of ENFJs

ENFJs base their decisions on personal values. They use their Feeling primarily externally, radiating warmth and energy. They look for and find the best in others and prize harmony and cooperation.

ENFJs are warmed by approval, responding with energy and devotion, and are especially sensitive to criticism and tension. They are likely to be

- Warm, compassionate, and supportive
- Loyal and trustworthy

ENFJs see meanings and connections and can be very insightful about people. They are curious about new ideas and stimulated by possibilities for contributing to the good of humanity. ENFJs are likely to

- Be imaginative and creative
- Like variety and new challenges

ENFJs naturally see the potential for growth in others and devote energy to helping them achieve it. They are sensitive facilitators. ENFJs take responsibility for organizing interactions of colleagues, friends, and family so that all are involved, harmony prevails, and people have fun.

How Others May See Them

ENFJs are energetic, enthusiastic, and very aware of others. Their genuine interest can usually draw out and involve even the most reserved person. They listen to and support others but also have very definite values and opinions of their own, which they will express clearly. ENFJs are energized by people and are socially adept. However, they also have a strong need for authentic, intimate relationships. They bring great enthusiasm and intensity to creating and maintaining these.

ENFJs like their lives to be organized and will work to bring closure to ambiguous relationships or situations. However, if people's needs conflict with schedules and rules, they will put people first.

Others usually see ENFJs as

- Sociable, personable, congenial, and gracious
- Expressive, responsive, and persuasive

Potential Areas for Growth

Sometimes life circumstances have not supported ENFJs in the development and expression of their favorite processes, Feeling and Intuition.

- If they have not developed their Feeling, their decisions may be inconsistent and poorly formulated. They may then accept the thoughts and opinions of others too readily.

- If they have not developed their Intuition, ENFJs may not see possibilities, making decisions too quickly without taking in enough information or considering factors beyond their own personal values.

If ENFJs don't find a place where they can use their gifts and be appreciated for their contributions, they usually feel frustrated and may

- Worry, feel guilty, and doubt themselves
- Become insistent and controlling in their desire for harmony
- Be overly sensitive to criticism, real or imagined

It is natural for ENFJs to give less attention to their less favored processes, Thinking and Sensing. If they neglect them too much, however, they may

- Make decisions based solely on personal values when logic is needed also
- Find it difficult to admit to problems or disagreements with people they care about
- Overlook details required to realize their ideals

When greatly stressed, ENFJs may find themselves suddenly and uncharacteristically critical and fault-finding with others. They generally keep these negative opinions to themselves, but they find such thoughts troubling and upsetting.

Lesson

6 *Culture*

Develop an understanding of how the culture we come from influences our world view through the varying ways it is reinforced. Those we work with now, and in the future, have a variety of cultural backgrounds that bring a wealth of experience and deep diversity. This promotes healthy discourse and appreciating this can improve an organization's practices.

Lesson

7 *Socialization*

Describe the differences between re-socialization and anticipatory socialization, how they are used in the military, and how they are an instrument of cultural reinforcement.

Lesson

8 *Values*

What we value, as internalized resulting from socialization, are the major drivers in our behavior. Recognizing different values in people from different backgrounds allows us to widen our perspective, and brings new ideas to the table.

READING 1

. . . David O. McKay taught, "The greatest battles of life are fought out daily in the silent chambers of the soul." If you win the battles there, if you settle the issues that inwardly conflict, you feel a sense of peace, a sense of knowing what you're about. And you'll find that the public victories—where you tend to think cooperatively, to promote the welfare and good of other people, and to be genuinely happy for other people's successes—will follow naturally.
—*Stephen Covey,* The Seven Habits of Highly Effective People *(1989)*

People who are self-aware, who have imagination and conscience, can see when the script they are living is not in harmony with their values—their life is not the product of their own design, but the result of a creation they have deferred to other people and circumstances. We need to approach our roles in life with values and directions clear, to rescript ourselves so the paradigms from which behavior and attitude flow are congruent with deepest values and in harmony with correct principles.
—*Milton Rokeach,* Understanding Human Values *(1979)*

When was the last time you thought about your values—those qualities or standards that you believe are desirable, worthy, and important? Can't remember? Maybe never? You're probably not alone. Most people have a set of values, but they don't think much about them. Instead, their lives resemble a collection of habits—habits that developed when a situation arose that needed to be resolved. Some people think about values only when they are faced with a crisis that requires immediate action.[1] Yet your values are directly related to the kind of person you are, your goals and aspirations, the way you behave, and the way you relate to other people.

This lesson helps you look at values in a number of ways. It begins with a definition of values and then explores the typical sources of our values. It also discusses the stages of values development and describes some ways of clarifying values and managing values conflicts.

What Are Values?

Values have been defined in many ways, and Schwartz & Bilsky's definition is summarized as, "values are (a) concepts or beliefs, (b) about desirable end states or behaviors, (c) that transcend specific situations, (d) guide selection or evaluation of behavior and events, and (e) are ordered by relative importance."[2] Values coincide with personal beliefs about what is good and just, right and wrong, ethical and unethical, moral and

---

[1] Leatz, C. A. (1993). *Career success/personal stress: How to stay healthy in a high-stress environment.* New York: McGraw Hill.
[2] Schwartz, S. H. & Bilsky, W. (1987). Toward a Universal Psychological Structure of Human Values. *Journal of Personality and Social Psychology, 53.* 551.

immoral. In this way, we find that values are important to our self-concept and personal identity, help us in achieving goal-directed behavior, and giving us a sense of purpose and direction in our lives. Values are important because they influence our perceptions and preferences and motivate us to act.[3] According to Williams, "Values are core conceptions of the desirable within every individual and society. They serve as standards or criteria to guide not only action but also judgment, choice, attitude, evaluation, argument, exhortation, [and] rationalization."[4]

Frankl based his theories of logotherapy on the human striving to find meaning in life.[5] But he cautioned that values do not drive a person—they pull rather than push. Implicit in the concept of pulling is the freedom of the individual to choose to accept or reject an idea. No one is driven to good behavior; in every instance we must decide to behave morally, not to satisfy some moral drive or to ease the conscience, but for the sake of some value to which we commit ourselves. The connections among beliefs, knowledge, and values are strong—changes in beliefs affect values and changes in values affect our perceptions of reality.[6]

The goals we set for ourselves, the plans we map out for our lives, result from our value systems, but aren't necessarily the same things as our value systems. Gaus offers this suggestion to help distinguish a plan of life from a value system: "The plan concerns the organization of commitments to act that flow from one's value system. . . . Valuings imply action commitments; one who adopts a plan of action has organized his activity in light of his comparative valuings, resources, and circumstances. Understood thus, plans do not directly determine or organize what one values, but rather how one's value system translates into efficient action in particular circumstances."[7]

Over the past decade, research in positive psychology led by Dr. Marty Seligman has provided a connection between values and what philosophers call virtues and character. The original core virtues as discussed by Aristotle are: wisdom, courage, humanity, justice, temperance, and transcendence. Character is the combination of values that act as psychological mechanisms driving behavior that defines our personal identity. The *Values in Action (VIA) Classification of Strengths* inventory measures 24 character strengths (values) that comprise most people's value systems.[8] When considering these character strengths, we find that all are desirable to some extent, but individually, we each identify more strongly with certain values. The VIA provides a method of assessing the degree to which we identify more or less with particular values. Organizes the character strengths by the virtue each supports.

[3] Hanna, S. L. (1995). *Person to person: Positive relationships don't just happen* (2nd ed.). Englewood Cliffs, NJ: Prentice Hall.

[4] Rokeach, M. (Ed.) (1979). *Understanding human values: Individual and societal.* New York: The Free Press.

[5] Frankl, V. E. (1963). *Man's search for meaning.* New York: Washington Square Press.

[6] Rokeach, M. (Ed.) (1979). *Understanding human values: Individual and societal.* New York: The Free Press.

[7] Gaus, G. F. (1990). *Value and justification: The foundations of liberal theory.* Cambridge: Cambridge University Press, 239.

[8] Park, N. (2004). Strengths and Positive Youth Development. *Annals of the American Academy of Political and Social Science, 591,* 40–54.

Sources of Values

While it is still debated as to the development of values and character, there are several researchers who continue to claim that there are biological factors that influence values and value development. The most compelling evidence is found in twin studies, which has found that behavior related to empathy and other prosocial behaviors are heritable in both adults and children.[9] Similarly, psychologists have found links between temperament/personality related to sociability and emotionality and values indicating a further biological component of values.[10] While this evidence supports biological factors, most experts agree that value development is influenced by both biology and culture.

We learn them from others—parents, families, peers, schools, religion, government, the media, etc. The primary sources of values for most of us are family and parents. The things our parents valued shaped both the way they behaved as parents and their expectations for the ways their children would behave. You can expect that your values will affect the way you raise your children, too. The strength of the influence of parental values can be seen in the parent messages that keep replaying in our minds, even well into adulthood: "A penny saved is a penny earned," "Vegetables are good for you," "Buckle up for safety." The values we learned from our parents are reflected in conscience, too. Many years after leaving home, a person can still feel guilty pangs about buying something on impulse or occasionally missing church—an indication that the individual's parents valued frugality and religion, and those values strongly influence that person's internal critic.

The value messages parents send can often be conflicting, as well. A child may hear that the parents value fairness and equality of all people, but when the child brings home a new friend of a different race, he or she may hear another message. It's no wonder that children are confused—and that confusion carries over when as adults they attempt to clarify values.[11]

Messages from television, radio, and advertisements are powerful influences on values, too. Just consider the value messages those media send about youth and body image. Is it any wonder that our society tends to devalue aging, or that so many of us are obsessed with diet, sometimes to the point that obsession becomes illness?

Our own experiences also influence the development of our values. Personally experiencing betrayal or dishonesty may clarify for us the degree to which we value loyalty and honesty. The strong support of parents and siblings or friends will reinforce for us the value of family and friendship.

Not only do we develop personal values, we also develop collective values that we share with others in the societies to which we belong—within families, on the job, in school, and within geopolitical groups like neighborhoods, towns, states, and nations. Research shows that we can find value differences related to race, ethnicity, gender, social class/occupation/education, immigrant status, age cohort, religion and nationality.[12] These value differences are important to not only understanding our own values, but also the values of those we work with in our diverse military.

---

[9] Matthews, K. A. Batson, C. D. Horn, & J. Rosenman, R. H. (1981). "Principles in his nature which interest him in the fortune of others...": The heritability of empathic concern for others. *Journal of Personality, 49,* 237–247.

[10] Roccas S., Sagive LSSH, Knafo A. (2002). The big five personality factors and personal values. *Personality and Social Psychology Bulletin, 28,* 789–801.

[11] Hanna, S. L. (1995). *Person to person: Positive relationships don't just happen* (2nd ed.). Englewood Cliffs, NJ: Prentice Hall.

[12] Hitlin, S. and Piliavin, J. A. (2004). Values: Reviving a dormant concept. *Annual Review of Sociology, 30,* 359–393.

Values Development

As we mature in other ways, we also mature in building our system of values. Values take time to develop; research into values clarification has identified three stages most people move through as they develop value systems: acceptance (prizing), preference (choosing), and commitment (acting).[13]

In the early stage of values development, we accept, prize, or cherish something largely because we have been influenced (by parents, media, experience, etc.) to value it. In the parallel stage of personal development, we are still largely focused on the external and tend to behave primarily in reaction to the actions of others. For example, a child of 6 or 7 identifies with going to church and considers it important only because it is important to his or her parents.

In the preference stage of values development, we choose to believe and behave in a certain way, not merely because of external influence, but because we have considered the alternatives and the consequences and have freely chosen to place value on the belief or behavior. This stage generally emerges between the ages of 8 and 16, when personal development is shifting from an external focus to an internal one. For example, at this stage a young person may value church attendance because the person enjoys it and wants to go.

In the final stage of values development, our values are clear and ingrained and we feel a strong commitment to them. At this stage, we are willing to act in accordance with our values and beliefs, consistently and regularly, and would be ready to take a stand to protect them. Most people are ready to commit to values by the time they reach adulthood (ages 16–23), when their life focus has crystallized. For example, at this stage a person may attend church consistently because she or he values religion and finds church services spiritually fulfilling. An adult who tells you he values going to church because that's "just what you're supposed to do" probably has not developed a firm commitment to religion as a value. He has remained in the acceptance phase of the values development process.

Changing Values

As we mature, our values may change. That doesn't mean that our core values shift dramatically, but that things that once seemed to shape our lives no longer exert as strong an influence. In their place have emerged new values (or perhaps they were always there, just not as powerful as they are now) that reflect the new direction our lives are taking. For example, a mother of young children may highly value a strong public school system and will lobby for strong schools and an elementary curriculum that challenges and encourages children. When that same woman is in her forties and her children are attending college, the passionate value she placed on strong elementary schools may have waned. She still may believe in the value of a public school system, but her actions may now reflect a stronger passion for worthwhile and accessible college programs that will prepare her grown children for successful life careers. Her early values haven't evaporated altogether—the basic belief in education hasn't gone away—but the shape of her values in that regard has changed as her life circumstances have changed.

People often find themselves achieving victories that are empty, successes that have come at the expense of things they suddenly realize were far more valuable to them. Peo-

---

[13] Simon, S. B., Howe, L. W., and Kirschenbaum, H. (1972). *Values clarification: A handbook of practical strategies for teachers and students.* New York: Hart.

ple from all walks of life—doctors, academicians, performers, politicians, business professionals, athletes, and plumbers—often struggle to achieve a higher income, more recognition, or a certain degree of professional competence, only to find that their drive to achieve the goal blinded them to the things that really mattered most and now are gone.[14]

Flexibility is vital to a strong and healthy value system, but strength doesn't imply unchanging, rigid values. Instead, it means we are able and willing to continually process values and in doing so, modify them or change their priority. Lack of flexibility makes us judgmental, closes doors, and dismisses the possibility that the value systems of others may be just as legitimate as our own. Without the flexibility to adjust our thinking, we may destroy good relationships or completely reject new relationships because the other person simply doesn't believe as we do.[15]

Managing Values Conflicts and Influencing the Values of Others

When our values coalesce to the point of clarity and action, we are ready to take a stand and act in accordance with them. Usually a stand emerges when our values are challenged, confronted, or attacked in some way. In the face of such a challenge (which may come from other people, the community, or new information we uncover about nature, people, or things), values that we might have held in the abstract suddenly are called forth in the form of concrete action. Say, for example, you value your environmental responsibility to pass the earth on relatively intact to future generations. You have only recently learned that the fluorocarbons in aerosol cans do serious damage to the ozone layer. So you take a stand to not use any products that come in aerosol cans. You act on that stand the next time you face a fierce flying insect and the only weapon available is a can of Raid. If you value your environmental responsibility strongly enough, you'll risk a sting rather than sending even a minute amount of fluorocarbons into the atmosphere.

Challenges sometimes evoke values we didn't realize we held dearly. For example, a young family has always spent time together on a regular summer vacation. This year, the oldest child is 10 years old and playing for the first time on a summer league softball team. It turns out that the scheduled games overlap the time the family had set aside for vacation. The family discusses the things it values that are relevant to this situation: sports play as a source of good health, teamwork as a means of learning to cooperate with and be responsible to others, as well as family togetherness and the mental and emotional benefits of a relaxing vacation. Ultimately, they take this stand: When they are in town, softball games get highest priority; but family trips are more important than attending every game.

We usually order our values hierarchically and use them to guide our behavior at certain moments. Because we view some values as more important than others, we often make trade-offs in our lives based on the relative importance we attach to certain values. For example, if you value intellectual development more than you value physical development, given a limited amount of time, you may spend it in the library studying rather than in the gym working out.[16] Values are so fundamental to human

[14] Covey, S. R. (1989). *The seven habits of highly effective people.* New York: Simon & Schuster.

[15] Hanna, S. L. (1995). *Person to person: Positive relationships don't just happen* (2nd ed.). Englewood Cliffs, NJ: Prentice Hall.

[16] Verderber, R. F., and Verderber, K. S. (2003). *Inter-act: Using interpersonal communication skills* (10th ed.). Belmont, CA: Wadsworth.

behavior that when our personal values are not congruent with our other value sets or the values of others, we may experience serious conflict and the stresses that result can be difficult to manage.

Ethics or values conflicts are not always framed in the context of right versus wrong. More often we are confronted with value dilemmas that present something that is right on both sides—and we can't do both right things at the same time. The rightness on each side reflects two of our core values in conflict with each other. People who have no core values can experience no ethical dilemmas—they don't value any rightness and so are unaware of the ethical universe in which value-driven people live.[17]

Interpersonal conflicts driven by values are the most difficult to resolve. Because values are so closely tied to beliefs, and because beliefs are largely subjective, when we find ourselves in conflict that stems from a fundamental difference in values, the result is likely to be a standoff. Neither party to a conflict is likely to relinquish his or her hold on values (especially those that have crystallized for us and to which we are firmly committed), so argument or moralizing will have little effect on the conflict and will most probably make it more intense. So how can you manage a values conflict? How can you influence the values of another?

Confrontation is not the answer. But more subtle approaches may work. Simply modeling the values you want to see others adopt can be a powerful strategy. If you truly value human dignity, for example, you'll walk away from conversations that turn to demeaning women or people of other races. Reinforcing the values you hold dear can also influence the values of others. If you and a co-worker are at odds because you strongly value cooperation in the workplace and your colleague seems to value only her own well-being, you may be able to gradually influence that person to value cooperation if you compliment her each time she demonstrates even the slightest willingness to be part of the team.

Sometimes you simply have to acknowledge that the other person's value system is different from yours. In some cases, the only resolution to a values-based conflict may be to agree to disagree and move beyond it.

Conclusion

We often form friendships by aligning ourselves with those who share our values; it is more difficult to develop an intense relationship with those whose fundamental values are different from our own. But just as we try to understand cultural differences that may initially seem to be barriers to interpersonal interactions, so too should we be open-minded enough to at least attempt to learn why someone else values things that we do not. Most likely we can find many common values in spite of differences on one or two value issues.

Values are fundamental to the way we interact with others. They are the foundation of the life goals we set for ourselves, the building blocks of self-concept and self-esteem, the guiding forces in our exertion of power and influence over others, the bases for many of the conflicts we experience (as well as the roots of conflict resolution). It is no wonder, then, that developing a value system is fundamental to interpersonal communication and interpersonal leadership.

[17] Kidder, R. M. (1994). *Shared values; troubled times: Global ethics for the twenty-first century.* E. N. Thompson Forum on World Issues, University of Nebraska–Lincoln. Lincoln, NE: Cooper Foundation and University of Nebraska–Lincoln.

Large Group Exercise: Cave Rescue

Adapted from Francis and Young, 1979.[18]

Purpose

To help you identify some of the things you value and to help you correlate actions to values.

You Will Need

Cave Rescue Briefing Sheet
Cave Rescue Biographical Sheet
Cave Rescue Ranking Sheet

Activity

Read the briefing sheet and become familiar with the situation you have been asked to help with. The biographical sheet is explained in the briefing. Use the ranking sheet as instructed.

When you have completed your ranking sheet individually, work with others in a small group to reach consensus about your rankings. Once your group has reached consensus, select someone to announce your decision and your rationale to the rest of the class.

Cave Rescue Briefing Sheet

You are a member of a research management committee responsible for administering research projects in the behavioral sciences at State University. You have been called to an emergency meeting because of a catastrophe in one of the projects for which the committee is responsible.

The project, which is a study of human behavior in confined spaces, is conducting an experiment in a remote part of the country. The experiment involves seven people who have been living underground in a cave system for several days. The group's only outside contact is via a radio link to a research station at the cave entrance. The volunteers in the cave have issued a call for help: They have been trapped by falling rocks, and water is slowly rising; they expect it will eventually fill the cave.

The only available rescue team reports that rescue will be extremely difficult and, with the equipment available, only one person can be brought out each hour. It is quite likely the rising water will drown some of the trapped volunteers before they can all be removed from the cave.

Through the radio link, the volunteers have been informed about the impossibility of rescuing everyone. They are unwilling to decide the sequence by which they will be rescued. Your research management committee must decide the order of rescue. Lifesaving equipment will arrive at the cave in about 50 minutes. By that time, you must provide the rescue team with the rescue sequence.

---

[18] Francis, D., and Young, D. (1979). *Improving work groups: A practical manual for team-building.* San Diego: University Associates.

The only available information about the trapped volunteers has been drawn from the project files. You'll find that information on the Cave Rescue Biographical Information Sheet. You can use any criteria you wish to help you make a decision.

Complete a Cave Rescue Ranking Sheet individually, then work with members of your group to reach a consensus about the best order of rescue. Once your group has made its decision, complete another Cave Rescue Ranking Sheet for the group and select a spokesperson to announce your decision and your rationale.

Cave Rescue Biographical Sheet

Helen: White, female, American, age 34. Married, homemaker, four children, aged 7 months to 8 years. Husband is city council member. Was a promising psychology student when she left university to marry. Lives in suburb near university. Hobbies are ice skating and cooking. Became involved in the volunteer project through association with Owen, another volunteer. Project coordinator suspects Helen and Owen have developed a covert sexual relationship.

Tozo: Female, Japanese, age 19. Single, sociology student at State University. Parents live in Tokyo, father is wealthy industrialist and national authority on traditional Japanese mime theater. Outstandingly attractive, has dated several men from the upper crust. Recently featured in TV documentary on Japanese women.

John: Black, male, American, age 37. Married, five children, aged 6 years to 19 years. Campus coordinator of Catholic Social Services at State University. Worked full time while attending school; earned master's degree in social work. Heavily involved with Black militant group for several years. Hobbies are camping with his family and photography.

Owen: White, male, American, age 47. Unmarried, physical education instructor at University High School. Served in Army right after high school, was infantry platoon leader in the first Iraq war, earned several distinguished decorations. Medical discharge due to serious leg wound (recovery complete except for occasional pains). Earned master's degree in physical education, using GI Bill benefits. Life is a bit unsettled, drinking problem. Hobbies: modifying and driving stock cars.

Paul: White, male, English, age 47. Divorced (six years), no children. Medical research scientist at University Hospital. Recognized world authority on treatment of rabies. Currently testing a new experimental, low-cost rabies treatment, but much of his research data are still in working notebooks. Hobbies are classical music and sailing. Some emotional difficulty related to divorce and ex-wife's recent remarriage. Twice convicted of indecent exposure (last occasion was 11 months ago).

Edward: White, male, American, age 59. Married, two grown children, seven grandchildren. General manager of small factory (71 employees) that produces rubber belts for machines. Recently negotiated a large contract for his company that, if signed, would create 85 new jobs for the company; will complete details when he returns to work. Socially and politically active; senior freemason and city council member. Hobbies: spelunking (cave exploration). Plans to write a book on the subject when he retires.

Jean: Black, female, Jamaican, age 72. Unmarried, no relatives. Living in U.S. since 1979, but has not sought American citizenship. Ph.D. in biological sciences; working with a government grant to explore biological organisms that live in caves. Most recent work with tree organisms has led to development of experimental vaccine that could be the forerunner to an AIDS vaccine. Recent Peabody Award winner from Stanford University. Assignment in current project: Study the behavior of people in confined spaces and gather microbes for future medical research.

Cave Rescue Values Sheet (Individual)

Instructions: Answer the 3 questions about each person. Then rank the seven people trapped in the cave in terms of the value of rescuing them. List numbers in the left-hand column. (Number 1 gets out first, etc.) Complete this sheet on your own.

#	Name	What I value about this person	What about this person has a neutral affect on me	What about this person might lower my ranking of them
3	Helen	• Stay at home mom • life is put together • volunteers	• left to marry • volunteers with Owen	• She is cheating 14 children • her own interests
6	Tozo	• Hot	• her age • her amount of wealth	• total sloot • doesn't psyco • Nothing substantial
1	John	• Married 15 children • Black	• Black militant group • Monogamy	• not much to offer • seems aggressive
(scribbled, 4)	Owen	• Army man • Injury	• war • no college • age	• drinking problem • not much to offer
7	Paul	• Cure for measles • volunteering	• (classical) music and siblings	• twe married, innocent • exposure
2	Edward	• Age • city council	• Big business	• old age • helpful
(scribbled, 5)	Jean	• PHD Biological Sciences • loves and people	• no U.S. citizenship	• old AF

Cave Rescue Ranking Sheet (Group)

As a group, you must arrive at consensus about your rankings. This doesn't mean you have to agree unanimously, but the majority of your group should be able to live with the final order you come up with. When you determine the order, select someone to present your decision to the class

	NAME	PRIMARY REASON FOR RANKING
1		
2		
3		
4		
5		
6		
7		

What procedures did you use to determine consensus?
What were the principal criteria you used to rank the trapped volunteers?

Foundations of Character

Courage "Courage is rightly esteemed the first of human qualities... because it is the quality which guarantees all others." — Winston Churchill Emotional strengths that involve the exercise of will to accomplish goals in the face of opposition, external or internal.

Integrity Speaking the truth but more broadly presenting oneself in a genuine way and acting in a sincere way; being without pretense; taking responsibility for one's feelings and actions

Bravery [Valor] Not shrinking from threat, challenge, difficulty, or pain; speaking up for what is right even if there is opposition; acting on convictions even if unpopular; includes physical bravery but is not limited to it.

Perseverance [Persistence] Finishing what one starts; persisting in a course of action in spite of obstacles; "getting it out the door"; taking pleasure in completing tasks.

Vitality [Zest, Enthusiasm, Vigor, Energy] Approaching life with excitement and energy; *not* doing things halfway or halfheartedly; living life as an adventure; feeling alive and activated.

Wisdom "The nation that will insist upon drawing a broad line of demarcation between the fighting man and the thinking man will find its fighting done by fools and its thinking done by cowards." — LtCol Sir William Butler Cognitive strengths that entail the acquisition and use of knowledge.

Love of Learning Mastering new skills, topics, and bodies of knowledge, whether on one's own or formally; obviously related to the strength of curiosity but goes beyond it to describe the tendency to add systematically to what one knows.

Ingenuity [Creativity] Thinking of novel and productive ways to conceptualize and do things; includes artistic achievement but is not limited to it.

Perspective Being able to provide wise counsel to others; having ways of looking at the world that make sense to oneself and to other people.

Curiosity [Interest, Novelty-seeking, openness to experience] Taking an interest in ongoing experience for its own sake; finding subjects and topics fascinating; exploring and discovering.

Open-mindedness [Judgment, Critical thinking] Thinking things through and examining them from all sides; not jumping to conclusions; being able to change one's mind in light of evidence; weighing all evidence fairly.

Justice "Justice is the first virtue of social institutions as truth is of systems of thought." — John Rawls Civic strengths that underlie healthy community life.

Fairness Treating all people the same according to notions of fairness and justice; *not* letting personal feelings bias decisions about others; giving everyone a fair chance.

Loyalty [Social responsibility, Citizenship, Teamwork] Working well as a member of a group or team; being loyal to the group; doing one's share.

Leadership: Encouraging a group of which one is a member to get things done and at the same time maintain good relations within the group; organizing group activities and seeing that they happen.

FIGURE **8.1** **Foundations of Character**[1]

[1] Modified from VIA Institute on Character. (2004). The VIA Classification of Character Strengths. retrieved from http://www.viacharacter.org/VIAINSTITUTE/Classification.aspx

Humanity "An individual has not started living until he can rise above the narrow confines of his individualistic concerns to the broader concerns of all humanity." — Martin Luther King, Jr. Interpersonal strengths that involve tending and befriending others.

Compassion [Kindness] Doing favors and good deeds for others; helping them; taking care of them.

Emotional Intelligence [Social Intelligence] Being aware of the motives and feelings of other people and oneself; knowing what to do to fit into different social situations; knowing what makes other people tick.

Gratitude Being aware of and thankful for the good things that happen; taking time to express thanks.

Love Valuing close relations with others, in particular those in which sharing and caring are reciprocated; being close to people.

Temperance "No [one] is fit to command another that cannot command him[or her]self." —William Penn Strengths that protect against excess.

Self-control [Self regulation] Regulating what one feels and does; being disciplined; controlling one's appetites and emotions.

Humility/Modesty Letting one's accomplishments speak for themselves; *not* seeking the spotlight; not regarding oneself as more special than one is.

Forgiveness and mercy Forgiving those who have done wrong; accepting the shortcomings of others; giving people a second chance; *not* being vengeful.

Prudence Being careful about one's choices; not taking undue risks; not saying or doing things that might later be regretted.

Transcendence "I have one life and one chance to make it count for something . . . I'm free to choose what that something is, and the something I've chosen is my faith. Now, my faith goes beyond theology and religion and requires considerable work and effort. My faith demands — this is not optional — my faith demands that I do whatever I can, wherever I am, whenever I can, for as long as I can with whatever I have to try to make a difference." — President Jimmy Carter Strengths that forge connections to the larger universe and provide meaning.

Spirituality [Religiousness, Faith, Purpose]: Having coherent beliefs about the higher purpose and meaning of the universe; knowing where one fits within the larger scheme; having beliefs about the meaning of life that shape conduct and provide comfort.

Optimism [Hope, Future-mindedness, Future orientation] Expecting the best in the future and working to achieve it; believing that a good future is something that can be brought about.

Appreciation of beauty and excellencee [Awe, Wonder, Elevation] Noticing and appreciating beauty, excellence, and/or skilled performance in various domains of life, from nature to art to mathematics to science to everyday experience.

Humor [playfulness] Liking to laugh and tease; bringing smiles to other people; seeing the light side; making not necessarily telling jokes.

FIGURE **8.1** **Foundations of Character**[1] *(Continued)*

[1] Modified from VIA Institute on Character. (2004). The VIA Classification of Character Strengths. retrieved from http://www.viacharacter.org/VIAINSTITUTE/Classification.aspx

READING 2

"Universal Human Values: Finding an Ethical Common Ground" Kidder. From "The Leader's Companion" Wren. The Free Press

Rushworth M. Kidder formerly served as senior columnist for *The Christian Science Monitor*. He is currently president of the Institute for Global Ethics. His most recent book is *Shared Values for a Troubled World: Conversations with Men and Women of Conscience*.

In the remote New Zealand village of Panguru, tucked into the mountains at the end of a winding gravel road, a Maori woman nearly a century old pauses for a moment as she talks about the moral values of her people. "This is God's country!" says Dame Whina Cooper with great feeling, gesturing toward the flowers blooming among the bird songs outside her modest frame house. "Only, we the people running it must be doing something wrong."

Halfway around the world, in a United Nations office perched under the eaves of a fifteenth-century building in Florence, a leading journalist from Sri Lanka is asked what will happen if the world enters the twenty-first century with the ethics of the twentieth. "I feel it will be disastrous," Varindra Tarzie Vittachi replies simply.

Midway between, in his well-appointed residence in San Jose, Costa Rica, former president Oscar Arias explains that our global survival "will become more complicated and precarious than ever before, and the ethics required of us must be correspondingly sophisticated."

Turn where you will in the world and the refrain is the same. The ethical barometer is falling, and the consequences appear to be grave. That, at least, is one of the impressions to be drawn from the two dozen individuals from 16 nations interviewed over the past few years by the Institute for Global Ethics.

These interviews did not seek to discover the ethical failings of various nations, but rather to find the moral glue that will bind us together in the twenty-first century. These voices speak powerfully of an underlying moral presence shared by all humanity—a set of precepts so fundamental that they dissolve borders, transcend races, and outlast cultural traditions.

There is a pressing need for shared values in our age of global interdependence without consensus. But there is one very real question unanswered: Is there in fact a single set of values that wise, ethical people around the world might agree on? Can there be a global code of ethics? If there is a common core of values "out there" in the world, it ought to be identifiable through examination of contemporary modes of thought in various cultures around the world. Can it be found?

On that topic, the two dozen "men and women of conscience" interviewed had a clear point of view. "Yes," they said, "there is such a code, and it can be clearly articulated." These interviewees were chosen not because they necessarily know more about ethics than their peers—although some do, having made it a lifelong study. Nor were they chosen because they are the single most exemplary person of their nation or community—though some could easily be nominated for that honor. They are, however, ethical thought-leaders within their different cultures, each viewed by his or her peers as a kind of ethical standard-bearer, a keeper of the conscience of the community, a center of moral gravity.

Each of the interviews began with a common question: If you could help create a global code of ethics, what would be on it? What moral values, in other words, would you bring to the table from your own culture and background?

In an ideal world, one would have assembled all the interviewees around a table, had each talk for an hour, had each listen intently to all the others, and finally had them arrive at a consensus. If they could have done so, here's the core of moral values upon which they probably would have agreed:

Love

Despite the concern of foundation executive James A. Joseph in Washington that "the L-word, Love," is falling sadly into disuse, it figured prominently in these interviews. "Love, yes," said children's author Astrid Lindgren in Stockholm. "This is the main word for what we need—love on all stages and with all people."

"The base of moral behavior is first of all solidarity, love, and mutual assistance," said former first lady Graça Machel of Mozambique. Buddhist monk Shojun Bando in Tokyo agreed, detailing three different kinds of love and insisting that "it shouldn't be that others should tell you to love others: It should just come of its own will, spontaneously." Or, as author Nien Cheng from China put it, "You cannot guide without love."

For tribal chief Reuben Snake of Nebraska, the central word is *compassion*. "We have to be compassionate with one another and help one another, to bold each other up, support one another down the road of life," he recalled his grandfather telling him. Thinking back on her dealings with a global spectrum of cultures at the United Nations, former ambassador Jeane Kirkpatrick in Washington noted that, no matter how severe the political differences, "there was a kind of assumption, on the part of almost everyone, that people would help one another at the personal level."

Truthfulness

Of the four these that form Harvard University ex-president Derek Bok's code of ethics, two center on truth. "You should not obtain your ends through lying and deceitful practices," he said, and you have a "responsibility to keep [your] promises." Astrid Lindgren put it with equal clarity when she spoke of the need to "be honest, not lying, not afraid to say your opinion."

Looking through the lens of science, the late economist Kenneth Boulding of Colorado also put "a very high value on veracity—telling the truth. The thing that gets you run out of the scientific community is being caught out telling a lie." Fortunately, said Bangladeshi banker Muhammad Yunus, the spread of technology makes it increasingly difficult for the truth to be hidden. In the future, "people will be forced to reveal themselves," he said. "Nothing can be kept hidden or secret—not in computers, not in the halls of government, nothing. People will feel much more comfortable when they're dealing in truth. You converge around and in truth."

Here, however, as with many of these global values, there was also a residue of concern—a fear that trust, which is central to honesty and truthfulness, seems to be falling into abeyance. "The idea that you ought to be able to trust somebody is out of fashion," worried Katharine Whitehorn, columnist for The Observer of London. That's a point seconded by corporate executive James K. Baker of Indiana. "Little by little," he said, "if we let that trust go out of our personal dealings with one another, then I think the system really begins to have trouble."

Fairness

Elevating the concept of justice to the top of his list, philosopher and author John W. Gardner of Stanford University said, "I consider that probably the number-one candidate for your common ground." By *justice*, he meant "fair play, or some word for even-handedness."

"Here, one could get caught up in the very complicated theories of social justice," warned James A. Joseph. "Or one could simply look at the Golden Rule. I relate fairness to treating other people as I would want to be treated. I think that [rule] serves humanity well. It ought to be a part of any ethic for the future."

For many, the concern for fairness goes hand in hand with the concept of equality. "The pursuit of equality is basic," said columnist and editor Sergio Muñoz of Mexico City and Los Angeles. "The people who come from Mexico and El Salvador have the same values, in my point of view, as the person who comes from Minnesota or from Alabama or from California—those basic principles that are common to all civilizations."

For some, like Joseph, the concept of fairness and equality focuses strongly on racial issues. Others, like author Jill Ker Conway from Australia, see the need for "greater equity between the sexes." Still others, like UNESCO Director-General Federico Mayor of Spain, see the problem as one of international relations: Despite the groundswell of interest in democracy arising within the former East Bloc nations, Westerners "have not reacted as humans, but only as economic individuals. . . . Even equity—the most important value in all the world—has collapsed."

Freedom

Very early in human history, said John Gardner, "the concept of degrees of freedom of my action—as against excessive constraints on my action by a tyrant or by military conquerors—emerged." Even the earliest peoples "knew when they were subjugated"—and didn't like it. That desire for liberty, he said, persists to the present as one of the defining values of humanity.

But liberty requires a sense of individuality and the right of that individual to express ideas freely, many of the interviewees said. "Without the principle of individual conscience, every attempt to institutionalize ethics must necessarily collapse" said Oscar Arias. "The effect of one upright individual is incalculable. World leaders may see their effect in headlines, but the ultimate course of the globe will be determined by the efforts of innumerable individuals acting on their consciences."

Such action, for many of these thinkers, is synonymous with democracy. "I think democracy is a must for all over the world," said Salim El Hoss, former prime minister of Lebanon. He defined the ingredients of democracy as "freedom of expression plus accountability plus equal opportunity." While he worried that the latter two are lacking in many countries, he noted that the first condition, freedom of expression, is increasingly becoming available to "all peoples."

Unity

As a counterbalance to the needs of individual conscience, however, stands the value that embraces the individual's role in a larger collective. Of the multitude of similar terms used for that concept in these interviews (*fraternity, solidarity, cooperation, community, group allegiance, oneness*) *unity* seems the most encompassing and the least open to misconstruction. For some, it is a simple *cri de coeur* in a world that seems close to coming un-done. "I want unity," said Dame Whina Cooper of New Zealand, adding that "God wants us to be one people." For Tarzie Vittachi of Sri Lanka, the idea of unity embraces a global vision capable of moving humanity from "unbridled competition" to cooperation. "That is what is demanded of us now: putting our community first, meaning the earth first, and all living things."

The problem arises when the common good is interpreted "by seeing the relation between the individual and the common in individualistic terms," said Father Bernard Przewozny of Rome. Carried to the extreme, individualism is "destructive of social life, destructive of communal sharing, destructive of participation," he said, adding that "the earth and its natural goods are the inheritance of all peoples."

Tolerance

"If you're serious about values," said John Gardner, "then you have to add tolerance very early—*very* early. Because you have to have constraints. The more you say, 'Values are important,' the more you have to say, 'There are limits to which you can impose your values on me.'"

"It is a question of respect for the dignity of each of us," said Graça Machel. "If you have a different idea from mine, it's not because you're worse than me. You have the right to think differently." Agreeing, Derek Bok defined tolerance as "a decent respect for the right of other people to have ideas, an obligation or at least a strong desirability of listening to different points of view and attempting to understand why they are held."

"You have your own job, you eat your own food," said Vietnamese writer and activist Le Ly Hayslip. "How you make that food is up to you, and how I live my life is up to me."

Reuben Snake traced the idea of tolerance back to a religious basis. "The spirit that makes you stand up and walk and talk and see and hear and think is the same spirit that exists in me—there's no difference," he said. "So when you look at me, you're looking at yourself—and I'm seeing me in you."

Abstracting from the idea of tolerance the core principle of respect for variety, Kenneth Boulding linked it to the environmentalist's urgency over the depletion of species. "If the blue whale is endangered, we feel worried about this, because we love the variety of the world," he explained. "In some sense I feel about the Catholic Church the way I feel about the blue whale: I don't think I'll be one, but I would feel diminished if it became extinct."

Responsibility

Oxford don A.H. Halsey placed the sense of responsibility high on his list of values because of its impact on our common future. "We are responsible for our grandchildren," he explained, "and we will make [the world] easier or more difficult for our grandchildren to be good people by what we do right here and now." This was a point made in a different way by Katharine White-horn, who noted that, while as a youth "it's fun to break away," it's very much harder to "grow up and have to put it together again."

For Nien Cheng, the spotlight falls not so much on the actions of the future as on the sense of self-respect in the present. "This is Confucius' teaching," she said. "You must take care of yourself. To rely on others is a great shame."

Responsibility also demands caring for others, Hayslip said. But, under the complex interactions of medicine, insurance, and law that exists in the West, "If you come into my house and see me lying here very sick, you don't dare move me, because you're not a doctor," she pointed out. "So where is your human obligation? Where is your human instinct to try to save me? You don't have it. You lost it, because there are too many rules."

Yet, paradoxically, "responsibility is not often mentioned in discussions of world politics or ethics," said Oscar Arias. "There, the talk is all of rights, demands, and desires." Human rights are "an unquestionable and critical priority for political societies and an indispensable lever for genuine development," he said. "But the important thing is not just to assert rights, but to ensure that they be protected. Achieving this protection rests wholly on the principle of responsibility."

Chicago attorney Newton Minow agreed. "I believe the basic reason we got off the track was that rights became more important than responsibilities, that individuals became more important than community interests. We've gotten to the point where everybody's got a right and nobody's got a responsibility."

At its ultimate, this sense of responsibility extends to the concept of the right use of force. "You shouldn't perpetrate violence," said Derek Bok simply, finding agreement with Jeane Kirkpatrick's insistence that "war is always undesirable" and that "any resort to force should be a very late option, never a first option."

Respect for Life

Growing out of this idea of the responsible use of force, but separate from and extending beyond it, is a value known most widely in the West from the Ten Commandments: Thou shalt not kill. For Shojun Bando, it is an inflexible principle: Even if ordered in wartime to defend his homeland by killing, he said, "I would refuse. I would say, 'I cannot do this.' "

Such an idea, expressed in today's peaceable Japan, may seem almost naive when examined through the lens of such war-riddled areas as the Middle East. Yet, Salim El Hoss took much the same view. "I was a prime minister [of Lebanon] for seven and a half years. I can't imagine myself signing a death penalty for anybody in the world. I think that is completely illegitimate, and I think that is the kind of thing a code of ethics should deal with."

Reuben Snake, noting that the North American Indians have a war-like reputation, said, "Probably the most serious shortcoming of tribal governments is their inability to effectively resolve conflict within the tribe and externally." He described earlier Indian traditions, however, in which great efforts were made by the tribal elders to prevent killing. That's a point with which Tarzie Vittachi—himself from the much-bloodied nation of Sri Lanka—felt perfectly at home. The first element of the Buddhist "daily prayer" under which he was raised, he recalled, is "I shall not kill." It is also central to the Ten Commandments of the Jewish decalogue under which Newton Minow was raised and which he said he still feels form the basis for the world's code of ethics.

Other Shared Values

There were, of course, other significant values that surfaced in these interviews. Nien Cheng, for instance, pointed to *courage*. "One should basically know what is right and what is wrong," she said, "and, when you know that, be courageous enough to stand for what is right."

Figuring strongly in Shojun Bando's pantheon was *wisdom*, which he defined as "attaining detachment, getting away from being too attached to things."

Whina Cooper put *hospitality* high on her list, recalling that her father said, "If you see any strangers going past, you call them—*Kia Ora*—that means to call them to come here." Astrid Lindgren put an emphasis on *obedience*—a quality that runs throughout the life of her most famous character, Pippi Longstocking, though usually in reverse.

Kenneth Boulding pointed to *peace*, which he defined simply as "well-managed conflict." Thinking of peace brought Salim El Hoss to the concept of stability. "Peace is equivalent to *stability*," he said, adding that "stability means a long-term perspective of no problems." These and other values, while they don't find broad support, had firm proponents among those we interviewed and deserve serious attention.

Other values mentioned included the burning public concerns for racial harmony, respect for women's place, and the protection of the environment. Many of the interviewees touched on them, and some elevated them to high priority. Speaking of the need for racial harmony, James Joseph put at the top of his list a sense of "respect for the cultures of other communities, respect for the need to begin to integrate into our collective memory appreciation of the contributions and traditions of those who are different." Jill Conway topped her list with a warning about the "increasing exploitation of women" around the world. And of the many human rights identified by Father Bernard Przewozny, the one to which he has dedicated his life is the "right to a healthy environment."

So what good is this code of values? It gives us a foundation for building goals, plans, and tactics, where things really happen and the world really changes. It unifies us, giving us a home territory of consensus and agreement. And it gives us a way—not the way, but *a* way—to reply when we're asked, "Whose values will you teach?" Answering this last question, as we tumble into the twenty-first century with the twentieth's sense of ethics, may be one of the most valuable mental activities of our time.

Part Two

Self-Leadership

Lesson

9 *Reflection*

Reflection is a tool to help foster healthy, analytic thinking. Frequent and effective systematic reflection is a necessary tool for leader development. It is a life skill that is, unfortunately underutilized and even under-appreciated in our "bias for action" military culture. We must understand this bias and strive to know when thoughtfulness is required pre-action and post-action.

READING 1

When we take the time to integrate action and reflection, we begin to behave differently. . . . As we become more purpose-centered, internally driven, other-focused, and externally open, we more fully integrate who we are with what we are doing. At this point, what we are doing enlarges our best self, and our best self enlarges what we are doing.

Here we will examine reflective action. It was Plato who once argued that the unexamined life is not worth living. To this someone once responded, "Yes, and the unlived life is not worth examining." Reflective action is a concept that combines both arguments. It is not easy to integrate both reflection and action. In the military for example, there is a tremendous imperative toward action. If we err between action and taking the time to reflect, we err on the side of action.

Given the bias toward action in modern life, let us begin our examination of the practice of reflective action from the other direction—from the viewpoint of a man who had chosen a life of reflection and contemplation.

In the military, we often become addicted to action. We develop organizational cultures that carry the expectations that people will come in early and leave late. We reinforce the compulsive patterns of type A personalities. We complain endlessly about the loss of balance in our lives and the pain of burnout. We assume that there is no place for reflection. We dare not speak of the need for spiritual awareness and personal integration. In this distorted world where we have institutionalized the split of action and reflection, we are trapped in the vortex of slow death. People often recognize the problem but lack the courage to do anything about it. They choose slow death over deep change.

Reflective Action

The positive tension of the state of reflective action. We can be so mindful and reflective that we become stagnant and inactive. On the other hand, and much more commonly in organizational life, we can be so active and energetic that we become mindless and unreflective.

The challenge is to be both reflective and active. We can do this by making a practice of regularly reflecting on what is happening in our lives. At first, we make time for contemplation when we are away from our usual tasks so as to increase our capacity for mindfulness during the tasks. Eventually we act and learn simultaneously. We are both mindful and energized while creating the life we want to live.

Practicing Reflective Action

Some Navy and Marine Corps officers have attributed "not making the same mistake twice" to their systematic method of maintaining a journal. Perhaps the most common way to integrate action and reflection is through the habit of journal writing. Some people record the events of each day in a process akin to diary writing by simply recording what happened during the day. *Reflective action requires more than just recording events.* It requires examination of who we are and how that matches with what we are doing. It often requires an exploration of the link between our present and our past.

While maintaining a journal serves many people as their method of reflection, there are several means of reflection one can use. *Systematically reflecting* refers to the manner or process of reflection that works best for you. Examples include meeting with teammates each week to discuss how practices have gone, using your daily Physical Training (PT) as time to think about the day's activities, or conversing with a friend to discuss your thoughts. An example from Plebe Summer is the daily Thoughts of the Day you completed each night. A good system of reflection might be to maintain a journal of all the leadership traits, both positive and negative, you have observed among the upper class. Periodically reflecting on these entries may help to avoid the traits you dislike and remind you of the traits you wish to exemplify.

Often times we reflect when it is natural or during times when it is most important to reflect. This type of reflection is an example of *natural reflection*. Generally after one has made a poor decision or made a mistake, time is spent trying to figure out why or how it could have been done better. While we have no way of knowing when these events will happen, the circumstances can compel us to think about the situation in a deep and meaningful way. This form of reflection can be very productive if we are objective in our assessment of the situation and we learn something positive from the experience.

Inserting some form of regularity or routine into one's reflection is an example of *recurrent reflection*. Recurrent reflection refers to *when* you reflect and not necessarily *how* you do so. Examples of this form of reflection are doing so every night before bed, during church, or during the ten minutes between third and fourth period. Some people find it important to maintain a formal schedule and like having a very specific time to spend in reflection. Putting aside time to think through the happenings of each day might serve useful in maintaining yourself as a reflective person that can act using lessons learned.

Being mindful of the past so that you can actively and energetically tackle future tasks embodies the idea of reflective action. Although many consider reflection to be a very personal and private process, reflection can be done *either alone or with others*. By asking for the help of a shipmate, friend or family member to think through why something happened, you will often find a different and potentially richer, point of view. In the fleet, junior officers are encouraged to seek the advice of the senior enlisted that have "been there and done that." By engaging others in reflecting on your daily life, you might find that you can avoid mistakes that have already been made by someone else.

READING 2

"Leadership Character: The Role of Reflection" Kail - Washington Post 3/9/2012

Some say experience is what you get when you don't get what you want. Perhaps. But I say experience is only as valuable as what we do with it.

Gaining *wisdom* from an experience requires reflection. In thinking back on the significant events of my life, experiences good and bad, it was the act of assigning meaning that has made all the difference for me. Reflection requires a type of introspection that goes beyond merely thinking, talking or complaining about our experiences. It is an effort to understand how the events of our life shape the way in which we see the world, ourselves and others. And it is essential for any leader.

Reflection is what links our performance to our potential. It is the process of properly unpacking ourselves as leaders for the good of others. We can't apply an abstract construct such as leading through crisis without experiencing what crisis does to us individually and collectively.

The concept of "reflection" may sound self involved, but it's actually just the opposite. By not reflecting, we engage in a narcissistic rationalization that makes us feel better about the events in our lives yet keeps us from learning from them. There is a natural tendency to attribute all our successes to ourselves and all our failures to forces beyond our control.

So where do you start? I find reflection often comes best through the help of a mentor who will ask seemingly simple questions, like: "What could you have done better, and why?" Or, "Did you do anything wrong?"

A little story: One time, I was very angry about being held responsible for consequences I considered beyond my control. I vented to a mentor about how unfairly I had been treated, and he responded by saying, "I see. This is really not your fault, is it?" I immediately felt comforted, and then he set the hook. "Eric, what would taking the blame off of you do for your soldiers?"

I didn't have to answer him. My anger turned to shame as I realized I had placed myself smack there at the center of importance. If my mentor had told me I was being selfish, I would have left his office angrier and even more isolated. Instead, he enabled me to reflect on how leadership is about moving forward for the good of those we lead, not about assigning or avoiding blame for our own self interests.

Encouraging reflection in your organization starts by being a good mentor yourself. I would caution, though, that assigning mentors doesn't work well—it's awkward and will only lead to frustration. Instead, be aware of those conversations in which others ask for your advice or want to run something by you. That's how mentorship begins. And like any other relationship built on trust, it begins slowly.

If you are fortunate enough to have someone seek out your mentorship, listen and challenge. No pithy advice will engage them in reflection as well as a simple, probing question can. Help them explore and assign meaning to their experiences. And remember, they came to see you about them, not you.

Col. Eric Kail is an Army field artillery officer who has commanded at the company and battalion levels. He is the course director of military leadership at the U.S. Military Academy at West Point. He holds a PhD in organizational psychology.

Disclaimer: The views expressed in this article are those of the author and do not reflect the official policy or position of the Department of the Army, Department of Defense or the U.S. Government.

Lesson

10 *Motivation and Goals*

Understand that people are motivated differently, and there are multiple methods available to motivate yourself, as well as those around you, especially the use of setting and communicating organizational goals.

READING 1

According to a widely accepted explanation of human behavior, people have needs and motives that propel them toward achieving certain goals. Needs and motives are closely related. A **need** is an internal striving or urge to do something, such as a need to drink when thirsty. It can be regarded as a biological or psychological requirement. Because the person is deprived in some way (such as not having enough fluid in the body), the person is motivated to take action toward a goal. In this case the goal might be simply getting something to drink.

A **motive** is an inner drive that moves a person to do something. The motive is usually based on a need or desire and results in the intention to attain an appropriate goal. Because needs and motives are so closely related, the two terms are often used interchangeably. For example, "recognition need" and "recognition motive" refer to the same thing.

Maslow's Need Hierarchy

The best-known categorization of needs is **Maslow's need hierarchy.** At the same time, it is the most widely used explanation of human motivation. According to psychologist Abraham H. Maslow, people strive to satisfy the following groups of needs in step-by-step order:

1. *Physiological needs* refer to bodily needs, such as the requirements for food, water, and sleep.
2. *Safety needs* refer to actual physical safety and to a feeling of being safe from both physical and emotional injury.
3. *Social needs* are essentially love or belonging needs. Unlike the two previous levels of needs, they center around a person's interaction with other people.
4. *Esteem needs* represent an individual's demand to be seen as a person of worth by others—and to him- or herself.
5. *Self-actualizing needs* are the highest level of needs, including the needs for self-fulfillment and personal development.

Notice the distinction between higher-level and lower-level needs. With few exceptions, higher-level needs are more difficult to satisfy. A person's needs for affiliation might be satisfied by being a member of a friendly work group. Yet to satisfy self-actualization needs, such as self-fulfillment, a person might have to develop an outstanding reputation in his or her company.

The need hierarchy implies that most people think of finding a job as a way of obtaining the necessities of life. Once these are obtained, a person may think of achieving friendship, self-esteem, and self-fulfillment on the job. When a person is generally satisfied at one level, he or she looks for satisfaction at a higher level. As Maslow describes it, a person is a "perpetually wanting animal." Very few people are totally satisfied with their lot in life, even the rich and famous.

The extent of need satisfaction is influenced by a person's job. Some construction jobs, for example, involve dangerous work in severe climates, thus frustrating both physiological and safety needs. Ordinarily there is much more opportunity for approaching self-actualization when a person occupies a prominent position, such as a top executive or famous performer. However, a person with low potential could approach self-actualization by occupying a lesser position. In the current era, workers at all levels are threatened with the frustration of security needs because so many companies reduce the number of employees to save money.

How do Maslow's needs and the other needs described in this lesson relate to self-motivation? First you have to ask yourself, "Which needs do I really want to satisfy?" After answering the question honestly, concentrate your efforts on an activity that will most likely satisfy that need. For instance, if you are hungry for power, strive to become a high-level manager or a business owner. If you crave self-esteem, focus your efforts on work and social activities that are well regarded by others. The point is that you will put forth substantial effort if you think the goal you attain will satisfy an important need.

How Does Goal Setting Work?[2]

Despite abundant goal-setting research and practice, goal-setting theories are surprisingly scarce. An instructive model was formulated by Locke and his associates. According to Locke's model, goal setting has four motivational mechanisms.

Goals Direct Attention

Goals direct one's attention and effort toward goal-relevant activities and away from goal-irrelevant activities. If, for example, you have a term project due in a few days, your thoughts and actions tend to revolve around completing that project. Scooter Store, which was included among the list of the 100 best companies to work for in America in 2004 by *Fortune,* uses this motivational function of goal setting on a daily basis. Every morning the company's managers assemble their workers in a 14-minute huddle to discuss the day's goals.

Goals Regulate Effort

Not only do goals make us selectively perceptive, they also motivate us to act. The instructor's deadline for turning in your term project would prompt you to complete it, as opposed to going out with friends, watching television, or studying for another course. Generally, the level of effort expended is proportionate to the difficulty of the goal.

Goals Increase Persistence

Within the context of goal setting, persistence represents the effort expended on a task over an extended period of time: It takes effort to run 100 meters; it takes persistence to run a 26-mile marathon. Persistent people tend to see obstacles as challenges to be overcome rather than as reasons to fail. A difficult goal that is important to an individual is a constant reminder to keep exerting effort in the appropriate direction. Annika Sorenstam is a great example of someone who persisted at her goal

---

[2] Kreitner, R. & Kinicki, A. (2007). *Organizational Behavior* (7th ed.). New York: McGraw-Hill.

of being the best female golfer in the world. She has won 62 tournaments since starting on the LPGA tour in 1994.

She already has qualified for the LPGA and World Golf Halls of Fame, has won a career Grand Slam, shot the only round of 59 in women's pro golf and has won six Player of the Year titles.

[In 2003] her new challenge was playing in a PGA Tour event, where she made a lasting impression but failed to make the cut. When it was over, she said she didn't care to compete in more men's tournaments but needed to move on.

Moving on meant winning two more LPGA majors. Just like Tiger Woods, major titles and a single-season Grand Slam have become her new focus.

"Nobody else has done it, so I think that says it all," she said. "But I like to set high goals, I like to motivate myself. If you believe it in your mind, I think you can do it."

Goals Foster the Development and Application of Task Strategies and Action Plans

If you are here and your goal is out there somewhere, you face the problem of getting from here to there. For example, the person who has resolved to lose 20 pounds must develop a plan for getting from "here" (his or her present weight) to "there" (20 pounds lighter). Goals can help because they encourage people to develop strategies and action plans that enable them to achieve their goals. By virtue of setting a weight-reduction goal, the dieter may choose a strategy of exercising more, eating less, or some combination of the two.

Setting Smart Goals

In accordance with available research evidence, goals should be "SMART." SMART is an acronym that stands for specific, measurable, attainable, results oriented, and time bound. Table 10-1 contains a set of guidelines for writing SMART goals. There are two additional recommendations to consider when setting goals. First, for complex tasks, [leaders] should train [subordinates] in problem-solving techniques and encourage them to develop a performance action plan. Action plans specify the strategies or tactics to be used in order to accomplish a goal.

Table 10-1 Guidelines for Writing SMART Goals

Specific	Goals should be stated in precise rather than vague terms. For example, a goal that provides for 20 hours of technical training for each [sailor and marine] is more specific than stating that a manager should send as many people as possible to training classes. Goals should be quantified when possible.
Measurable	A measurement device is needed to assess the extent to which a goal is accomplished. Goals thus need to be measurable. It also is critical to consider the quality aspect of the goal when establishing measurement criteria. For example, if the goal is to complete a managerial study of methods to increase productivity one must consider how to measure the quality of this effort. Goals should not be set without considering the interplay between quantity and quality of output.
Attainable	Goals should be realistic, challenging, and attainable. Impossible goals reduce motivation because people do not like to fail. Remember, people have different levels of ability and skill.
Results oriented	[Command] goals should focus on desired end-results that support the [Navy's] vision. In turn, an individual's goals should directly support the accomplishment of [command] goals. Activities support the achievement of goals and are outlined in action plans. To focus goals on desired end-results, goals should start with the word to followed by verbs such as *complete, acquire, produce, increase,* and *decrease.* Verbs such as *develop, conduct, implement,* or *monitor* imply activities and should not be used in a goal statement.
Time bound	Goals specify target dates for completion.

SOURCE: Kinicki, A.J. (2005). *Performance Management Systems.* Superstition Mt., AZ: Kinicki and Associates Inc.

READING 2

"Understanding and Influencing Follower Motivation," reprinted from *Leadership: Enhancing the Lessons of Experience*, edited by Richard L. Hughes, Robert C. Ginnett and Gordon S. Curphy (1993), by permission of McGrawHill Companies.

Richard L. Hughes has a Ph.D. in clinical psychology and heads the Department of Behavioral Sciences and Leadership at the United States Air Force Academy. Robert C. Ginnett has a Ph.D. in organizational behavior from Yale University and is currently deputy department head for leadership programs and counseling at the United States Air Force Academy. Gordon Curphy's graduate work was in industrial/organizational psychology. He was an associate professor at the Air Force Academy, and is now a senior consultant at Personnel Decisions, Inc.

Many people believe the most important quality of a good leader is the ability to motivate others to accomplish group tasks. The importance of motivation as a component of output is suggested in findings from diverse work groups that most people believe they could give as much as 15 percent or 20 percent more effort at work than they now do with no one, including their own bosses, recognizing any difference. Perhaps even more startling, these workers also believed they could give 15 percent or 20 percent *less* effort with no one noticing any difference. Moreover, variation in the output of jobs varies significantly across leaders and followers. Hunter, Schmidt, and Judiesch estimated the top 15 percent of the workers for a particular job produced from 20 to 50 percent more output than the average worker, depending on the complexity of the job. What can leaders and followers do to enhance the motivation to perform? . . .

According to Kanfer, **motivation** is anything that provides *direction, intensity*, and *persistence* to behavior. Another definition considers the term *motivation* a sort of shorthand to describe choosing an activity or task to engage in, establishing the level of effort to put forth on it, and determining the degree of persistence in it over time. Like preferences and personality traits, motivation is not directly observable; it must be inferred from behavior. For example, if one person regularly assembles twice as many computers as any other person in his work group—assuming all have the same abilities, skills, and resources—then we likely would say this first person is more motivated than the others. We use the concept of motivation to explain differences we see among people in the energy and direction of their behavior. . . .

Few topics of human behavior have been the subject of so many books and articles as that of motivation. So much has been written about motivation that a comprehensive review of the subject is beyond the scope . . . [here]. This section will, however, overview several major approaches to understanding work motivation, as well as address their implications for followers' satisfaction and performance. (See for more comprehensive reviews.) It is important for leadership practitioners to become familiar with these major approaches, which offer a variety of perspectives and ideas for influencing followers' decisions to choose, exert effort, or resist an activity. Additionally, through such understanding, leadership practitioners may recognize that some motivation theories are more applicable in certain situations, or for producing certain outcomes, than others. . . .

Need Theories

The two major need theories include Maslow's hierarchy of needs and Alderfer's existence-relatedness-growth (ERG) theory. These two theories assume all people share a common set of basic needs. **Needs** refer to internal states of tension or arousal, or uncomfortable states of deficiency people are motivated to change.

Maslow's Hierarchy of Needs

According to Maslow, people are motivated to satisfy five basic sorts of needs. These include the need to survive physiologically, the need for security, the need for affiliation with other people, the need to feel self-esteem, and the need for self-actualization. Maslow's conceptualization of needs is usually represented by a triangle with the five levels of needs arranged in a hierarchy called, not surprisingly, the **hierarchy of needs**. According to Maslow, any person's behavior can be understood primarily as directed effort to satisfy one particular level of need in the hierarchy. Which level happens to be motivating one's behavior at any time depends on whether "lower" needs have been satisfied. According to Maslow, lower level needs must be satisfied before the next higher level would become salient in motivating behavior.

As an example, if Eric's salary were sufficient to meet his physiological needs, and his job security and retirement plan were sufficient to meet his security needs, neither of these two needs would serve to energize and direct his behavior. However, if he were in a secluded position on an assembly line and could not talk with others or be part of a close work group, he may still feel unfulfilled in his needs for affiliation and belongingness. This may cause him to put a lot of effort into forming friendships and socializing at work.

Maslow said higher-level needs like those for self-esteem or self-actualization would not become salient (even when unfulfilled) until lower needs were satisfied. Thus, a practical implication of his theory is that leaders may only be successful in motivating follower behavior by taking account of the follower's position on the need hierarchy. For example, it might be relatively inefficient to try to motivate our lonely assembly-line worker by appealing to how much pride he would take in a job well done (i.e., to his self-esteem); Maslow said only *after* one feels part of a social group will such motives become energizing. At all levels of the hierarchy, the leader should watch for mismatches between his motivational efforts and the followers' lowest unsatisfied needs.

ERG Theory

Alderfer's **existence-relatedness-growth (ERG) theory** has several similarities to Maslow's hierarchy of needs. In the terms of ERG theory, existence needs basically correspond to Maslow's physiological and security needs; relatedness needs are like

Maslow's social and esteem needs; and growth needs are similar to the need for self-actualization. Beyond those similarities, however, are two important differences.

First, Alderfer reported that people sometimes try to satisfy more than one need at the same time. For example, even though a follower's existence needs may not be entirely satisfied, she may still be motivated to grow as a person. Second, he claimed frustration of a higher-level need can lead to efforts to satisfy a lower-level need. In other words, a follower who is continually frustrated in achieving some need might "regress" and exert effort to "satisfy" a lower need that already has been satisfied. For example, if the nature of work on an assembly line repeatedly frustrates Eric's need for relatedness with others, he may eventually stop trying to satisfy these needs at work and regress to demanding more pay—an existence need—and might, then, try to satisfy the relatedness need outside of work. Alderfer called this the **frustration-regression hypothesis**.

Concluding Thoughts on Need Theories

Although both Maslow's and Alderfer's need theories have played an important historical role in our understanding of motivation, they do have certain limitations. For one thing, neither theory makes specific predictions about what an individual will do to satisfy a particular need. In the example above, Eric may exert considerable effort to establish new friendships at work, try to make friends outside of work, or even spend a lot of money on a new car or stereo equipment (the frustration-regression hypothesis). The theories' lack of specificity and predictive power severely limits their practical applicability in organizational, school, or team settings. On the other hand, awareness of the general nature of the various sorts of basic human needs described in these two theories seems fundamentally useful to leaders. . . .

Cognitive Theories

The . . . cognitive theories we will describe here are concerned primarily with clarifying the conscious thought processes people use when deciding how hard or long to work toward some task or goal.

Equity Theory

As the name implies, **equity theory** emphasizes the motivational importance to followers of fair treatment by their leaders. It assumes that people value fairness in leader-follower exchange relationships. Followers are said to be most satisfied when they believe that what they put into an activity or job and what they get out of it are roughly equivalent to what others put into and get out of it. Equity theory proposes a very rational model for how followers assess these issues. Followers presumably reach decisions about equitable relationships by assigning values to the four elements then comparing the two ratios. In looking at the specific elements in each ratio, personal outcomes refer to what one is receiving for one's efforts, such as pay, job satisfaction, opportunity for advancement, and personal growth. Personal inputs refer to all those things one contributes to a job such as time, effort, knowledge, and skills.

A key aspect of equity theory is that contains *two* ratios. Judgments of equity are always based on comparison to some reference group. It is the *relationship* between *the two ratios* that is important in equity theory, not the absolute value of either one's own outcomes or inputs, or those of others, considered by themselves. What matters most is the comparison between one's own ratio and that of a reference group such as one's co-workers or workers holding similar jobs in other organizations. For example, there may be many people who make more money than a particular follower; they may also, however, work longer hours, have more skills, or have to live in undesirable geographic locations to do so. In other words, although their outcomes are greater, so are their inputs, and thus the ratios may still be equal; there is equity.

In essence, equity theory does not try to evaluate "equality of inputs" or "equality of outcomes." It is concerned with "fairness" of inputs relative to outcomes. The perception of inequity creates a state of tension and an inherient pressure for change. As long as there is general equality between the two ratios, there is no motivation (at least based on inequity) to change anything, and people are reasonably satisfied. If, however, the ratios are significantly different, a follower will be motivated to take action likely to restore the balance. Exactly what the follower will be motivated to do depends on the direction of the inequality. Adams suggested six ways people might restore balance: (*a*) changing their inputs; (*b*) changing their outcomes; (c) altering their self-perceptions; (*d*) altering their perceptions of their reference group; (*e*) changing their reference group; or, if all else fails, (*f*) leaving the situation. Thus, if a follower believed her ratio was lower than her co-worker's, she may reduce her level of effort or seek higher pay elsewhere. Research has shown that perceptions of underpayment generally resulted in actions in support of the model, but perceptions of overpayment did not. Instead of working harder in an over-payment condition (to make their own ratio more equitable), subjects often rationalized that they really deserved the higher pay.

Expectancy Theory

First described by Tolman, **expectancy theory** has been modified for use in work settings. It involves two fundamental assumptions: (*a*) Motivated performance is the result of conscious choice and (*b*) people will do what they believe will provide them the highest (or surest) rewards. Thus, expectancy theory, like equity theory, is a highly rational approach to understanding motivation. It assumes that people act in ways that maximize their expectations of attaining valued outcomes and that reliable predictions of behavior are possible if the factors that influence those expectations can be quantified. In this model, there are three such factors to be quantified. The first two are probability estimates (expectancies), and the third is a vector sum of predicted positive and negative outcomes.

The first probability estimate is the **effort-to-performance expectancy**. Like all probabilities, it ranges from no chance of the event occurring to an absolute certainty of it occurring; or, in decimal form, from 0.0 to 1.0. Here, the follower estimates the likelihood of performing the desired behavior adequately, assuming she puts forth the required effort. The second probability estimate is the **performance-to-outcome expectancy**. In this case, our follower estimates the likelihood of receiving a reward,

TABLE 10.2	Motivators and Hygiene Factors of the Two-Factor Theory	

MOTIVATORS	HYGIENE FACTORS
Achievement	Supervision
Recognition	Working conditions
The work itself	Co-workers
Responsibility	Pay
Advancement and growth	Policies/procedures
	Job security

SOURCE: Adapted from Herzberg, *Work and the Nature of Man* (Cleveland, Ohio: World Publishing, 1966).

given that she achieves the desired level of performance. This is a necessary step in the sequence since it is not uncommon for people actually to do good work yet not be rewarded for it (e.g., someone else may be the teacher's pet). Finally, the follower must determine the likely outcomes, assuming that the previous conditions have been met, and determine whether their weighted algebraic sum (**valence**) is sufficiently positive to be worth the time and effort. To put it more simply, expectancy theory says that people will be motivated to do a task if three conditions are met; (1) They *can* do the task, (2) they will be rewarded if they do it, and (3) they value the reward. . . .

Situational Approaches

These approaches place considerably more emphasis on how the situation affects motivation. In other words, these approaches emphasize the leader's role in changing various aspects of the situation in order to increase followers' motivational levels. The three theories that emphasize situational influences in motivation are Herzberg's two-factor theory, the job characteristics model, and the operant approach.

Herzberg's Two-Factor Theory

Herzberg developed the **two-factor theory** from a series of interviews he conducted with accountants and engineers. More specifically, he asked what satisfied them about their work and found that their answers usually could be sorted into five consistent categories. Furthermore, rather than assuming what dissatisfied people was always just the opposite of what satisfied them, he also specifically asked what dissatisfied people about their jobs. Surprisingly, the list of satisfiers and dissatisfiers represented entirely different aspects of work.

Herzberg labeled the factors that led to *satisfaction* at work motivators, and he labeled the factors that led to *dissatisfaction* at work hygiene factors. The most common motivators and hygiene factors can be found in Table 10.2. According to the two-factor theory, efforts directed toward improving hygiene factors will not increase followers' motivation. No matter how much leaders improve working conditions, pay, or sick-leave policies, for example, followers *will not* exert any additional effort or persist any longer at a task. For example, followers will probably be no more motivated to do a dull and boring job merely by being given pleasant office furniture. On the other hand, followers may be asked to work in conditions so poor as to create dissatisfaction, which can distract them from constructive work.

Given limited resources on the leader's part, the key to increasing followers' effort levels according to two-factor theory is to just adequately satisfy the hygiene factors while maximizing the motivators for a particular job. It is important for working conditions to be adequate, but it is even more important (for enhancing motivation) to provide plenty of recognition, responsibility, and possibilities for advancement. In the words of Fred Herzberg, "if you don't want people to have Mickey Mouse attitudes, then don't give them Mickey Mouse work" (unpublished comments). . . .

The Job Characteristics Model

According to the **job characteristics model**, jobs or tasks having certain kinds of characteristics provide inherently greater motivation and job satisfaction than others. Hackman and Oldham said that followers will work harder and be more satisfied if their tasks are meaningful, provide ample feedback, allow considerable latitude in deciding how to accomplish them, and require use of a variety of skills. The Hackman and Oldham model is based on five critical job characteristics: task identity, task significance, feedback, autonomy, and skill variety.

Note that while a job high in all these characteristics might seem intrinsically motivating, this model is not just another way of looking at intrinsic motivation. *Individuals* differ in their intrinsic motivation, whereas the job characteristics model says some *jobs* are, by their nature, more motivating and satisfying than others.

Actually, individual differences also play an important role in the job characteristics model. In this case the critical individual difference is called **growth-need strength,** which refers to the degree to which an individual is motivated by the need to fulfill herself (in Maslow's terms, to increase one's self-esteem or self-actualization). Hackman and Oldham said that individuals with high growth-need strength especially desire jobs high on the five characteristics in the model; they are even more motivated and satisfied than others with such jobs, and even less motivated and satisfied than others with jobs very low on those characteristics. Thus, if leaders were to follow the tenets of the job characteristics model to increase followers' satisfaction

---

TABLE 10.3 Schedules of Reinforcement

Continuous: When rewards are given every time a person manifests a specific response. An example would be giving a golfer praise every time he broke par.

Fixed ratio: When rewards are given after a certain number of responses occur. For example, a coach may give her players a reward every time they shoot 100 free throws before practice.

Fixed interval: When rewards are given after a fixed period of time has elapsed, such as a weekly or monthly paycheck.

Variable ratio: When rewards are administered on a variable basis, but on average after a certain number of responses have occurred. An example would be a worker who gets rewarded after successfully assembling as few as 10 or as many as 20 computers, but on average the worker receives reinforcement after an average of 15 computers have been assembled.

Variable interval: Similar to the variable ratio schedule, except in this case rewards are administered after an average amount of time has elapsed. A worker might get a reward after 3, 8, or 1 days of good work, but on average receives a reward once a week.

and motivation, then they would hire followers with high growth-need strength, and they would restructure followers' jobs to have more favorable task characteristics.

The Operant Approach

The **operant approach** focuses on modifying rewards and punishments in order to change the direction, intensity, or persistence of *observable behavior*. It will help at the outset of this discussion to define several terms. A **reward** is any consequence that *increases* the likelihood that a particular behavior will be repeated. For example, if a student receives an A on a science project, then she will be more likely to work hard on the next science project. **Punishment** is the administration of an aversive stimulus or the withdrawal of something desirable, each of which *decreases* the likelihood a particular behavior will be repeated. Thus, if a child loses his allowance for talking back to his parents, then he will be less likely to do so again in the future. Both rewards and punishments can be administered in a contingent or noncontingent manner. **Contingent** rewards or punishments are administered as consequences of a particular behavior. Examples might include giving a runner a medal immediately after she won a race or grounding a teenage son after he comes home late. **Noncontingent** rewards and punishments are not associated with a particular behavior and might include receiving the same monthly paycheck even after working considerably less hard than the month before or getting a better parking slot because of seniority rather than performance. Rewards and punishments can also be administered using different schedules, such as those found in Table 10.3. Finally, behaviors that are not rewarded will eventually be eliminated through the process of **extinction**.

Research evidence has consistently shown that the operant approach is a very effective way of modifying followers' motivation and performance levels. Other evidence has shown that rewards were more strongly related to satisfaction and performance than was punishment, and that contingent rewards and punishments were more strongly related to satisfaction and performance than noncontingent rewards and punishments.

Although these findings paint an encouraging picture of the practical utility of the operant approach, implementing it correctly in a work setting can be difficult. Using operant principles properly to improve followers' motivation and hence performance requires following several steps. First, leaders need to *clearly specify* what behaviors are important. Second, leaders need to determine if those behaviors are currently being punished, rewarded, or ignored. Believe it or not, sometimes followers are actually rewarded for behavior that leaders are trying to extinguish and are punished for behavior that leaders want to increase. For example, followers may get considerable positive attention from peers by talking back to the leader or by violating dress codes. Similarly certain overly competitive employees may be promoted ahead of their peers (by walking over their backs, we might say), even when management's rhetoric extols the need for cooperation and teamwork. It also may be the case that leaders sometimes just ignore the very behaviors they would like to see strengthened. An example here would be if a leader consistently failed to provide reward when followers produced high-quality products despite the leader's rhetoric always emphasizing the importance of quality.

Third, leaders need to find out what followers actually find rewarding and punishing. Leaders should *not* make the mistake of assuming that followers will find the same things rewarding and punishing as they do, nor should they assume that all followers will find the same things to be rewarding and punishing. What may be one follower's punishment may be another follower's reward. For example, some followers may dislike public attention and actually exert *less* effort after being publicly recognized; other followers may find public attention to be extremely rewarding. Fourth, leaders need to be wary of creating perceptions of inequality and decreasing intrinsic motivation when administering individually tailored rewards. Fifth, leaders should not limit themselves to administering organizationally sanctioned rewards and punishments. Using a bit of ingenuity, leaders can often come up with an array of potential rewards and punishments that are effective, inexpensive, and do not violate company policies. Finally, because the administration of noncontingent consequences has relatively little impact, leaders should administer rewards and punishments in a contingent manner whenever possible.

Concluding Thoughts on Situational Approaches to Motivation

The two-factor theory, the job characteristics model, and the operant approach all make one important point that is often overlooked in other theories of motivation: By changing the situation, leaders can enhance followers' motivation, performance, and satisfaction. Unfortunately, the same approaches tend to pay too little attention to the importance of needs, individual difference variables, and cognitive processes in the direction, intensity, and persistence of followers' behaviors (with the exception of growth-need strength in the job characteristics model). Perhaps the best strategy for leaders is to recognize that some motivational theories are more applicable to some situations than others, and to be flexible in the types of motivational interventions they use. However, leaders will only be able to adopt a flexible motivation intervention strategy if they become familiar with the strengths and weaknesses of the different theories and approaches. Just as a carpenter can more effectively build a house by using a variety of tools, a leader can be more effective by using a variety of motivational interventions to resolve work problems.

READING 3

"Intrinsic and Extrinsic Motivation; Classic Definitions and New Directions" Ryan and Deci. Contemporary Educational Psychology. 2000 Jan 25 (1)

To be motivated means to be moved to do something. A person who feels no impetus or inspiration to act is thus characterized as unmotivated, whereas someone who is energized or activated toward an end is considered motivated. Most everyone who works or plays with others is, accordingly, concerned with motivation, facing the question of how much motivation those others, or oneself, has for a task, and practitioners of all types face the perennial task of fostering more versus less motivation in those around them. Most theories of motivation reflect these concerns by viewing motivation as a unitary phenomenon, one that varies from very little motivation to act to a great deal of it.

Yet, even brief reflection suggests that motivation is hardly a unitary phenomenon. People have not only different amounts, but also different kinds of motivation. That is, they vary not only in level of motivation (i.e., how much motivation), but also in the orientation of that motivation (i.e., what type of motivation). Orientation of motivation concerns the underlying attitudes and goals that give rise to action—that is, it concerns the why of actions. As an example, a student can be highly motivated to do homework out of curiosity and interest or, alternatively, because he or she wants to procure the approval of a teacher or parent. A student could be motivated Address correspondence and reprint requests to Richard Ryan, University of Rochester, to learn a new set of skills because he or she understands their potential utility or value or because learning the skills will yield a good grade and the privileges a good grade affords. In these examples the amount of motivation does not necessarily vary, but the nature and focus of the motivation being evidenced certainly does.

Intrinsic motivation is defined as the doing of an activity for its inherent satisfactions rather than for some separable consequence. When intrinsically motivated a person is moved to act for the fun or challenge entailed rather than because of external prods, pressures, or rewards. The phenomenon of intrinsic motivation was first acknowledged within experimental studies of animal behavior, where it was discovered that many organisms engage in exploratory, playful, and curiosity-driven behaviors even in the absence of reinforcement or reward (White, 1959). These spontaneous behaviors, although clearly bestowing adaptive benefits on the organism, appear not to be done for any such instrumental reason, but rather for the positive experiences associated with exercising and extending ones capacities.

Although intrinsic motivation is clearly an important type of motivation, most of the activities people do are not, strictly speaking, intrinsically motivated. This is especially the case after early childhood, as the freedom to be intrinsically motivated becomes increasingly curtailed by social demands and roles that require individuals to assume responsibility for nonintrinsically interesting tasks. In schools, for example, it appears that intrinsic motivation becomes weaker with each advancing grade.

Extrinsic motivation is a construct that pertains whenever an activity is done in order to attain some separable outcome. Extrinsic motivation thus contrasts with intrinsic motivation, which refers to doing an activity simply for the enjoyment of the activity itself, rather than its instrumental value. However, unlike some perspectives that view extrinsically motivated behavior as invariantly nonautonomous, SDT proposes that extrinsic motivation can vary greatly in the degree to which it is autonomous. For example, a student who does his homework only because he fears parental sanctions for not doing it is extrinsically motivated because he is doing the work in order to attain the separable outcome of avoiding sanctions. Similarly, a student who does the work because she personally believes it is valuable for her chosen career is also extrinsically motivated because she too is doing it for its instrumental value rather than because she finds it interesting. Both examples involve instrumentalities, yet the latter case entails personal endorsement and a feeling of choice, whereas the former involves mere compliance with an external control. Both represent intentional behavior, but the two types of extrinsic motivation vary in their relative autonomy.

Lesson

11 *Purpose*

By understanding the "why" for things, from mundane tasks to large scale operations, missions etc., and communicating it to the organization, leaders are more able to affect the motivation and commitment of their followers to the desired end-state.

Part Three

Leading Others

Lesson

12 *Civility*

By conducting ourselves in a manner that demonstrates respect and models civility to others, we ensure that we continue to develop the healthy relationships that are the foundation of leadership.

READING 1

CAPT James A. Campbell, USN (RET)
Class of 1972 Distinguished Military Professor for Character Education

Plebe Summer is over! Today you move to your new company area, from 6th wing to 1st wing ... bummer. And WOW, all that stuff! You never realized how much you were issued since you didn't use most of it over the summer. And on top of that, you have to move a computer too! You need to get some things at the Mid Store for cleaning and maybe some deodorant ... you'll definitely need some after this move. You decide to go after breakfast.

Your shoes are looking good; they should, since you spent about an hour on them last night! But just as you're heading out the door, your roommate blows by you and wipes out the toe of your left shoe. "Sorry, man," he shouts over his shoulder as he beats you out the door. There's no time to change shoes so you'll have to risk it at formation. "No chance," you mumble as you chop into the P-way. "I'm screwed." Sure enough, you get flamed on by your 2/C and put on "All Calls." Nice. He didn't have to beat you out the door. Did you see a smirk on his face?

Having been ordered to change shoes by your Squad Leader, you arrive to your squad table late to find no seats ... thanks again, roommate! You finally find a seat at another company's table and request permission to come aboard. As the Firstie stares at you, she grudgingly grants permission. She wants to know why you're late, and you try the obligatory "No excuse, Ma'am." It doesn't work. She wants the real reason. You retell the story, and she asks to see the shoes you are wearing, which aren't your best. Of course, that draws another flame session while standing at attention, and as you take your seat, you note that most of the food is gone. "I guess it doesn't matter anyway," you think to yourself as breakfast ends and you're all dismissed. You can pick up some snacks in the Mid Store, along with the deodorant, in your brief few minutes of free time before the big move.

You're unable to find your favorite deodorant so you ask one of the attendants (a high schooler just working for the summer) if there might be some in the back. He responds, "What you see is what you get." Fair enough—what's the big deal anyway? Deodorant is deodorant, right? This guy isn't interested in helping you anyway; he turns away and continues flirting with one of the other female workers. You grab some deodorant and a snack and go to checkout. You give the clerk your Mid Store card. He gives you an icy stare and the words: "Don't you have cash? I'm new here and not sure how to charge your card." The hits just keep on coming!

After the cashier finally figures out how to charge your account (while you endure the heated stares from the mids waiting in line behind you), you head back to your room, already dreading the task of schlepping your stuff from one side of the world to the other.

As you chop back to your room, each greeting of "Good morning, Sir" or "Good morning, Ma'am" is returned with either a wordless stare or something mumbled unintelligibly. It's then that you think about your lessons over the summer, the preaching about "brothers and sisters in arms," "one team, one fight," and being "professional." Did you miss something? Was that all a bunch of fluff? So much for brothers and sisters in arms, you think. I'm treated like crap around here. What a fine Navy day so far, and it is not even 0830!

Any or all of the above story sound familiar? If so, then you have experienced a lack of *civility*. In the next few pages, let's try to identify this concept called civility, its connection to leadership, specifically military leadership, and how you can work to establish a habit of civility while at the Naval Academy.

Stephen Carter, the author of the book, *Civility: Manners, Morals, and the Etiquette of Democracy*, defines civility as the "**. . . sum of the many sacrifices we are called to make for the sake of living together. When we pretend that we travel alone, we can also pretend that these sacrifices are unnecessary.**" Carter considers integrity and civility absolutely necessary for us to function in our roles as human beings, and I would add, in our roles as commissioned officers. Integrity, as you have learned, helps align our moral compass. Civility, then, provides us the tools to interact with others on this journey called life. Civility is not just manners, but an attitude of dignity and respect for our fellow citizens and for ourselves. What does civility look like in the routine of day-to-day business? Consider the following story.

> In one of my far-too-few shore tours, I had the pleasure of traveling to England and Scotland in 1998 to work with members of the Royal Navy's submarine force as they prepared to launch their final Vanguard-class ballistic missile submarine. The missile, missile launch, and fire control systems were ours, so the United States had oversight for the operational testing and acceptance of that submarine's missile-related systems. My primary point of contact was a captain in the Royal Navy named Marcus. Marcus was the poster child for the English gentleman, as suave and refined as 007. Most of my travel in the United Kingdom was by rail, which would have been unusual in the United States. As I rode the train, I was struck by a sign located by each seat, requesting that passengers respect their fellow passengers and not use cell phones. Interestingly enough, I did not see anyone using a cell phone until one day when Marcus and I boarded the train in Bath to travel to London. Marcus' cell phone rang. To my amazement, he answered it! I was dumbfounded; I could also sense the stares from several passengers. Marcus, the ultimate gentleman, had breached the code of civility on this particular journey! Before I could collect my thoughts, a gentleman a few seats away rose and approached Marcus as he was talking. The gentleman leaned in, saying nothing, and pointed to the sign about cell phone use. Then he left. It was now Marcus' turn to be dumbfounded. He immediately terminated the call and was immensely embarrassed, not believing he had been so inconsiderate. He apologized profusely to those near him for his rudeness.
>
> I was struck by several things during that short event, including the concept itself: respect your fellow passengers on this ride. The issue was resolved with no one raising their voice (or a finger); in fact, there was no conversation at all, and the "perpetrator" apologized to those around him. The civility of that event remains with me to this day. I suspect that it might not have been so memorable had it occurred in the United States—or maybe memorable for other reasons. How have your cell phone experiences compared to this one?

Now let's consider the concept of civility in connection with leadership. The following two stories are about military leaders with whom you should be familiar. But these stories are not about combat. These stories both occur in the post-Civil War period of 1865 and had far-reaching consequences.

The first involves the Confederate surrender at Appomattox:

> On the morning of April 9, 1865, [MGEN Joshua] Chamberlain learned of the desire by Lee to surrender the Army of Northern Virginia when a Confederate staff officer approached him under a flag of truce. "Sir," he reported to Chamberlain, "I am from General John Gordon. General Lee desires a cessation of hostilities until he can hear from General Grant as to the proposed surrender." The next day, Chamberlain was summoned to Union headquarters where Major General Charles Griffin informed him that of all the officers in the Federal Army, General Grant had selected Chamberlain to preside over the ceremony of the surrender and parole of the Confederate infantry at Appomattox Court House on April 12.
>
> Thus Chamberlain was responsible for one of the most poignant scenes of the Civil War. As the Confederate soldiers marched down the road to surrender their arms and colors, Chamberlain, on his own initiative, ordered his men to come to attention and "carry arms" as a show of respect. Chamberlain described what happened next:
>
> "The gallant John B. Gordon, at the head of the marching column, outdoes us in courtesy. He was riding with downcast eyes and more than pensive look; but at this clatter of arms he raises his eyes and instantly catching the significance, wheels his horse with that superb grace of which he is master, drops the point of his sword to his stirrup, gives a command, at which the great Confederate ensign following him is dipped and his decimated brigades, as they reach our right, respond to the 'carry.' All the while on our part not a sound of trumpet or drum, not a cheer, nor a word nor motion of man, but awful stillness as if it were the passing of the dead."
>
> Chamberlain's salute to the Confederate soldiers was unpopular with many in the North, but he defended his action in his memoirs, *The Passing of the Armies*. Many years later, Gordon, in his own memoirs, called Chamberlain "one of the knightliest soldiers of the Federal Army."[1]

The second story is about Robert E. Lee in Richmond:

> The scene is St. Paul's Episcopal Church in Richmond, Virginia—April 1865. The nation had been recently and nearly completely destroyed by the cataclysm of civil war. The social fabric, particularly of the South, had been torn. People resented change and the agents of change. A recently-freed African American man observed the service from the rear of the church. When it was time for communion, he walked to the rail to receive alongside the church's white parishioners. The congregation was aghast.
>
> This seemingly small matter ran completely counter to anything almost anyone in that church had experienced—or would even tolerate. The minister and other communicants were stunned and didn't move.
>
> Just then, a grandfatherly yet ramrod straight gentleman rose from a pew near the front. Robert E. Lee, the man called "the greatest soldier in the history of the English-speaking peoples" by Winston Churchill, understood the situation immediately. He knelt beside the man and both received communion. In an instant a situation was diffused, and more importantly, a message was sent to the congregation, the community, and entire region that change, positive change, was inevitable.

[1] Joshva Chamberlain. (n.d.). Retrieved from http://en.wikipedia.org/wiki/Joshua_Chamberlain# Appomattox

While Lee's actions on that Sunday morning did not themselves end the struggle for the civil rights of African Americans, for that struggle continues today, but that message and the message of rapprochement with the laws and ideals of former enemies became the starting point for healing a nation. Lee would continue to urge his former soldiers to put away their arms and ill will toward the United States. He was, in many regards, singularly responsible for thousands of former Confederate soldiers' (and the generations that followed) willingness to reintegrate fully into American life.[2]

Is there a common thread that runs through each of the stories of Chamberlain, Lee, and my friend Marcus? I would offer that, when you look at their actions and consider Carter's definition of civility, that thread would be "sacrifice." Each man placed the needs and feelings of others ahead of his own in the choices he made. They sacrificed their own desires and egos in deference to others. For Chamberlain and Lee, after a bloody, protracted civil war with families divided and many destroyed, their acts of civility were profound and far-reaching. These were men of high visibility and impeccable reputation, and the ripple-effect of their singular acts did much to restore a divided country. For Marcus, he sacrificed his desire to save face and admitted his error to those around him. His act also had a ripple effect, just not of the same magnitude. Each, by the power of their position and example, were able to influence others, which is the ultimate end state of leadership—the art of influencing others.

At this point, you may be thinking, "But we are training to be combat leaders. Do I extend acts of civility to the enemy?" The short answer to the question is yes. History is replete with examples of civility on the battlefield, among combatants on the same side and those who were considered enemies. A developed habit of civility, based on respect, is not weakness, but rather an attitude that can keep one's soul intact in spite of the horrors of combat. The following is from the book (and movie by the same name) *A Bridge Too Far*. As the Allies were driving to cross the Rhine into Germany, the British had unknowingly run headlong into a crack Panzer force at the bridge in the Dutch city of Arnhem and were in the process of being annihilated. The German commander, General Model, at the request of the British, allowed a cease fire to extract the British wounded into German field hospitals and bury their dead before recommencing the battle. In today's environment, this action would seem to be unachievable and maybe it is; however, this topic of honorable conduct on the battlefield will be addressed in more depth in your ethics course next year.

Great stories, but how can we put this concept of civility into practice on a daily basis here at the Naval Academy? Considering that we are servants of the nation, it is appropriate to look at Carter's "etiquette of democracy.[3]" I have not listed all of the tenets (Carter has fifteen), but putting these five to work each day will have a significant impact on those with whom you share this journey at the Naval Academy.

1) **Our duty to be civil toward others does not depend on whether we like them or not.**
   Remember the words of Coach Boone in *Remember the Titans* as he exhorts his players to come together, become a team, and overcome the social pressures of integration: "I don't care if you like each other, but you will respect each other." He knew, like we all do, that we will never like all of our coworkers, teammates, company mates, or shipmates, but if any organiza-

[2] Horn, S.F. (1949). *The Robert E. Lee Reader*. New York, NY: Konecky & Konecky, 462.
[3] Carter, S.L (1999). *Civility*. New York, NY: Basic Books, 277–285.

tion, command, or team is to succeed, its people must work together. The ability to do that is built on a foundation of respect for each other and the trust that develops from that respect.

2) **Civility requires that we sacrifice for strangers, not just for people we happen to know.**

Consider the terms military *service* or community *service*. Each of these concepts represents, at its heart, doing something for a person or group of people that you do not personally know and for which you receive nothing. Start small. You will never know all of your classmates, but consider what you might sacrifice for the betterment of the class. Then expand your sacrifice for the betterment of the Brigade, then the Navy, then your fellow citizens. Civility, sacrifice, and service all presuppose an obligation to a larger and mostly anonymous group of fellow citizens.

3) **Civility has two parts: generosity, even when it is costly, and trust, even when there is risk.**

This tenet of civility is a little more difficult. Consider the first part: generosity. Since you have little money right now, one thing you can be generous with is your time. Some would consider that time is a more valuable resource than money. I am one of those people. We can always write a larger check because we can get more money. But you cannot give more time, because once expended it is gone, never to be recouped. We all are only issued 24 hours per day—both the rich and the poor. To determine your values, check where you spend your time. The second part is even more difficult. It is very hard at this point in time to do what is implied here: to trust that the judgment of others is as good as your own. As you acquire more seniority and responsibility, you will find more and more people have their hands on the control stick of your life. Never more obvious was this to me than in command of a submarine. You learn to trust your people—at great risk to yourself. No one said that being civil was easy.

4) **Civility requires that we listen to others with knowledge of the possibility that they are right and we are wrong.**

This is the intellectual virtue of humility and one of the foundations of critical thinking. Intellectual humility depends on recognizing that you should not claim to know more than you do and that someone else may know more. Knowing and admitting when one is wrong is not weakness nor does it weaken your authority. Quite the converse—it will enhance the trust that your Sailors and Marines have in your leadership. You should endeavor, however, through study and experience to develop your competence so that the times you are wrong are few. When you are in error, admit it.

5) **Civility requires that we express ourselves in ways that demonstrate our respect for others.**

Carter's summary is most appropriate: "We show respect for ourselves and others when we trouble ourselves to think carefully about what we say, rather than grabbing for the first expletive that comes to mind." Demeaning someone in an effort to raise your acceptance in a group is neither civil nor an indication of a good leader. Those around you will wonder what you think and say about them when they are not around. The foundation of trust will erode, eventually undermining your leadership and team-building efforts.

In summary, civility, sacrifice, and leadership are inextricably linked. Civility and effective leadership can only be achieved if we are willing and able to sacrifice *our* wants and needs to the wants and needs of *others*, whether they are your peers, fellow citizens, or your Sailors and Marines. Civility as an attitude of selflessness and sacrifice is not a sign of weakness. On the contrary, acts of civility strengthen bonds and build trust between people, teams, organizations, and cultures. Being civil, when circumstances and human nature dictate otherwise, takes more self-control and inner strength than giving in to the temptation of the moment. Lord Moran, in his landmark book, *The Anatomy of Courage,* observes ". . . namely that a man of character in peace becomes a man of courage in war. He cannot be selfish in peace and yet be unselfish in war. Character, as Aristotle taught, is a habit, the daily choice of right instead of wrong; it is a moral quality which grows to maturity in peace and is not suddenly developed on the outbreak of war. If you know a man in peace, you know him in war."

Alexis deTocqueville once noted "America is great because America is good ... when America ceases to be good, it will cease to be great." In order to remain good, we must start with learning how to be good to each other—to be civil.

READING 2

"The Reasons for Civility" Gerson. www.townhall.com
"We are not enemies, but friends."
— Abraham Lincoln

WASHINGTON—With Americans shocked into reflection on the desperate, divisive tone of their politics, it is worth asking: Why, other than upbringing, should we be civil in the first place?

In the Western tradition, one answer has been rooted in epistemology—the limits of knowledge. Citizens, in this view, should not be arrogant or intolerant about their political, moral and religious views because no one has the right to be certain of his or her views. What our public life needs is more ambiguity, agnosticism and detachment. The humble are less strident, more peaceful.

This argument is made by a certain kind of campus relativist, who views the purpose of education as the systematic cultivation of doubt. But it is also reflected in the conservative tradition, which is suspicious of ideological certainties that lead to radical social experiments. Both the liberal and conservative variants of this epistemological modesty can be traced back to classical liberal thinkers such as John Locke, whose overriding concern was to prevent wars of opinion, particularly religious wars. If no one believed their opinions were absolutely true, there would be less incentive to attack or coerce others. In the absence of harmful certainty, society would operate by barter and compromise.

But there is a second, very different argument for civility—this one rooted in anthropology. The Christian and natural law traditions assert that human beings are equal and valuable, not because of what they think but because of who they are. Even when badly mistaken, their dignity requires respect for their freedom and conscience. A society becomes more just and civil as more people are converted to this moral belief in human dignity and reflect that conviction in their lives and laws.

Without a doubt, doubt is useful and needed at the margins of any ideology. The world is too complex to know completely. Many of our judgments are, by nature, provisional. Those who are immune to evidence, who claim infallibility on debatable matters, are known as bores—or maybe columnists.

Yet doubt becomes destructive as it reaches the center of a belief and becomes its substitute. A systematic skepticism may keep us from bothering our neighbor. It does not motivate a passion to fight for his or her dignity and rights. How do ambiguity and agnosticism result in dreams of justice, in altruism and honor, in sacrifices for the common good? What great reformers of American history can be explained by their elegant ambivalence?

The holiday just past demonstrates the limits of a political philosophy founded on doubt. Martin Luther King Jr. did not oppose segregation because its supporters were too doctrinaire. He opposed segregation because it was an insult to the nature of human beings. He did not seek to lessen passions by exposing ambiguity. He sought to persuade Americans of a superior moral belief—to convert them to the ideals of their own founding. The intensity of his convictions led him to be a firebrand, a leader, a martyr. Yet he argued for peaceful, civil methods because even oppressors had dignity and value, and thus the hope of redemption.

Moral conviction is not a synonym for arrogance. Both of the paths to civility call for humility. A civility based on doubt demands an appreciation for our own ignorance. A civility grounded in human dignity requires us to bow before a principle greater than ourselves—the belief that others count and matter as much as ourselves. The latter is more difficult to cultivate, but more lasting and important.

So what is the source of America's current civility problem? Is there too much immodest conviction? Or is there too little regard for the value and dignity of others?

There is no reason that both answers can't be "yes." But the second challenge is primary. We need a robust civility that allows for deep and honest disagreements instead of explaining those differences away. In the long run, this is only achievable if Americans believe that their fellow citizens deserve respect, even when they hold absurd political beliefs.

It is not a coincidence that the first draft of the American ideal begins with a statement of anthropology, asserted without epistemological modesty. "We hold these truths to be self-evident, that all men are created equal." It is this belief—not the absence of belief—that provides the most compelling reason for civility. We are not enemies, but friends.

Michael Gerson writes a twice-weekly column for The Post on issues that include politics, global health, development, religion and foreign policy. Michael Gerson is the author of the book "*Heroic Conservatism*" and a contributor to Newsweek magazine.

TOWNHALL DAILY: Be the first to read Michael Gerson's column. *Sign up today* and receive Townhall.com daily lineup delivered each morning to your inbox.

READING 3

"Psychology: Civility Starts with Each of Us" Smith. *Capital Gazette. 10 March 2010*

As part of her annual Oscar awards special, Barbara Walters recently interviewed actress Sandra Bullock, who starred in the movie "The Blind Side" about Baltimore Ravens offensive tackle Michael Oher. When asked what she would do if her chief competitor, Meryl Streep, won the acting award over her, Bullock replied, "I'd beat the—out of her!"

Of course, Bullock was kidding, but her reply is representative of our current society, where it sometimes seems that we have lost our ability to be civil toward others. It appears that people from all walks of life have lost their desire or even their ability to interact civilly with others. This is often the case among our political and business leaders, as well as our perceived "role models" in the sports and entertainment fields.

It is now commonplace for leaders and celebrities in our society to generate new scandals while displaying emotional tantrums that include name-calling, obscene gestures and a philosophy that degrades others who do not see things the same way. This has led social scientists to wonder where "civility" has gone and whether or not it is important. Besides the coarsening of our society where incivility leads to the expression of potentially hurtful, raw, unfiltered emotional expression, there may also be a much larger cost.

When we consider what civility actually is, we realize that it is more than just protecting people's feelings and being nice—not that there is anything wrong with that. Civility is far more than being polite and well-mannered. Civility means respecting other people as unique, thoughtful, intelligent, capable human beings in their own right. It is an essential ingredient for meaningful discourse and the complete understanding of complex situations where different points of views are held. It is impossible to compromise on anything or to come up with creative and unique solutions unless civility and an open tolerance of ideas is encouraged.

Alternatively, incivility breeds harshness, intolerance and ultimately a suppression of meaningful dialogue. **It is literally impossible to have a meaningful exchange of differing ideas without patience and interest in other points of view.** This seems to be apparent in our own national dialogue, or attempts at dialogue, regarding the possibility of nationalized government-run health care. Clearly, many people feel that their ideas are not being heard or fully considered. The purpose of debate over this or any important public policy should be to increase our understanding of the situation, not to "win" the argument.

Many have wondered how we have come so far from civility in such a short period of time. One prevailing explanation is that we now live in a **society of instant or rapid gratification,** and that people are simply accustomed to "getting their way." In modern society there is a subtle narcissism that may develop from our ability to move through life gratifying many of our wishes almost instantly—as if the world should constantly conform to our desires and expectations. Fast food, music and entertainment at the touch of a button, remote controls, cell phones, garage door openers, etc. may be having more of an effect on the primitive part of our brain than we realize. The theory goes that when we are denied what we want—such as total agreement on our perspective—then we feel entitled to have the equivalent of an adult temper tantrum.

Another contributor to incivility may be the general **emotional imbalance** that the human condition now involves. This theory suggests that human beings in the modern world are badly out of sync with their natural needs. Being unbalanced due to our modern work schedules, poor diet and nutrition, exposure to various toxins and other life stresses leave us grasping for a sense of personal validation and control over our lives.

A modern life of stress and fear can leave us intolerant of viewpoints other than our own because we view them as threatening rather than enriching. Inversely, the more physically and emotionally balanced we are, the better we are able to deal with things not to our immediate liking. Sadly, intolerance can be found in our homes as well. With divorce rates approaching 50 percent and family conflict common, it is apparent that tolerance in close interpersonal relationships may also be hard to find. In relationship problems it is often the case that people are finding it harder and harder to compromise or to "agree to disagree" on life perspectives. There is always hope that we can return civility to our society and public discourse. To restore civility the change must begin with each one of us, because the most effective way to restore civility is to behave civilly.

Starting with our own relationships, we need to reach down inside and **find our sense of tolerance, wisdom and compassion in order to overcome our tendency to be critical and judgmental of others.** We need to model the type of civility we seek in others as well as hold our public officials and even our entertainment figures to the same standard. By speaking with our votes, how we spend our money and engaging in civil discourse ourselves, we can slowly shift the momentum back to a more civil society.

After all, civility is rooted in respect for other human beings, and that's a principle we can all agree on.

READING 4

"Servant Leadership" Greenleaf. Excerpt from *Servant Leadership* 1977. From "The Leader's Companion" Wren. The Free Press

Robert Greenleaf developed his theory of servant leadership while an executive at AT&T, and subsequently lectured at Harvard Business School, Dartmouth College, and the University of Virginia. He founded The Center for Applied Ethics, now known as the Robert K. Greenleaf Center.

Servant and leader—can these two roles be fused in one real person, in all levels of status or calling? If so, can that person live and be productive in the real world of the present? My sense of the present leads me to say yes to both questions. This lesson is an attempt to explain why and to suggest how.

The idea of *The Servant as Leader* came out of reading Hermann Hesse's *Journey to the East*. In this story we see a band of men on a mythical journey, probably also Hesse's own journey. The central figure of the story is Leo who accompanies the party as the *servant* who does their menial chores, but who also sustains them with his spirit and his song. He is a person of extraordinary presence. All goes well until Leo disappears. Then the group falls into disarray and the journey is abandoned. They cannot make it without the servant Leo. The narrator, one of the party,' after some years of wandering finds Leo and is taken into the Order that had sponsored the journey. There he discovers that Leo, whom he had known first as *servant*, was in fact the titular head of the Order, its guiding spirit, a great and noble *leader*.

One can muse on what Hesse was trying to say when he wrote this story. We know that most of his fiction was autobiographical, that he led a tortured life, and that *Journey to the East* suggests a turn toward the serenity he achieved in his old age. There has been much speculation by critics on Hesse's life and work, some of it centering on this story which they find the most puzzling. But to me, this story clearly says that *the great leader is seen as servant first*, and that simple fact is the key to his greatness. Leo was actually the leader all of the time, but he was servant first because that was what he was, *deep down inside*. Leadership was bestowed upon a man who was by nature a servant. It was something given, or assumed, that could be taken away. His servant nature was the real man, not bestowed, not assumed, and not to be taken away. He was servant first.

I mention Hesse and *Journey to the East* for two reasons. First, I want to acknowledge the source of the idea of *The Servant as Leader*. Then I want to use this reference as an introduction to a brief discussion of prophecy.

Fifteen years ago when I first read about Leo, if I had been listening to contemporary prophecy as intently as I do now, the first draft of this piece might have been written then. As it was, the idea lay dormant for eleven years until, four years ago, I concluded that we in this country were in a leadership crisis and that I should do what I could about it. I became painfully aware of how dull my sense of contemporary prophecy had been. And I have reflected much on why we do not hear and heed the prophetic voices in our midst (not a new question in our times, nor more critical than heretofore).

I now embrace the theory of prophecy which holds that prophetic voices of great clarity, and with a quality of insight equal to that of any age, are speaking cogently all of the time. Men and women of a stature equal to the greatest of the past are with us now addressing the problems of the day and pointing to a better way and to a personeity better able to live fully and serenely in these times.

The variable that marks some periods as barren and some as rich in prophetic vision is in the interest, the level of seeking, the responsiveness of the hearers. The variable is not in the presence or absence or the relative quality and force of the prophetic voices. Prophets grow in stature as people respond to their message. If their early attempts are ignored or spurned, their talent may wither away.

It is *seekers*, then, who make prophets, and the initiative of any one of us in searching for and responding to the voice of contemporary prophets may mark the turning point in their growth and service. But since we are the product of our own history, we see current prophecy within the context of past wisdom. We listen to as wide a range of contemporary thought as we can attend to. Then we *choose* those we elect to heed as prophets—*both old and new*—and meld their advice with our own leadings. This we test in real-life experiences to establish our own position. . . .

One does not, of course, ignore the great voices of the past. One does not awaken each morning with the compulsion to reinvent the wheel. But if one is *servant*, either leader or follower, one is always searching, listening, expecting that a better wheel for these times is in the making. It may emerge any day. Any one of us may find it out from personal experience. I am hopeful.

I am hopeful for these times, despite the tension and conflict, because more natural servants are trying to see clearly the world as it is and are listening carefully to prophetic voices that are speaking *now*. They are challenging the pervasive injustice with greater force and they are taking sharper issue with the wide disparity between the quality of society they know is reasonable and possible with available resources, and, on the other hand, the actual performance of the whole range of institutions that exist to serve society.

A fresh critical look is being taken at the issues of power and authority, and people are beginning to learn, however haltingly, to relate to one another in less coercive and more creatively supporting ways. A new moral principle is emerging which holds that the only authority deserving one's allegiance is that which is freely and knowingly granted by the led to the leader in response to, and in proportion to, the clearly evident servant stature of the leader. Those who choose to follow this principle will not casually accept the authority of existing institutions. *Rather, they will freely respond only to individuals who are chosen as leaders because they are proven and trusted as servants.* To the extent that this principle prevails in the future, the only truly viable institutions will be those that are predominantly servant-led.

I am mindful of the long road ahead before these trends, which I see so clearly, become a major society-shaping force. We are not there yet. But I see encouraging movement on the horizon.

What direction will the movement take? Much depends on whether those who stir the ferment will come to grips with the age-old problem of how to live in a human society. I say this because so many, having made their awesome decision for autonomy and independence from tradition, and having taken their firm stand against injustice and hypocrisy, find it hard to convert themselves into *affirmative builders* of a better society. How many of them will seek their personal fulfillment by making the hard choices, and by undertaking the rigorous preparation that building a better society requires? It all depends on what kind of leaders emerge and how they—we—respond to them.

My thesis, that more servants should emerge as leaders, or should follow only servant-leaders, is not a popular one. It is much more comfortable to go with a less demanding point of view about what is expected of one now. There are several undemanding, plausibly-argued alternatives to choose. One, since society seems corrupt, is to seek to avoid the center of it by retreating to an idyllic existence that minimizes involvement with the "system" (with the "system" that makes such withdrawal possible). Then there is the assumption that since the effort to reform existing institutions has not brought instant perfection, the remedy is to destroy them completely so that fresh new perfect ones can grow. Not much thought seems to be given to the problem of where the new seed will come from or who the gardener to tend them will be. The concept of the servant-leader stands in sharp contrast to this kind of thinking.

Yet it is understandable that the easier alternatives would be chosen, especially by young people. By extending education for so many so far into the adult years, the normal participation in society is effectively denied when young people are ready for it. With education that is preponderantly abstract and analytical it is no wonder that there is a preoccupation with criticism and that not much thought is given to "What can I do about it?"

Criticism has its place, but as a total preoccupation it is sterile. In a time of crisis, like the leadership crisis we are now in, if too many potential builders are taken in by a complete absorption with dissecting the wrong and by a zeal for instant perfection, then the movement so many of us want to see will be set back. The danger, perhaps, is to hear the analyst too much and the artist too little.

Albert Camus stands apart from other great artists of his time, in my view, and deserves the title of *prophet*, because of his unrelenting demand that each of us confront the exacting terms of our own existence, and, like Sisyphus, *accept our rock and find our happiness in dealing with it*. Camus sums up the relevance of his position to our concern for the servant as leader in the last paragraph of his last published lecture, entitled Create Dangerously:

> One may long, as I do, for a gentler flame, a respite, a pause for musing. But perhaps there is no other peace for the artist than what he finds in the heat of combat. "Every wall is a door," Emerson correctly said. Let us not look for the door, and the way out, anywhere but in the wall against which we are living. Instead, let us seek the respite where it is—in the very thick of battle. For in my opinion, and this is where I shall close, it is there. Great ideas, it has been said, come into the world as gently as doves. Perhaps, then, if we listen attentively, we shall hear, amid the uproar of empires and nations, a faint flutter of wings, the gentle stirring of life and hope. Some will say that this hope lies in a nation, others, in a man. I believe rather that it is awakened, revived, nourished by millions of solitary individuals whose deeds and works every day negate frontiers and the crudest implications of history. As a result, there shines forth fleetingly the ever-threatened truth that each and every man, on the foundations of his own sufferings and joys, builds for them all. . . .

Who Is the Servant-Leader?

The servant-leader is servant first—as Leo was portrayed. It begins with the natural feeling that one wants to serve, to serve *first*. Then conscious choice brings one to aspire to lead. That person is sharply different from one who is *leader* first, perhaps because of the need to assuage an unusual power drive or to acquire material possessions. For such it will be a later choice to serve—after leadership is established. The leader-first and the servant-first are two extreme types. Between them there are shadings and blends that are part of the infinite variety of human nature.

The difference manifests itself in the care taken by the servant first to make sure that other people's highest priority needs are being served. The best test, and difficult to administer, is: Do those served grow as persons? Do they, *while being served*, become healthier, wiser, freer, more autonomous, more likely themselves to become servants? *And*, what is the effect on the least privileged in society; will they benefit, or, at least, not be further deprived? . . .

All of this rests on the assumption that the only way to change a society (or just make it go) is to produce people, enough people, who will change it (or make it go). The urgent problems of our day—the disposition to venture into immoral and senseless wars, destruction of the environment, poverty, alienation, discrimination, overpopulation—are here because of human failures, individual failures, one person at a time, one action at a time failures.

If we make it out of all of this (and this is written in the belief that we will make it), the "system" will be whatever works best. The builders will find the useful pieces wherever they are, and invent new ones when needed, all without reference to ideological coloration. "How do we get the right things done?" will be the watchword of the day, every day. And the context of those who bring it off will be: all men and women who are touched by the effort grow taller, and become healthier, stronger, more autonomous, *and* more disposed to serve.

Leo the *servant*, and the exemplar of the *servant-leader*, has one further portent for us. If we may assume that Hermann Hesse is the narrator in *Journey to the East* (not a difficult assumption to make), at the end of the story he establishes his identity. His final confrontation at the close of his initiation into the Order is with a small transparent sculpture: two figures joined together. One is Leo, the other is the narrator. The narrator notes that a movement of substance is taking place within the transparent sculpture.

> I perceived that my image was in the process of adding to and flowing into Leo's, nourishing and strengthening it. It seemed that, in time . . . only one would remain: Leo. He must grow, I must disappear.
>
> As I stood there and looked and tried to understand what I saw, I recalled a short conversation that I had once had with Leo during the festive days at Bremgarten. We had talked about the creations of poetry being more vivid and real than the poets themselves.

What Hesse may be telling us here is that Leo is the symbolic personification of Hesse's aspiration to serve through his literary creations, creations that are greater than Hesse himself; and that his work, for which he was but the channel, will carry on and serve and lead in a way that he, a twisted and tormented man, could not—except as he created.

Does not Hesse dramatize, in extreme form, the dilemma of us all? Except as we venture to create, we cannot project ourselves beyond ourselves to serve and lead.

To which Camus would add: *Create dangerously*!

Lesson

13 *Social Influence*

Gain a foundational understanding of the various means of influencing others, and understanding the dangers with which they are associated. Leaders not only influence followers, but followers also influence leaders. Begin understanding basic tools for influence/inspiration/persuasion - necessary for effective leadership communication and team building.

READING 1

Social psychologists have considered three major categories of social influence: conformity, compliance, and obedience. The amount of overt social pressure associated with these categories escalates as one moves from conformity to compliance and, finally, to obedience. **Conformity** involves changing one's behavior to match the responses or actions of others, to fit in with those around us. Before a party or concert, you might ask, "What will people be wearing?" Imagine showing up in shorts and a T-shirt when everyone else is wearing formal clothing, or imagine appearing in formal wear when everyone else is dressed casually. The discomfort most of us would feel in such situations gives you some sense of the strength of the desire to fit in. Conformity can occur without overt social pressure; no one may ever have to take you aside to say, "You're dressed inappropriately," but you may still voluntarily leave to change into an outfit that looks less out of place.

Compliance refers to the act of changing one's behavior in response to a direct request. The request may come from sources as distinct as friends ("C'mon, have a beer and forget your studying!"), salespeople ("You should sign now because we can't guarantee this model will be here tomorrow"), charities ("St. Mary's Food Bank needs your contributions to feed the poor this Thanksgiving. Please give"), or panhandlers on the street ("Hey buddy, can you spare $3.75 for a cup of cappucino?"). As in the case of a restroom sign asking you to wash your hands before leaving, the requester need not be physically present to exert pressure to comply.

Obedience is a special type of compliance that involves changing one's behavior in response to a directive from an authority. A boss may require employees to work overtime, a military officer may command soldiers to attack the enemy, or a police officer may order drivers to take a detour. In directing others to obey, typically exert the most overt attempts at influence.

Before considering the factors that motivate us to yield to social influence pressures, let's explore conformity, compliance, and obedience in greater depth by examining a classic piece of research into each process. These pieces of research are noteworthy in that each revealed more impact of social influence than nearly anyone expected and each stimulated a tradition of investigation that continues today (Blass, 2000; Cialdini, 2001; Levine, 1999).

Conformity: Asch's Research on Group Influence

Group pressure can lead people to conform even when contradictory evidence is right before their eyes. This phenomenon was investigated in a series of experiments conducted by Solomon Asch (1956). Asch was interested not only in the submission of individuals to group forces but also in the capacity of people to act independent of conformity pressures.

To investigate these processes of conformity and independence, Asch asked college students in groups of eight to match the lengths of different lines. The task was not difficult. In the control condition, in which there was no group pressure pushing toward wrong choices, 95% of the participants got all of 12 line matches right. For those in the experimental condition, however, the situation changed.

They were faced with a social consensus that contradicted their own eyes. Before making their own judgments, they heard five other students (who were actually confederates of the experimenter) unanimously agree on an answer that was clearly wrong. Did they stick to their guns and give the right answers or did they go along with the crowd? only 25% of these participants ignored the group's obvious errors and gave only correct answers. The other 75% went against the evidence of their senses and conformed to some extent. Although no one went along every single time, one individual conformed on 11 of the 12 choices.

What was going on in the minds of the participants when they heard the whole group make judgments that seemed plainly wrong? One participant, who stayed independent of group pressure, became embarrassed, whispering to a neighbor at one point, "I always disagree, darn it." When the experiment was over and he was asked whether he thought the entire group was wrong, he turned to them and said, "You're *probably* right, but you *may* be wrong!" He was "exultant and relieved" when the true nature of the experiment was disclosed to him. Although he hadn't buckled under group pressure, even he had been led to doubt his own judgment. The participant who conformed 11 out of 12 times (more than any other participant) claimed later that he was swayed by the seeming confidence of the other group members. He said he actually came to believe that they were right, thinking that he alone had fallen victim to some sort of "illusion." Asch's research demonstrated that people faced with strong group consensus sometimes go along even though they think the others may be wrong. In addition, they sometimes believe that the others are right, doubting the evidence of their own senses if the members of their group seem confident enough.

Asch obtained his results among students who were strangers convened for a short experiment. Think how much more potent the social pressure might be when those confident others are members of one's own circle, whose goodwill is treasured. And imagine how much more potent the pressure might become within groups like religious cults, in which the members are often taught to suppress their individuality and are counseled daily on the importance of blind faith in the group's beliefs. Two months before the Heaven's Gate commune members committed suicide in 1997, they spent several thousand dollars for a high-powered telescope because they had heard rumors about a small object (which they suspected was a spaceship) that appeared to be trailing Comet Hale-Bopp. When they complained to the salesman that the telescope showed them no trace of the mysterious object, he explained that there never was a trailing object, only a rumor based on a blip of static in one very early and poor-quality image of the comet. How did they respond to this direct evidence against their group's unanimous and firmly held beliefs about a spaceship carrying their extraterrestrial contacts? They decided to continue believing in the spaceship's existence but to stop looking at the evidence: They turned in the telescope for a refund (Ferris, 1997).

Compliance: The "Foot-in-the-Door" Technique

The term *foot-in-the-door* refers to door-to-door salespeople getting one foot in the door as a way to gain full entry. The psychological underpinnings of this technique were investigated in a clever series of experiments by Jonathan Freedman and Scott Fraser (1966). To address their question, "How can a person be induced to do something he would rather not do?" Freedman and Fraser left the laboratory to conduct field experiments.

In one experiment, 156 housewives in Palo Alto, California, were called on the phone and asked to do something the researchers guessed that most people would rather not do: allow a team of six men from a consumer group to come into their home for two hours "to enumerate and classify all the household products you have." The women were told that the men would need full freedom to go through the house exploring cupboards and storage spaces. Few women (only 22%) complied if this was all they were asked. However, another group of women was contacted twice, once with a small request designed simply to get a "foot in the door"—they were asked to answer a series of eight questions about household soaps (such as "What brand of soap do you use in your kitchen sink?"). It was such a minor favor that nearly everyone agreed. Three days later, these women were contacted by the same consumer group, but now with the larger, home-visit request. Under these circumstances, 52% of the women agreed to allow the team of men to rummage through their cupboards and closets for two hours.

Can people be influenced like this in everyday life? And how can social psychologists find out? Most of social psychology's knowledge of human behavior comes from controlled laboratory experiments, which offer an excellent way to understand the *causes* of that behavior. But these experiments have their drawbacks. For instance, laboratories are artificial settings where responding might not occur as it would in daily life. Therefore, social scientists sometimes employ other methods that are better able to capture behavior as it normally takes place. One such method is the field experiment, in which researchers perform controlled experimentation in naturally occurring settings, as Freedman and Fraser did to study the foot-in-the-door tactic. A second method doesn't require controlled experimentation at all. Instead it involves the careful observation of people as they act and interact in natural situations.

Obedience: Milgram's Shock(ing) Procedure

Political leaders, military commanders, police officers, high school principals, store managers, and parents issue commands that produce obedience on a daily basis. Social psychologist Stanley Milgram wanted to see how far the obedience-inducing power of authority could be extended. Would you obey orders from a researcher you had never before met if he or she asked you to deliver painful, potentially deadly electric shocks to an innocent victim? And if so, what would the victim have to say to get you to stop obeying such orders?

In a well-known series of studies done decades ago, Milgram (1974) placed advertisements in local newspapers to solicit participants for a "memory experiment" at Yale University. Suppose that one of those studies was being conducted today and that you signed up to participate. Here's what you'd encounter: Upon your arrival at the laboratory, you'd be introduced to another participant (actually a confederate of the experimenter). After hearing that the research would examine the effects of punishment on memory, you'd be assigned to the Teacher role and the other participant to the Learner role in the study. You'd be informed that, as part of your duties, you'd have to deliver a series of electric shocks to the Learner. At this point, the Learner would mention that he had been treated for a heart condition and express concern about the dangers of receiving electric shocks. To this, the experimenter would reply that, although painful, the shocks would produce "no permanent tissue damage."

The experimenter would then take you both to the next room, where the nervous Learner would be strapped into an apparatus looking eerily like an electric chair. That accomplished, you'd be ushered into an experimental room and shown a menacing shock-delivery machine with shock levers ascending from 15 to 450 volts. Each group of four shock levers would be assigned a progressively more frightening label, ranging from

"Slight shock" through "Moderate," "Strong," "Very strong," "Intense," "Extreme intensity," to "Danger: Severe shock." A final pair of levers (for the 435- and 450-volt shocks) would apparently deliver shocks so intense that the English language had no words to describe them adequately, as they carried only the stark label "XXX."

Before beginning, you would receive an unpleasant sample shock of 45 volts to give you an idea of what the Learner would be experiencing. You'd then be instructed to deliver a shock to the Learner every time he erred on a memory task, advancing to the next higher shock lever with every new mistake. With each error and each more punishing shock, the confederate would voice increasingly desperate cries of pain. At first, he'd simply cry out, "Ugh." At 120 volts, he would shout out, "Hey, this really hurts!" At 150 volts, he'd plead to be released:

> That's all! Get me out of here. I told you I had heart trouble. My heart's starting to bother me now. Get me out of here, please. My heart's starting to bother me. I refuse to go on. Let me out.

Would you continue or stop? If you tried to stop, the experimenter would prod you by saying, "Please continue." If you failed to obey, the experimenter would insist, "The experiment requires that you continue." If you persisted in your disobedience, he'd state, "It is absolutely essential that you continue." Finally, he would demand, "You have no choice; you must go on."

If you continued to follow orders and deliver the shocks, the Learner's appeals would become more agonized and desperate. Finally, he'd burst into a litany of pleas, demands, and shrieks:

> Let me out of here. Let me out of here. My heart's bothering me. Let me out, I tell you. Let me out of here. Let me out of here. You have no right to hold me here. Let me out! Let me out! Let me out! Let me out of here! Let me out! Let me out!

Should that not be enough to convince you to resist the experimenter's orders, things would suddenly change. When you delivered the next shock, you'd hear nothing from the Learner's chamber. If you asked the experimenter to see if the Learner was all right, he'd refuse, saying instead, "Treat no response as a wrong response, and deliver the next higher level of shock." For the final eight shocks—into the "Danger" category and the region marked "XXX"—the Learner, once so vocal in his pain would be deadly silent.

How likely would you and other participants like you be to follow orders to go all the way to 450 volts? Before publishing his study, Milgram described the procedures to 40 psychiatrists at a leading medical school and asked them to predict the results. They expected that fewer than 4% of Milgram's subjects would continue once the Learner stopped answering and that only 0.01% would go all the way to the end. Sadly, the psychiatrists greatly underestimated the power of obedience to authority. More than 80% of the participants continued past the Learner's refusal to answer. Even more remarkably, 65% persisted to the end—defying an innocent victim's repeated screams and enduring his subsequent ominous silence—simply because the "boss" of the study commanded it. What's more, these high levels of obedience have remained steady when researchers have repeated Milgram's procedures in more recent years (Blass, 1999).

Milgram conducted an elaborate series of follow-up studies. In one, he explored the extent to which his results were due to the scientific credibility of Yale University, where the study took place. He rented office space in a rundown section of Bridgeport, Connecticut, and ran the same procedures again. Surprisingly, a large proportion of participants (48%) obeyed the researcher's orders even under these questionable circumstances, indicating that his findings were not limited to university-based authorities. But how do we know that it was authority influence rather than some other factor—the desire to release pent-up aggression, for instance—that caused Milgram's subjects to behave so cruelly?

The evidence supporting the obedience to authority explanation is strong. First, it's clear that, without the researcher's directive to continue, the participants would have ended the experiment quickly. They hated what they were doing and agonized over their victim's agony. They implored the researcher to let them stop. When he refused, they went on, but in the process they trembled, perspired, shook, and stammered protests and additional pleas for the victim's release. In addition to these observations, Milgram provided even more convincing evidence for the interpretation of his results in light of obedience to authority. In a later experiment, for instance, he had the researcher and the victim switch scripts so that the researcher told the Teacher to stop delivering shocks to the victim, while the victim insisted bravely that the Teacher continue. The result couldn't have been clearer: 100% of the participants refused to give one additional shock when it was merely the fellow participant who demanded it. These results would hardly be expected if participants' principal motive was to release aggressive energy rather than to follow an authority.

If, as Milgram's research indicates, a majority of people will deliver painful shocks to a heart patient on the orders of a research scientist who has no real authority over them, it becomes less surprising that soldiers have killed innocent civilians and that cult members will kill themselves at the direction of more personally relevant authority. More recent work has examined disturbing levels of unethical obedience in organizations (Darley, 2001). For example, personnel managers may discriminate against certain racial groups when instructed to do so by an authority (Brief, Buttram, & Dukerich, 2001). But *why* do people obey? What goals are served by this and the other forms of social influence?

Authority

The most striking research evidence for the influence of legitimate authority comes from the Milgram obedience study. But the tendency to defer to an authority arises in many more situations than the laboratory setting that Milgram constructed (Blass, 1991; Miller, Collins, & Brief, 1995). What's more, the behaviors influenced in these situations range from the ordinary to the dramatic (Sabini & Silver, 1982). In the realm of ordinary behaviors, we can find deference to authority in something as commonplace as the tone of voice one uses in a conversation. Communication researchers who study what happens in conversations have learned that people shift their voice and speech styles toward the styles of individuals in positions of power and authority (Giles & Coupland, 1991; Pittam, 1994). One study explored this phenomenon by analyzing interviews on the *Larry King Live* television show. When King interviewed guests having great social standing and prestige (for instance, George Bush, Bill Clinton, and Barbra Streisand), his voice style changed to match theirs. But when he interviewed guests of lower status and prestige (for instance, Dan Quayle, Spike Lee, and Julie Andrews), he remained unmoved, and their voice styles shifted to match his (Gregory & Webster, 1996).

As Milgram's findings demonstrated, people also follow an authority's lead in situations involving much more dramatic consequences than changes in voice. Consider, for example, the catastrophic consequences of a phenomenon that airline industry officials have labeled "captainitis" (Foushee, 1984). Accident investigators from the Federal Aviation Administration have recognized that an obvious error by a flight captain often goes uncorrected by other crewmembers and results in a crash. It seems that, because of the captain's authority position, crewmembers either fail to notice or fail to challenge the mistake. They appear to assume that if the captain said it, it must be right.

Think back throughout your schooling, when your English teachers corrected your writing style, you probably took their criticisms into account in your next paper. That was no doubt the case for multiple reasons. First, like many authorities, teachers have power over you. They can affect your grade in the class, your standing in school, your chances for a good position after graduation, and so on. For such reasons alone, it makes good sense to follow their directions. Bur there's a second reason. Like many authorities, teachers are experts on the subject at hand. If they say that a sentence you've written is awkward, you're likely to *believe* it and to change in order to improve your writing in general. In short, following the advice of authorities helps us choose rapidly and correctly. Although some authorities are in a position to force us into obedience, it's more interesting to consider how effective they can be without the power to reward or punish—when what they have instead is **expert power**, the power that comes from acknowledged competence in the matter at hand (French & Raven, 1959; Kozlowski & Schwartzwald, 2001).

Authorities as Experts An authority's expert power can have a strong effect on compliance because it serves our strong motivation to choose correctly. Milgram (1965, p. 74) claimed that his subjects' obedience occurred not simply through overt pressure but, as well, "by the uncritical acceptance of the experimenter's definition of the situation." When authorities are presumed to know best, following their lead becomes a sensible thing. This helps explain why less educated individuals are more obedient to authority (Hamilton, Sanders, & McKearney, 1995; Milgram, 1974): They tend to presume that authorities know more than they do.

Because following an expert's direction is normally wise, and because authorities are frequently experts, we often use authority as a decision-making heuristic (shortcut). Assuming that an authority knows best can be an efficient way of deciding, because we don't have to think hard about the issues ourselves; all we have to do to be right is accept the authority's advice. But unthinking reliance on authority can be dangerous, too. This shortcut approach can lead us to respond to the symbols rather than the substance of genuine authority (Bushman, 1984).

The results of a study conducted by a team of physicians and nurses revealed the force that one such symbol—the mere title Dr.—has in the medical arena. Hospital nurses received a phone call from a man they'd never met but who identified himself as the doctor of a patient on their floor. He then ordered them to give twice the maximum acceptable dosage of a drug to that patient. Ninety-five percent obeyed and had to be stopped on their way to the patient's room with the unsafe drug dosage in their hands (Hofling, Brotzman, Dalrymple, Graves, & Pierce, 1966). A follow-up study asked nurses to recall a time when they'd obeyed a doctor's order that they considered inappropriate and potentially harmful to a patient. Those who admitted such incidents (46%) attributed their actions to their beliefs that the doctor was a legitimate and expert authority in the matter—the same two features of authority that appear to account for obedience in the Milgram procedure (Blass, 1999; Krackow & Blass, 1995). Incidents of this deference to the symbols of authority continue to occur. A 17-year-old convinced nurses at a Virginia hospital to carry out twelve treatments on six patients by misrepresenting himself as a doctor on the phone.

Authorities as Agents of Influence It should come as no surprise that influence professionals frequently try to harness the power of authority by touting their experience, expertise, or scientific recognition: "Fashionable clothiers since 1841," "Babies are our business, our only business," "Four out of five doctors recommend the ingredients in . . . ," and so on. There's nothing wrong with such claims when they're real, because we usually want to know who is an authority on a topic and who isn't, it helps us choose correctly. The problem comes when we are subjected to phony claims of this sort. When we aren't thinking hard, as is often the case when confronted by authority symbols, we can be easily steered in the wrong direction by false authorities—those who aren't authorities at all but who merely present the aura of authority. For instance, people are more willing to perform a variety of unusual actions (to pick up a paper bag on the street, stand on the other side of a Bus Stop sign, put money in someone else's parking meter) if directed to do so by someone wearing a security guard's or firefighter's uniform; moreover, they are more likely to do so unquestioningly (Bickman, 1974; Bushman, 1984).

In sum, authorities are formidable sources of social influence. One reason is that they are often expert. Consequently, following their directions offers us a shortcut route to choosing correctly. However, when we defer to authority orders or advice too readily, we risk performing actions that may be unethical or unwise. Let's turn now to a second major principle that people use to help them achieve the goal of choosing correctly, social validation.

READING 2

Power, Influence, and Influence Tactics" Hughes, Ginnett, and Curphy. *Leadership: Enhancing the Lessons of Experience* 1993 Richard D Irwin, Inc. From "The Leader's Companion" Wren. The Free Press

Richard L. Hughes has a Ph.D. in clinical psychology and heads the Department of Behavioral Sciences and Leadership at the United States Air Force Academy. Robert C. Ginnett has a Ph.D. in organizational behavior from Yale University and is currently deputy department head for leadership programs and counseling at the United States Air Force Academy. Gordon Curphy's graduate work was in industrial/organizational psychology. He was an associate professor at the Air Force Academy, and is now a senior consultant at Personnel Decisions, Inc.

One cannot understand leadership without understanding the concepts of power, influence, and influence tactics. Many people use these concepts synonymously but it may be useful to distinguish among power, influence, and influence tactics. **Power** has been defined as the capacity to produce effects on others or the potential to influence. **Influence** can be defined as the change in a target agent's attitudes, values, beliefs, or behaviors as the result of influence tactics. **Influence tactics** refer to one person's actual behaviors designed to change another person's attitudes, beliefs, values, or behaviors. Although power, influence, and influence tactics are typically examined from the leader's perspective, it is important to remember that followers can also wield a considerable amount of power and influence, and that followers also use a variety of influence tactics to change the attitudes, values, beliefs, and behaviors of their leaders. Leadership practitioners can improve their effectiveness by reflecting on the types of power they and their followers have and the types of influence tactics that they may use or that may be used on them. . . .

A Taxonomy of Social Power

French and Raven identified five sources, or bases, of power by which an individual can potentially influence others. These five sources include one that is primarily a function of the leader; one that is a function of the relationship between leaders and followers; one primarily a function of the leader and the situation; one primarily a function of the situation; and finally, one that involves aspects of all three elements. The five bases of power are organized from the leader's perspective, yet it is important to note that followers also have varying amounts of power they can use to resist a leader's influence attempts. Because both leaders and followers can use all five bases of power to influence each other, this section describes the bases of power from both the leader's and followers' perspectives. Understanding these bases of power from both perspectives can help leadership practitioners be more effective, because these bases can be used (a) to help determine why subordinates and superiors may successfully resist different influence attempts and (b) to improve the potential amount of influence leadership practitioners can have with subordinates and superiors. The following is a more detailed discussion of French and Raven's five bases of social power.

Expert Power. Expert power is the power of knowledge. Some people are able to influence others through their relative expertise in particular areas. A surgeon may wield considerable influence in a hospital because others are dependent on her knowledge, skill, and judgment, even though she may not have any formal authority over them. A mechanic may be influential among his peers because he is widely recognized as the best in the city. A longtime employee may be influential because his "corporate memory" provides a useful historical perspective to newer personnel. Legislators who are expert in the intricacies of parliamentary procedure, athletes who have played in championship games before, and soldiers who have been in combat before are valued for the "lessons learned" and wisdom they can share with others.

Because expert power is a function of the amount of knowledge one possesses relative to the rest of the members of the group, it is possible for followers to have considerably more expert power than leaders in certain situations. For example, new leaders often possess less knowledge of the jobs and tasks performed in a particular work unit than the followers do, and in this case the followers can potentially wield considerable influence when decisions are made regarding work procedures, new equipment, or the hiring of additional workers. Probably the best advice for leaders in this situation is to ask a lot of questions and perhaps seek additional training to help fill this knowledge gap. So long as different followers have considerably greater amounts of expert power, it will be difficult for a leader to influence the work unit on the basis of expert power alone.

Referent Power. One way to counteract the problems stemming from a lack of expertise is to build strong interpersonal ties with subordinates. Referent power refers to the potential influence one has due to the strength of the relationship between the leader and the followers. When people admire a leader and see her as a role model, we say she has referent power. For example, students may respond positively to advice or requests from teachers who are well liked and respected, while the same students might be unresponsive to less popular teachers. This relative degree of responsiveness is primarily a function of the strength of the relationship between the students and the different teachers. We knew one young lieutenant who had enormous referent power with the military security guards working for him due to his selfless concern for them, evident in such habits as bringing them hot chocolate and homemade cookies on their late-night shifts. The guards, sometimes taken for granted by other superiors, understood and valued the extra effort and sacrifice this young supervisor put forth for them. When Buddy Ryan was fired as head coach of the Philadelphia Eagles football team, many of the players expressed fierce loyalty to him. One said, "We'd do things for Buddy that we wouldn't do for another coach. I'd sell my body for Buddy" (Associated Press, January 9, 1991). That is referent power.

It is important to note that the relationships between leaders and followers take time to develop and often limit the actions leaders may take in a particular leadership situation. For example, a leader who has developed a strong relationship with a follower may be reluctant to discipline the follower for poor work or chronic tardiness, as these actions could disrupt the nature of the relationship between the leader and the follower. Thus, referent power is a two-way street; the stronger the relationship, the more influence leaders and followers exert over each other. Moreover, just as it is possible for leaders to develop strong relationships with followers and, in turn, acquire more referent power, it is also possible for followers to develop strong relationships with other followers and acquire more referent power. Followers with relatively more referent power than their peers are often the spokespersons for their work units and generally have more latitude to deviate from work-unit norms. Followers with little referent power have little opportunity to deviate from group norms. For example, in an episode of the television show "The Simpsons," Homer Simpson was fired for wearing a pink shirt to work (everybody else at the Springfield nuclear power plant had always worn white shirts). Homer was fired partly because he "was not popular enough to be different."

Legitimate Power. Legitimate power depends on a person's organizational role. It can be thought of as one's formal or official authority. Some people make things happen because they have the power or authority to do so. The boss can assign projects; the coach can decide who plays; the colonel can order compliance with uniform standards; the teacher assigns the homework and awards the grades. Individuals with legitimate power exert influence through requests or demands deemed appropriate by virtue of their role and position. In other words, legitimate power means a leader has authority because he or she has been assigned a particular role in an organization (and the leader has this authority only as long as he or she occupies that position and operates within the proper bounds of that role).

It is important to note that legitimate authority and leadership are not the same thing. Holding a position and being a leader are not synonymous, despite the relatively common practice of calling position holders in bureaucracies the leaders. The head of an organization may be a true leader, but he also may not be. Effective leaders often intuitively realize they need more than legitimate power to be successful. Before he became president, Dwight Eisenhower commanded all Allied troops in Europe during World War II. In a meeting with his staff before the Normandy invasion, Eisenhower pulled a string across a table to make a point about leadership. He was demonstrating that just as you can pull a string, not push it, officers must lead soldiers and not "push" them from the rear.

It is also possible for followers to use their legitimate power to influence leaders. In these cases, followers can actively resist a leader's influence attempt by only doing work specifically prescribed in job descriptions, bureaucratic rules, or union policies. For example, many organizations have job descriptions that limit both the time spent at work and the types of tasks and activities performed. Similarly, bureaucratic rules and union policies can be invoked by followers to resist a leader's influence attempts. Often the leader will need to change the nature of his or her request or find another way to resolve the problem if these rules and policies are invoked by followers. If this is the case, then the followers will have successfully used legitimate power to influence their leader.

Reward Power. Reward power involves the potential to influence others due to one's control over desired resources. This can include the power to give raises, bonuses, and promotions; to grant tenure; to select people for special assignments or desirable activities; to distribute desired resources like computers, offices, parking places, or travel money; to intercede positively on another's behalf; to recognize with awards and praise; and so on. Many corporations use rewards extensively to motivate employees. At McDonald's, for example, there is great status accorded the "All-American Hamburger Maker," the cook who makes the fastest, highest-quality hamburgers in the country. At individual fast-food restaurants, managers may reward salespersons who handle the most customers during rush periods. Tupperware holds rallies for its salespeople. Almost everyone wins something, ranging from pins and badges to lucrative prizes for top performers. Schools pick "teachers of the year" and professional athletes are rewarded by selection to all-star teams for their superior performance.

The potential to influence others through the ability to administer rewards is a joint function of the leader, the followers, and the situation. Leaders vary considerably in the types and frequency in which they mete out rewards, but the position they fill also helps to determine the frequency and types of rewards administered. For example, employees of the month at Kentucky Fried Chicken are not given new cars; the managers of these franchises do not have the resources to offer such awards. Similarly, leaders in other organizations are limited to some extent in the types and frequency in which they can administer awards. Nevertheless, leadership practitioners can enhance their reward power by spending some time reflecting on the followers and the situation. Often a number of alternative or innovative rewards can be created, and these rewards, along with ample doses of praise, can help a leader overcome the constraints his or her position puts on reward power.

Although using the power to administer rewards can be an effective way to change the attitudes and behaviors of others, there are several situations where a leader's use of reward power can be problematic. For example, the perception that a company's monetary bonus policy is handled equitably may be as important in motivating good work (or avoiding morale problems) as the amount of the bonus itself. Moreover, a superior may mistakenly assume that a particular reward is valued when it is not. This would be the case if a particular subordinate were publicly recognized for her good work when she actually dislikes public recognition. Leadership practitioners can avoid the latter problem by developing good relationships with subordinates and administering rewards that they, not the leader, value.

Another potential problem with reward power is that it may produce compliance but not other desirable outcomes like commitment. In other words, subordinates may perform only at the level necessary to receive a reward and may not be willing to put forth the extra effort needed to make the organization better. An overemphasis on rewards as "payoff" for performance may also lead to resentment and feelings by workers of being manipulated, especially if it occurs in the context of relatively cold and distant superior-subordinate relationships. Extrinsic rewards like praise, compensation, promotion, privileges, and time off may not have the same effects on behavior as intrinsic rewards such as feelings of accomplishment, personal growth, and development. There is evidence under some conditions extrinsic rewards can even decrease intrinsic motivation toward a task and make the desired behavior less likely to persist when extrinsic rewards are not available. Overemphasis on extrinsic rewards may instill an essentially contractual or economic relationship between superiors and subordinates, diluting important aspects of the relationship like mutual loyalty or shared commitment to higher ideals.

All these cautions about reward power should not cloud its usefulness and effectiveness, which is very real. As noted previously, top organizations make extensive use of both tangible and symbolic rewards in motivating their workers. Furthermore, some of the most important rewards are readily available to all leaders—sincere praise and thanks to others for their loyalty and work. The bottom line is that leadership practitioners can enhance their ability to influence others based on reward power if they (*a*) determine what rewards are available, (*b*) determine what rewards are valued by their subordinates, and (*c*) establish clear policies for the equitable and consistent administration of rewards for good performance.

Finally, because reward power is partly determined by one's position in the organization, some people may believe followers have little, if any, reward power. This may not be the case. If followers have control over scarce resources, then they may use the administration of these resources as a way of getting leaders to act in the manner they want. Moreover, followers may reward their leader by putting out a high level of effort when they feel their leader is doing a good job, and they may put forth less effort when they feel their leader is doing a poor job. By modifying their level of effort, followers may in turn modify a leader's attitudes and behaviors. And when followers compliment their leader (e.g., for running a constructive meeting), it is no less an example of reward power than when a leader compliments a follower. Thus, leadership practitioners should be aware that followers can also use reward power to influence leaders.

Coercive Power. Coercive power, the opposite of reward power, is the potential to influence others through the administration of negative sanctions or the removal of positive events. In other words, it is the ability to control others through the fear of punishment or the loss of valued outcomes. Like reward power, coercive power is partly a function of the leader, but the situation often limits the coercive actions a leader can take. Examples of coercive power include policemen giving tickets for speeding, the army court-martialing AWOL soliders, a teacher detaining disruptive students after school, employers firing lazy workers, and parents spanking children. Even presidents resort to their coercive powers. Historian Arthur Schlesinger, Jr., for example, described Lyndon Johnson as having a "devastating instinct for the weaknesses of others." Lyndon Johnson was familiar and comfortable with the use of coercion; he once told a White House staff member, "Just you remember this. There's only two kinds at the White House. There's elephants and there's ants. And I'm the only elephant."

Coercive power, like reward power, can be used appropriately or inappropriately. It is carried to its extreme in harsh and repressive totalitarian societies. One of the most tragic instances of coercive power was in the cult led by Jim Jones, which tragically and unbelievably self-exterminated in an incident known as the Jonestown massacre. Virtually all of the 912 who died there drank, at Jones's direction, from large vats of a flavored drink containing cyanide. The submissiveness and suicidal obedience of Jones's followers during the massacre was due largely to the long history of rule by fear Jones had practiced. For example, teenagers caught holding hands were beaten, and adults judged slacking in their work were forced to box for hours in marathon public matches against as many as three or four bigger and stronger opponents. Jim Jones ruled by fear, and his followers became self-destructively compliant.

Perhaps the preceding example is so extreme that we can dismiss its relevance to our own lives and leadership activities. On the other hand, it does provide dramatic reminder that reliance on coercive power has inherent limitations and drawbacks. This is not to say the willingness to use disciplinary sanctions is never necessary. Sometimes it is.

Informal coercion, as opposed to the threat of formal punishment, can also be used to change the attitudes and behaviors of others. Informal coercion is usually expressed implicitly, and often nonverbally, rather than explicitly. It may be the pressure employees feel to donate to the boss's favorite charity, or it may be his glare when they bring up an unpopular idea. One of the most common forms of coercion is simply a superior's temperamental outbursts. The intimidation of a leader's poorly controlled anger is usually, in its long-term effects, a dysfunctional style of behavior for leaders.

It is also possible for followers to use coercive power to influence their leader's behavior. For example, a leader may be hesitant to take disciplinary action against a large, emotionally unstable follower. Followers can threaten leaders with physical assaults, industrial sabotage, or work slowdowns and strikes, and these threats can serve to modify a leader's behavior. In all likelihood, followers will be more likely to use coercive power to change their leader's behavior if they have a relatively high amount of referent power with their fellow co-workers. This may be particularly true if threats of work slow-downs or strikes are used to influence a leader's behavior.

Concluding Thoughts About French and Raven's Power Taxonomy. There has been considerable research addressing French and Raven's3 taxonomy of power, and generally the findings indicate that leaders who relied primarily on referent and expert power had subordinates who were more motivated and satisfied, were absent less, and performed better. However, Yukl12 and Podsakoff and Schriesheim have criticized these findings, and much of their criticism centers on the instrument used to assess a leader's bases of power. Recently, Hinkin and Schriesheim have developed an instrument that overcomes many of the criticisms, and future research should more clearly delineate the relationship between the five bases of power and various leadership effectiveness criteria.

Even though much research to date about the five bases of power may be flawed, three generalizations about power and influence still seem warranted. First, effective leaders typically take advantage of all their sources of power. They understand the relative advantages and disadvantages of the different power sources, and they selectively emphasize one or another depending on their particular objectives in a given situation. Second, whereas leaders in well-functioning organizations have strong influence over their subordinates, they are also open to being influenced by them. High degrees of reciprocal influence between leaders and followers characterize the most effective organizations.5 Third, leaders vary in the extent to which they share power with subordinates. Some leaders seem to view their power as a fixed resource that, when shared with others (like cutting a pie into pieces), reduces their own portion. They see power in zero-sum terms. Other leaders see power as an expandable pie. They see the possibility of increasing a subordinate's power without reducing their own. Needless to say, which view a leader subscribes to can have a major impact on the leader's support for power-sharing activities like delegation and participative management. Support for them is also affected by the practice of holding leaders responsible for subordinates' decisions and actions as well as their own. It is, after all, the coach or manager who often gets fired when the team loses. . . .

Leader Motives

People vary in their motivation to influence or control others. McClelland called this the **need for power**, and individuals with a high need for power derive psychological satisfaction from influencing others. They seek positions where they can influence others, and they are often involved concurrently in influencing people in many different organizations or decision-making bodies. In such activities they readily offer ideas, suggestions, and opinions, and also seek information they can use in influencing others. They are often astute at building trusting relationships and assessing power networks, though they can also be quite outspoken and forceful. They value the tangible signs of their authority and status as well as the more intangible indications of others' deference to them. Two different ways of expressing the need for power have been identified: **personalized power** and **socialized power**. Individuals who have a high need for personalized power are relatively selfish, impulsive, and uninhibited, and lacking in self-control. These individuals exercise power for their own self-centered needs, not for the good of the group or the organization. Socialized power, on the other hand, implies a more emotionally mature expression of the motive. Socialized power is exercised in the service of higher goals to others or organizations and often involves self-sacrifice toward those ends. It often involves and empowering rather than autocratic style of management and leadership. . . .

Findings concerning both the need for power and the motivation to manage have several implications for leadership practitioners. First, not all individuals like being leaders. One reason may be that some have a relatively low need for power or motivation to manage. Because these scores are relatively stable and fairly difficult to change, leaders who do not enjoy their role may want to seek positions where they have few supervisory responsibilities.

Second, a high need for power or motivation to manage does not guarantee leadership success. The situation can play a crucial role in determining whether the need for power or the motivation to manage is related to leadership success. For example, McClelland and Boyatzis found the need for power to be related to leadership success for nontechnical managers only, and Miner found motivation to manage was related to leadership success only in hierarchical or bureaucratic organizations.

Third, in order to be successful in the long term, leaders may have to have both a high need for socialized power and a high level of activity inhibition. Leaders who impulsively exercise power merely to satisfy their own selfish needs will probably be ineffective in the long term.

Finally, it is important to remember that followers as well as leaders differ in the need for power, activity inhibition, and motivation to manage. Certain followers may have stronger needs or motives in this area. Leaders may need to behave differently toward these followers than they might toward followers having a low need for power or motivation to manage. . . .

Influence Tactics

Whereas power is the capacity or potential to influence others, influence tactics are the actual behaviors used by an agent to change the attitudes, opinions, or behaviors of a target person. Kipnis and his associates accomplished much of the early work on the types of influence tactics one person uses to influence another, and developed the Profile of Organizational Influence Strategies (POIS) to assess these behaviors. Several methodological problems, however, limit the usefulness of this instrument. For example, influence tactics are evaluated only from the perspective of the influencing agent; the target's perceptions are ignored. Others, fortunately, have developed an alternative measure of influence tactics: the Influence Behavior Questionnaire, or IBQ. The IBQ is completed by both agents and targets, and appears to be a more valid instrument than the POIS. The following is a more detailed discussion of the tactics assessed by the IBQ.

Types of Influence Tactics

The IBQ is designed to assess nine types of influence tactics. **Rational persuasion** occurs when an agent uses logical arguments or factual evidence to influence others. Agents make **inspirational appeals** when they make a request or proposal designed to arouse enthusiasm or emotions in targets. **Consultation** occurs when agents ask targets to participate in planning an activity, and **ingratiation** occurs when the agent attempts to get you in a good mood before making a request. Agents use **personal appeals** when they ask another to do a favor out of friendship, whereas influencing a target through the exchange of favors is labeled **exchange**. **Coalition tactics** are different from consultation in that they are used when agents seek the aid or support of others to influence the target. Threats or persistent reminders used to influence targets are known as **pressure tactics**, and **legitimizing tactics** occur when agents make requests based on their position or authority.

Influence Tactics and Power

As alluded to throughout this . . . [selection], a strong relationship exists between the powers possessed by agents and targets, and the type of influence tactic used by the agent to modify the attitudes, values, or behavior of a target. Because leaders with relatively high amounts of referent power have built up close relationships with followers, they may be more able to use a wide variety of influence tactics to modify the attitudes and behaviors of their followers. For example, leaders with a lot of referent power could use inspirational appeals, consultations, ingratiation, personal appeals, exchanges, and even coalition tactics to increase the amount of time a particular follower spends doing work-related activities. Note, however, that leaders with high referent power generally do not use legitimizing or pressure tactics to influence followers since by threatening followers leaders risk some loss of referent power. Leaders who have only coercive or legitimate power may be able to use only coalition, legitimizing, or pressure tactics to influence followers. In this case, coalition tactics are just pressure tactics one step removed, as these leaders can threaten other followers with disciplinary action if they do not persuade a fellow follower to change his attitudes or behavior.

Other factors also can affect the choice of influence tactics. People typically use hard tactics (i.e., the legitimizing or pressure tactics of the IBQ) when an influencer has the upper hand, when she anticipates resistance, or when the other person's behavior violates important norms. People typically use soft tactics (e.g., ingratiation) when they are at a disadvantage, when they expect resistance, or when they will personally benefit if the attempt is successful. People typically use rational tactics (i.e., the exchange and rational appeals tactics of the IBQ) when parties are relatively equal in power, when resistance is not anticipated, and when the benefits are organizational as well as personal. . . .

Concluding Thoughts about Influence Tactics

In the above discussion, an implicit lesson for leaders is the value of being conscious of what influence tactics one uses and what effects are typically associated with each tactic. Knowledge of such effects can help a leader make better decisions about her manner of influencing others. It might also be helpful for leaders to think more carefully about why they believe a particular influence tactic might be effective. Research indicates that some reasons for selecting among various possible influence tactics lead to successful outcomes more frequently than others. More specifically, thinking an act would improve an employee's self-esteem or morale was frequently associated with successful influence attempts. On the other hand, choosing an influence tactic because it followed company policy and choosing one because it was a way to put a subordinate in his place were frequently mentioned as reasons for unsuccessful influence attempts. In a nutshell, these results suggest that leaders should pay attention not only to the actual influence tactics they use—to *how* they are influencing others—but also to *why* they believe such methods are called for. It is consistent with these results to conclude that influence efforts intended to build others up more frequently lead to positive outcomes than influence efforts intended to put others down.

Summary

This.... [selection] has defined power as the capacity or potential to exert influence; influence tactics as the behaviors used by one person to modify the attitudes and behaviors of another; and influence as the degree of change in a person's attitudes, values, or behaviors as the result of another's influence tactic. Because power, influence, and influence tactics play such an important role in the leadership process, this.... [selection] provides ideas to help leadership practitioners improve their effectiveness. Leadership practitioners can help themselves become more effective by reflecting on their leadership situation and considering the relative amounts of the five bases of social power both they and their followers possess. By reflecting on their bases of power, leadership practitioners can better understand how they can affect followers and how they can expand the amount of power they possess. In addition, the five bases of power also provide clues as to why subordinates are able to influence leaders and successfully resist leaders' influence attempts.

Leaders also may gain insight about why they may not enjoy their job by considering their own need for power or motivation to manage, or may better understand why some leaders exercise power selfishly by considering McClelland's concepts of personalized power and activity inhibition....

Although power is an extremely important concept, having power is relatively meaningless unless a leader is willing to exercise it. The exercise of power occurs primarily through the influence tactics leaders and followers use to modify the attitudes and behaviors of each other. The types of influence tactics used seem to depend on the amount of different types of power possessed, the degree of resistance expected, and the rationale behind the different influence tactics. Because influence tactics designed to build up others are generally more successful than those that tear down others, leadership practitioners should always consider why they are using a particular influence attempt before they actually use it. By carefully considering the rationale behind the tactic, leaders may be able to avoid using pressure and legitimizing tactics and to find ways to influence followers that build them up rather than tear them down. Being able to use influence tactics that modify followers' attitudes and behaviors in the desired direction at the same time they build up followers' self-esteem and self-confidence should be a skill all leaders strive to master.

Lesson

14 *Integrity*

Doing what is right, and being willing to defend our actions, even at the sacrifice of ourselves, is the essence of integrity. By consistently acting with integrity and communicating the purpose behind those actions, it fosters respect in the leadership relationship.

READING 1

"Integrity" Carter. P. 7, 10-12. Excerpts from *The Rules about the Rules*.

When I refer to integrity, I have something very simple and very specific in mind. Integrity, as I will use the term, requires three steps: (1) *discerning* what is right and what is wrong; (2) *acting* on what you have discerned, even at personal cost; and (3) *saying openly* that you are acting on your understanding of right from wrong. The first criterion captures the idea of integrity as requiring a degree of moral reflectiveness. The second brings in the ideal of an integral person as steadfast, which includes the sense of keeping commitments. The third reminds us that a person of integrity is unashamed of doing the right. I will explain more about why I have chosen this as my definition; but I hope that even readers who quarrel with my selection of the term *integrity* to refer to the form of commitment that I describe will come away from the book understanding why the concept itself, whatever it may be called, is a vital one.

The word *integrity* comes from the same Latin root as *integer* and historically has been understood to carry much the same sense, the sense of *wholeness*: a person of integrity, like a whole number, is a whole person, a person somehow undivided. The word conveys not so much a single-mindedness as a completeness; not the frenzy of a fanatic who wants to remake all the world in a single mold but the serenity of a person who is confident in the knowledge that he or she is living rightly. The person of integrity need not be a Gandhi but also cannot be a person who blows up buildings to make a point. A person of integrity lurks somewhere inside each of us: a person we feel we can trust to do right, to play by the rules, to keep commitments. Perhaps it is because we all sense the capacity for integrity within ourselves that we are able to notice and admire it even in people with whom, on many issues, we sharply disagree.

Indeed, one reason to focus on integrity as perhaps the first among the virtues that make for good character is that it is in some sense prior to everything else: the rest of what we think matters very little if we lack essential integrity, the courage of our convictions, the willingness to act and speak in behalf of what we know to be right. In an era when the American people are crying out for open discussion of morality—of right and wrong—the ideal of integrity seems a good place to begin. No matter what our politics, no matter what causes we may support, would anybody really want to be led or followed or assisted by people who *lack* integrity? People whose words we could not trust, whose motives we didn't respect, who might at any moment toss aside everything we thought we had in common and march off in some other direction?

The Three Steps

Integrity, I should explain before proceeding, is not the same as honesty, although honesty obviously is a desirable element of good character as well. From our definition, it is clear that one cannot have integrity without also displaying a measure of honesty. But one can be honest without being integral, for integrity, as I define it, demands a difficult process of discerning one's deepest understanding of right and wrong, and then further requires action consistent with what one has learned. It is possible to be honest without ever taking a hard look inside one's soul, to say nothing of taking any action based on what one finds. For example, a woman who believes abortion is murder may state honestly that this is what she thinks, but she does not fulfill the integrity criteria unless she also works to change abortion law. A man who believes in our national obligation to aid the homeless cannot claim to be fulfilling the criteria unless he works to obtain the aid he believes is deserved—and perhaps provides some assistance personally.

All too many of us fall down on step 1: we do not take the time to discern right from wrong. Indeed, I suspect that few of us really know just what we believe—what we value—and, often, we do not really want to know. Discernment is hard work; it takes time and emotional energy. And it is so much easier to follow the crowd. We too often look the other way when we see wrongdoing around us, quite famously in the widely unwitnessed yet very unprivate murder of Kitty Genovese thirty years ago. We refuse to think in terms of right and wrong when we elect or reject political candidates based on what they will do for our own pocketbooks. On the campuses, too many students and not a few professors find it easier to go along with the latest trends than to risk the opprobrium of others by registering an objection. Indeed, social psychologists say that this all too human phenomenon of refusing to think independently is what leads to mob violence. But a public-spirited citizen must do a bit of soul-searching—must decide what he or she most truly and deeply believes to be right and good—before it is possible to live with integrity.

The second step is also a tough one. It is far easier to know what one believes—to know, in effect, right from wrong—than it is to do something about it. For example, one may believe that the homeless deserve charity, but never dispense it; or one may think that they are bums who should not be given a dime, yet always dig into one's pockets when confronted. We Americans have a remarkable capacity to say one thing and do another, not always out of true hypocrisy but often out of a lack of self-assurance. We see this in our politics, where nobody wants to be the one to say that the retirees who receive Social Security payments are, for the most part, receiving not a return on an investment but direct subventions from the payments being made by today's workers toward their own retirements—which, if done by a private investment firm, would be an illegal pyramid scheme. The late legal scholar Robert Cover illustrated the point quite powerfully when he examined the puzzling question of how avowedly antislavery judges in the early nineteenth century could hand down obviously proslavery decisions. Equally puzzling to many political activists is their inability to recruit support from people they know to be committed to their causes, who frequently explain that they simply do not want to get involved.

But in order to live with integrity, it is sometimes necessary to take that difficult step—to get involved—to fight openly for what one believes to be true and right and good, even when there is risk to oneself. I would not go so far as to insist that morally committed citizens living integral lives must fight their way through life, strident activists in behalf of all their beliefs; but I worry deeply about the number of us who seem happy to drift through life, activists in behalf of none of our beliefs.

This leads to the third step, which seems deceptively simple, but is often the hardest of all: the person truly living an integral life must be willing to say that he or she is acting consistently with what he or she has decided is right. When the statements of a person of integrity are the result of discernment, of hard thought, we treat them as reliable, even when they are indicators of the future—"You've got the job" or "Till death do us part." But forthrightness also matters because people of integrity are willing to tell us *why* they are doing what they are doing. So it does not promote integrity for one to cheat on taxes out of greed but to claim to be doing it as a protest; indeed, it does not promote integrity to do it as a protest unless one says openly (including to the Internal Revenue Service) that that is what one is doing. It does not promote integrity to ignore or cover up wrongdoing by a co-worker or family member. And it does not promote integrity to claim to be doing the will of God when one is actually doing what one's political agenda demands.

This third step—saying publicly that we are doing what we think is right, even when others disagree—is made particularly difficult by our national desire to conform. Most of us want to fit in, to be accepted, and admitting to (or proudly proclaiming) an unpopular belief is rarely the way to gain acceptance. But if moral dissenters are unwilling to follow the example of the civil rights movement and make a proud public show of their convictions, we as a nation will never have the opportunity to be inspired by their integrity to rethink our own ideas.

This last point bears emphasis. Integrity does not always require following the rules. Sometimes—as in the civil rights movement—integrity requires *breaking* the rules. But it also requires that one be open and public about both the fact of one's dissent and the reasons for it. A person who lives an integral life may sometimes reach moral conclusions that differ from those of the majority; displaying those conclusions publicly is a crucial aspect of the wholeness in which integrity consists.

READING 2

"Integrity" Carter. P. 20-24 Excerpts from *The Rules about the Rules*.

Discernment: Antigone's Integrities

Our admiration for this capacity to sacrifice *all* for the sake of principle is a vital part of our more general admiration of integrity. Let us take a moment now to consider one of the most famous examples of this in literature: Sophocles's play *Antigone*.

The facts are quickly told. The ruler of Thebes, Creon, has decreed that no citizen who dies fighting for the city-state's enemies may be buried; instead, the corpse must be left to rot. In due time, Creon's own nephew, Polynieces, turns against the city and is slain outside the walls. The king insists on imposing the punishment he previously decreed, refusing permission for burial. His niece, Antigone, acting out of love, defies her uncle and buries her brother according to tradition. A furious Creon has the unrepentant Antigone walled up in a cave; when at last he changes his mind and has the cave opened, he finds that she has committed suicide. Query: Who showed the greater integrity?

Many a high-schooler or college freshman has struggled with this question. Let us struggle along with them. First, consider the possibility that King Creon, in his unbending insistence on punishing even his own nephew, acts with more integrity than Antigone. Creon is hardly a sympathetic character, but he is clear and steadfast in doing what he believes to be right. He plays no favorites, making no exception even for his own flesh and blood. As for Antigone, she evidently made no protest when the punishment was carried out against ordinary citizens of Thebes, but only when the burial of her brother was forbidden; she asserts no principle (other than familial love) to undergird her protest.

In this Antigone is like many of the Americans who protested with such vehemence when a judge in Singapore sentenced a young American to a caning—a flogging, really—for vandalism, an offense that some in the United States consider relatively minor. The reason the protesters were like Antigone is that the ground of protest seemed to be so narrow: Treat your own citizens as you like, but you may not so treat one of ours! (No wave of revulsion has ever swept America at the way that Singapore treats its own people.) And, so stated, the objection turns out to be an argument not against brutality generally but against brutality to Americans, thus losing a good deal of its moral force.

The same may be said of Antigone: her argument, directed only at her brother, loses the universalism that might make it sound in justice, at least to the modern ear. And yet it is plain to the most casual reader of the play that Sophocles means us to see Creon as the villain and Antigone as one to be admired. Consider how Sophocles builds the dramatic tension as Creon begins to have second thoughts. First his own son, Haemon, Antigone's betrothed, urges him to release her and is furious when he will not. Then Teiresias, a prophet, shows up to warn Creon: "Stubbornness and stupidity are twins." When Creon, at last convinced, rushes off to free Antigone, he is too late. She has hanged herself. Haemon, in a rage, tries to kill his father and, missing, kills himself instead. A distraught Creon returns to the palace, haunted by the Chorus, which taunts him: "You have learned justice, though it comes too late." And then he learns that his wife, Eurydice, has killed herself in despair over the death of her son. Creon cries out, "This is my guilt, all mine."

But is Creon right that the guilt is all his? If he was in his way too unbending, might we not say the same of Antigone? After all, had she submitted to the law, there would have been no tragic string of suicides. Indeed, it is fair to say that the horrible ending arose from the *combination* of her stubbornness and Creon's. The philosopher Martha Nussbaum (following Hegel) points out that "Antigone, like Creon, has engaged in a ruthless simplification of the world of value which effectively eliminates conflicting obligations." So why is Antigone to be more admired?

Part of the answer comes from the conversation between Creon and the Chorus that I just quoted. Creon, on reflection, sees his error. The Chorus's position—and, I think, the reader's—must be that Creon should have thought all this out in advance. His moral error came in not being sufficiently reflective before announcing his rule. Antigone, by contrast, holds a lengthy conversation with her sister, Ismene, *before* embarking on her defiance of the king. We know that she has reflected long and hard on both right and wrong and the consequences of her action because we see her do it. So our admiration for Antigone probably stems at least in part from our realization that she, unlike Creon, *is* morally reflective, and that she undertakes this process of reflection *before* deciding what to do.

Thinking matters through before we act is always difficult and often consumes a significant part of our time. But it simply is not possible to be a person of integrity without doing it. On this point, many different moral sources agree. Socrates, of course, thought the unexamined life not worth living. Such very different contemporary philosophers as John Rawls and Bernard Williams, by exalting dialogue, necessarily exalt reflection as well. But reflection is not merely for philosophers; it is for all of us. For example, when the *Catechism of the Catholic Church* turns to the issue of conscience, it enjoins individuals to follow the dictates of conscience but also concedes that conscience can be in error—usually because the conscience "remains in ignorance." The *Catechism* continues: "Ignorance can often be imputed to personal responsibility. This is the case when a man 'takes little trouble to find out what is true and good, or when conscience is by degrees almost blinded through the habit of committing sin.' In such cases, the person is culpable for the evil he commits."

Why is the person culpable? Because it is his own fault that he is morally ignorant. He either is stuck in "the habit of committing sin" or—what is, for the student of integrity, both much more important and much worse—he has not taken the trouble "to find out what is true and good"; that is to say, he has not engaged in moral reflection before choosing a course of action.

Discernment and Risk

Doing right in preference to wrong implies that one will do so even in the presence of risk. This surely accounts for our respect for this century's twin icons of nonviolent resistance, Mohandas Gandhi and Martin Luther King, Jr., both of whom were open and public and loving in their successful battles against oppressive authority.

Their example continues to inspire people who love democracy—literally around the world. As I write these words, the government of Myanmar (formerly Burma) has just yielded to intense international pressure and released from six years of house arrest Daw Aung San Suu Kyi, who won the 1991 Nobel Peace Prize for her struggle to democratize her nation and was punished for it. Also as I write, the government of China has just released Harry Wu, who spent nineteen years in Chinese prisons for his prodemocracy work but became a U.S. citizen in 1994. Since changing citizenship, Wu has often returned to China (sometimes under assumed names) to gather information about human rights abuses. Finally, the Chinese government arrested Wu, only to turn around and release him after an international outcry—fresh evidence that faith moves mountains.

Faith—the faith that we are right—also enables us to take risks for what we most deeply believe to be good and true, and that is what all of these people did. If for the sake of the right they stood in harm's way, they did so by personal choice, a choice that the rest of us can only admire. The philosopher Lynne McFall has argued that there is no integrity without risk of loss: "A person of integrity is willing to bear the consequences of her convictions, even when this is difficult, that is, when the consequences are unpleasant." And if we are never tested, we never really know how deeply we believe: "Where there is no possibility of its loss, integrity cannot exist." In short, we can never really know whether we are acting from deep and steadfast principles until those principles are tested.

McFall's point is well taken, not only as a matter of moral philosophy but as a matter of human personality: we admire most those who stand up for their beliefs when they have something to lose. Much of the Biblical narrative is built around such steadfastness. Thus, Abraham accepts God's command to sacrifice his son Isaac, and Job refuses, in the face of endless tribulations, to abandon his faith (or, as he puts it, his "integrity" [Jb. 27:5]). And secular examples abound. Thus, Bobby Fischer, the tempestuous American genius who was world chess champion from the time of his victory over Boris Spassky in 1972 until his resignation in 1975, was to many observers a spoiled and irritating brat, but there was no denying his integrity. Indeed, had he possessed less integrity, he might well have been champion a good deal sooner. In 1967, he was comfortably alone in first place at the midpoint of the Interzonal Tournament—one of several tournament and match hurdles that championship aspirants must leap—when he withdrew in protest after the organizers insisted that he play a game on his sabbath. Most of us, I suspect, with the championship at stake, would have ignored the sabbath and played the game. But Fischer stuck to his principles, was disqualified from the tournament (which he almost certainly would have won), and had to begin the hard climb to the championship anew three years later.

Of course, we admire more those who risk more. That is why Barbara Fritchie is an American hero (at least to Yankees), whether or not, as legend has it, the ninety-five-year-old widow actually resisted Confederate General Stonewall Jackson's September 1862 invasion of Frederick, Maryland, with the words attributed to her by the poet John Greenleaf Whittier: "'Shoot, if you must, this old gray head, / But spare your country's flag,' she said." Jackson supposedly responded: "Who touches a hair on yon gray head / Dies like a dog! March on!"

But whether or not the story of Barbara Fritchie (who was, at least, a real person) is true, our admiration for her is plainly admiration of her willingness to make the ultimate sacrifice for her beliefs. She was in that sense a thorough patriot, not in our deplorable modern sense of somebody who wants to escape the force of law while telling everybody else how to be a good American, but in the traditional sense of somebody who simply loves her country enough—or, as Whittier would have it, loves *our* country enough—that she will stand and die for its flag.

Like the first-century Jews who faced down Petronius, Antigone, too, offers the ultimate sacrifice—not for her city, perhaps, but for her family and her belief in the right. Certainly she meets McFall's test, for she is "willing to bear the consequences of her convictions, even . . . when the consequences are unpleasant." And Antigone's willingness to face death, even if the fact that it is suicide deprives it of some of its moral resonance, surely is a part of the reason why we admire her.

READING 3

"How Princes Should Keep Faith" Machiavelli. Excerpt from *The Prince* (1513) trans. Thompson (1813) New York: Limited Editions Club, 1954. From "The Leader's Companion" Wren. The Free Press

> Niccolo Machiavelli (1469–1527) was trained as a humanist and served as an active diplomat for Florence. He was exiled, and there wrote his most famous work, *The Prince,* a classic on the pragmatic use of power. While *The Prince* addresses winning and maintaining individual power by any means necessary, his other famous work, the *Discourses,* describes the advantages of a republic.

Every one understands how praiseworthy it is in a Prince to keep faith, and to live uprightly and not craftily. Nevertheless, we see from what has taken place in our own days that Princes who have set little store by their word, but have known how to overreach men by their cunning, have accomplished great things, and in the end got the better of those who trusted to honest dealing.

Be it known, then, that there are two ways of contending, one in accordance with the laws, the other by force; the first of which is proper to men, the second to beasts. But since the first method is often ineffectual, it becomes necessary to resort to the second. A Prince should, therefore, understand how to use well both the man and the beast. . . .

. . . a prudent Prince neither can nor ought to keep his word when to keep it is hurtful to him and the causes which led him to pledge it are removed. If all men were good, this would not be good advice, but since they are dishonest and do not keep faith with you, you, in return, need not keep faith with them; and no prince was ever at a loss for plausible reasons to cloak a breach of faith. . . .

It is necessary, indeed, to put a good colour on this nature, and to be skilful in simulating and dissembling. But men are so simple, and governed so absolutely by their present needs, that he who wishes to deceive will never fail in finding willing dupes. . . .

A Prince should therefore be very careful that nothing ever escapes his lips which is not. . . . the embodiment of mercy, good faith, integrity, humanity, and religion. . . .

It is not essential, then, that a Prince should have all the good qualities which I have enumerated above, but it is most essential that he should seem to have them; I will even venture to affirm that if he has and invariably practises them all, they are hurtful, whereas the appearance of having them is useful. Thus, it is well to seem merciful, faithful, humane, religious, and upright, and also to be so; but the mind should remain so balanced that were it needful not to be so, you should be able and know how to change to the contrary.

And you are to understand that a Prince, and most of all a new Prince, cannot observe all those rules of conduct in respect whereof men are accounted good, being often forced, in order to preserve his Princedom, to act in opposition to good faith, charity, humanity, and religion. He must therefore keep his mind ready to shift as the winds and tides of Fortune turn, and, as I have already said, he ought not to quit good courses if he can help it, but should know how to follow evil courses if he must. . . .

Moreover, in the actions of all men, and most of all of Princes, where there is no tribunal to which we can appeal, we look to results. Wherefore if a Prince succeeds in establishing and maintaining his authority, the means will always be judged honourable and be approved by every one. For the vulgar are always taken by appearances and by results, and the world is made up of the vulgar, the few only finding room when the many have no longer ground to stand on.

A certain Prince of our own days, whose name it is as well not to mention, is always preaching peace and good faith, although the mortal enemy of both; and both, had he practised them as he preaches them, would, oftener than once, have lost him his kingdom and authority.

Lesson

15 *Loyalty*

By keeping ourselves, as well as our peers, seniors, and subordinates loyal to the commitments we have made and the values, behaviors, and expectations of the organization we are a part of, we foster increased devotion not only in ourselves, but in those we influence.

READING

"The Greatest Threat Facing the Army Profession" Johnson. Military Review. September-October 2013

IT'S ABOUT THE men next to you. That's it. That's all it is." This is the closing note of the movie *Blackhawk Down*, delivered by Sgt. 1st Class Norm "Hoot" Gibson (Eric Bana's Special Forces role). The line encompasses an idea with which most Americans—and all service members—are familiar. He's talking about loyalty.

Framing loyalty as the bonds between soldiers facing conflict together is a common way for us to think about loyalty in the military—particularly when we are applying it to the Army. It is a conception of loyalty that has been explored to explain why American soldiers fight, or the need for esprit de corps, or the strength of traumatic combat experiences.

Often, though, the loyalty felt between comrades is just the loyalty most easily understood and communicated—and we, as the Army Profession, *must* communicate loyalty. It is an Army Value, first in the mnemonic acronym LDRSHIP. The definition we officially provide is—

> Bear true faith and allegiance to the U.S. Constitution, the Army, your unit and other soldiers. Bearing true faith and allegiance is a matter of believing in and devoting yourself to something or someone. A loyal soldier is one who supports the leadership and stands up for fellow soldiers. By wearing the uniform of the U.S. Army you are expressing your loyalty. And by doing your share, you show your loyalty to your unit.[1]

This explanation states what the Army Profession expects of new members. It gives them a structure by which to arrange their loyalties. Yet, too many American soldiers come away from the Army Values with the wrong ideas about loyalty. Not understanding, and not living by, the values we profess is the greatest danger facing the Army Profession in the next decade.

As human beings, we naturally feel the strongest emotional bonds—we *feel* loyal—to those closest to us. Our emotional ties evoke a strong sense of loyalty to family, to the team on the field, to the local gang, or to the military unit.[2] This loyalty is the default setting—the one our American culture reinforces with movies like *Saving Private Ryan*, with television like *Band of Brothers*, and with the endless echo chamber of the media. Military scholars often revert to the same default.

In "Why They Fight," Dr. Leonard Wong, et al., agree heartily with historian S.L.A. Marshall's observations about loyalty. In *Men Against Fire*, Marshall wrote, "I hold it to be one of the simplest truths of war that the thing which enables an infantry soldier to keep going with his weapons is the near presence or the presumed presence of a comrade. . . . He is sustained by his fellows primarily and by his weapons secondarily." When Marshall observed that "Men do not fight for a cause but because they do not want to let their comrades down," the Army War College authors went further. They argued that, in this modern era, American soldiers often "go to war" for larger reasons of ideology: patriotism, altruism, and the like. These men and women put their trust in the larger Army to frame the strategic direction of the war, but they place their loyalty with their comrades.[3]

So? What's Wrong With This?

The problem is that we give credence, throughout the Army Profession, to the notion of a "conflict of loyalties." Drill, small group, and platform instructors have spent so much energy hammering home to aspiring professionals the credo of loyalty to the men and women "next to you" that, in the hierarchy created by the Army's official definition, the last "level" of loyalty has gained primacy in our minds.

Couple that primacy developed from training and instruction with our emotional tendencies and, all too often, this small-unit loyalty becomes *the* value. Capt. Walter Sowden and Sgt. Maj. David Stewart take note of this in their paper "The Dilemma of Competing Loyalties in the Profession of Arms." In the past decade, the Army Profession has suffered through a serious public infraction of the Army Ethic on average once a year—and the decision or action occurred in a small, cohesive, *loyal* unit.[5]

The tolerance American men and women have for toxic leaders within the profession evinces the dynamic of competing loyalties: men and women who bide their time and hold their tongues in the face of incredible disrespect because they do not want to appear *disloyal*. That desire influenced subordinates to tolerate Lt. Gen. Patrick O'Reilly's common threats to "choke" those around him and Col. Frank Zachar's oft-voiced threats to stick an ice pick in the eye of the disloyal.[6] Army professionals *feel* the need to be loyal, Lt. Gen. Walter Ulmer writes. "Subordinates are reluctant to identify their boss as toxic. They feel a loyalty and do not want to embarrass their unit."[7] All too often Army professionals choose not to speak—when a superior is wrong, when a superior is unethical, when a superior is toxic—because of the cultural power of loyalty.[8]

Our training and education system reinforces this conception of loyalty so often as men and women enter the profession that it becomes an active part of their identity. It becomes part of the culture, a given element of an Army professional's emotional composition—he or she is loyal to their comrades, their battle buddies, their unit, first, last, always.[9]

This is important. It's great for cohesion, for fighting spirit, for esprit de corps. It is terrible for ensuring that the Army Profession is stewarded into the next decade. This all-important loyalty to the small group can be in conflict to loyalty to the Army, to true faith and allegiance to the U.S. Constitution.

Because identity and emotional ties will easily overwhelm the intangible idea of allegiance to ideals, this conflict is rarely resolved. Behavior economist Dan Ariely in *The Upside of Irrationality* discussed something called "self-herding"; we make decisions based upon the actions we have taken and the decisions we made in the past—based on our ideas about who we are.[10] To consult the high ideals embodied in the Constitution is too hard, and as psychologist Daniel Kahneman's "law of least effort" observes, "Laziness is built deep into our nature."[11] Too few Americans have read the Constitution, and digested the values and principles expressed, for the power of their oath to override the emotional tie to their ranger-buddy.

However, loyalty is not an expression only of emotion. It is also a function of identity. In his *Sociology of Loyalty*, James Connor wrote, "Our loyalties furnish identity."[12] We are loyal to the things most closely tied to our identity. The problem is that, today, too much of the *identity* of an Army professional is built around the emotional bond of loyalty between fighting men on the field of battle, until it has power far from the battlefield. While we need that emotional connection for esprit de corps, we also need to step away from it and carefully reinforce an identity that venerates the Constitution.

> *We are loyal to the things most closely tied to our identity. The problem is that, today, too much of the identity of an Army professional is built around the emotional bond of loyalty between fighting men on the field of battle, until it has power far from the battlefield.*

Constructing this identity is a career-long process. Dr. Pauline M. Kaurin delivered a paper at the Joint Services Conference on Professional Ethics in 2006, saying, "Rather than seeing identity as a possession, identity [even for the most senior Army professionals] "is something one is in the process of cultivating, leaving open the possibility of changing, evolving and altering one's identity in response to either individual or social influences and concerns (or both.)"[13]

As Army professionals, we must recognize that the key element of our identity is our sworn oath to support and defend, to bear true faith and allegiance to, the Constitution of the United States of America. Sharing an identity centered on the Constitution builds more expansive ties than the insular, yet tight-knit bonds of combat. Bonds forged to support an ideal rather than forged in shared hardship or firefights allow for an institutional trust that suffers otherwise. As Michael Wheeler wrote for the Air University Review—

> [This] is a different view of how loyalty can be inspired, in a manner such that the military goal of discipline can be achieved along with the social goal of having soldiers who are also reflective, morally sensitive men. This conception of loyalty is one of loyalty inspired by trust, where that trust resides in the moral integrity of the commander.[14]

That trust is the foundation of the Army Profession. If we purposefully build and continuously refine identities centered upon a desire to "establish Justice, insure [sic] domestic Tranquility, provide for the common defense, promote the general Welfare, and secure the Blessings of Liberty to ourselves and our Posterity."[15]

- We will have no more conflicts of loyalty. Either a decision, an action, will reflect our true faith and allegiance, or it will not. If our smaller groups take action counter to the Constitution, it is that group that is disloyal.
- We will more clearly understand our duty to strive for excellence in supporting and defending the Constitution and the mission defined within it.
- We will not wonder how to treat people with respect, but recognize that every person has intrinsic worth and we must recognize their dignity.
- We will not wonder what it means to offer selfless service, but recognize we derive fulfillment and worth from *serving* the American people in a unique profession with individual expertise.
- We will not debate honor, but know that it is a reverence for honesty, candor, and the truth.
- We will strive every day for enough courage to live these values openly, with integrity, admitting our shortcomings, but striving.

We are working toward an achievable goal. Striving to be Army professionals, worthy of trust and sworn to support and defend the Constitution of the United States of America. *MR*

NOTES

1. See http://www.army.mil/values/>.
2. Simon Keller, *The Limits of Loyalty* (Cambridge University Press, 2007), 31; James Connor, *The Sociology of Loyalty* (New York: Springer, 2007), 44, 69.
3. Leonard Wong, Thomas A. Kolditz, Raymond A. Millen, Terrence M. Potter, "Why They Fight: Combat Motivation in the Iraq War," *US Army War College's Strategic Studies Initiative* (Carlisle Barracks, PA, 2003). The Marshall quote is from page 2, and the authors' argument is on page 19.
4. Walter J. Sowden and David L. Stewart, "The Dilemma of Competing Loyalties in the Profession of Arms," Paper Submission: Fort Leavenworth Ethics Symposium "Applying the Military Ethic Across the Spectrum of Operations" (Fort Leavenworth, KS, 7-10 November 2011), 19.
5. Sowden and Stewart, 3. The authors cite the following to support their claim: the Guantanamo Bay (Gitmo), Abu Ghraib (2003), Ltc. West (2003), Ltc. Sassaman/ Samarra (2004), Pat Tilman (2004); Haditha (U.S. Marines in 2005), Bagram Airfield (2005), Hamdania (U.S. Marines in 2006), Mahmudiyah/Black Hearts (2006), Operation Iron Triangle (2006), Baghdad Canal Killings (2007), "Kill Team" (2010) incidents, and the rash of senior commanders (Army and Navy) being relieved over the past year (2011).
6. Inspector General, "Report of Investigation, Lt. Gen. Patrick J. O'Reilly, U.S. Army, Missile Defense Agency," Alexandria, VA, 2 May 2012; Joe Gould, "Germanybased colonel relieved of duty," *Army Times*, 6 March 2011, <http://www.armytimes.com/news/2011/03/army-report-finds-toxic-command-climate-zachar-030611w/>.
7. Walter F. Ulmer Jr., "Toxic Leadership: What Are We Talking About?" *Army* June (2012): 50.
8. Fred Kaplan, *The Insurgents: David Petraeus and the Plot to Change the American Way of War* (Simon and Schuster: New York, 2013), 190. Kaplan illustrates this point when he records that "[Maj. Gen. Peter] Chiarelli wasn't the protesting or resigning type. He'd signed on to this assignment, to this war. He valued the Army's hierarchy and its ethos of loyalty. He gnashed his teeth over Casey nearly every day, but always spoke up on his behalf and never'at least at the time'spoke out against him."
9. Sowden and Stewart, 18.
10. Dan Ariely, *The Upside of Irrationality: The Unexpected Benefits of Defying Logic* (Harper Perennial: New York, 2010), 262.
11. Daniel Kahneman, *Thinking, Fast and Slow* (Farrar, Straus and Giroux: New York, 2011), 35.
12. Connor, 51.
13. Pauline M. Kaurin, "Identity, Loyalty and Combat Effectiveness: A Cautionary Tale," JSCOPE (2006), 2, <http://isme.tamu.edu/JSCOPE06/Kaurin06.html>.
14. Michael O. Wheeler, "Loyalty, Honor, and the Modern Military," *Air University Review*, May-June (1973): 4.
15. The Constitution of the United States.

Lesson

16 *Ownership*

Similar to loyalty, ownership requires that one show and articulate their buy-in to their organization, taking orders that come down the chain of command as their own, even when they are unfavorable.

READING 1

Damn Exec[1]

The Norfolk wind was streaking the water of Hampton Roads as Commander Martin K. Speaks, U.S. Navy, Commanding Officer of the USS Bowens (DD-891), stepped from his car, slammed the door, and straightened his cap. As he approached the pier head, a Sailor stepped from the sentry hut and saluted.

"Good morning, Captain."

"Good morning, Kowalski," answered Commander Speaks. He took pleasure in the fact that he knew the Sailor's name. Kowalski was a good Sailor. He had served his entire first cruise in the *Bowens* and did his work well.

The Captain noticed that, over his blues, Kowalski wore a deck force foul weather jacket, faded, frayed, dirty, and spotted with red lead. "Little chilly this morning," said the Captain as he walked by. "Yes sir, sure is," replied the Sailor with his usual grin.

As the Captain approached his quarterdeck, there was the usual scurrying of people, and four gongs sounded. "Bowens arriving," spoke the loudspeaker system, and Lieutenant (j.g.) Henry Graven, U.S. Naval Reserve, gunnery officer and the day's command duty officer, came running to the quarterdeck. Salutes and cheerful "Good mornings" were exchanged, and the Captain continued to his cabin.

Lieutenant Graven looked over the quarterdeck and frowned. "Let's get this brightwork polished, chief."

"It's already been done once this morning, sir," replied the OD.

"Well, better do it again. The Exec will have a fit if he sees it this way," said Graven.

"Yes sir," answered the OD.

As soon as Graven had left, the OD turned to his messenger, "Go tell the duty boatswain's mate that Mr. Graven wants the brightwork done over again on the quarterdeck."

Later that morning, Captain Speaks was going over some charts with the ship's executive officer, Lieutenant Commander Steven A. Lassiter, U.S. Navy. The Captain had just finished his coffee and lighted a cigarette. "Steve, I noticed our pier sentry in an odd outfit this morning. He had a foul weather jacket on over his blues; it looked pretty bad."

"Yes sir. Well, it gets cold out there, and these deck force boys have mighty bad-looking jackets," the Exec said.

The Captain felt the Exec had missed his point and said, "Oh, I realize they have to wear a jacket, but for a military watch like that, I'd like to see them wear pea coats when it's cold."

Lieutenant Graven was talking with a third-class boatswain's mate on the fantail when the quarterdeck messenger found him. When told that the executive officer wanted to see him, Graven ended his discussion with, "There, hear that? He proba-

---

[1] Landersman, S. D. (1965). Damn Exec. *Proceedings of the U.S. Naval Institute.*

bly wants to see me about the brightwork. I don't care how many men it takes to do it, the Exec told me to be sure to get that brightwork polished every morning."

The executive officer indicated a chair to Graven and asked: "How's it going these days?"

Lassiter had always liked Graven, but in the past few months, since he had taken over as senior watch officer, Graven seemed to have more problems than usual.

"Okay, I guess," Graven replied with a forced grin. He knew that things were not as they used to be. It seemed strange, too, because everyone on the ship had been so glad to be rid of the previous senior watch officer, that "damn" Lieutenant Dumphy. The junior officers even had a special little beer bust at the club to celebrate Dumphy's leaving and Graven's "fleeting up" to senior watch officer. Now the Exec was always after him. The junior officers didn't help much either, always complaining about the Exec. Maybe the Exec was taking over as "the heel" now that Dumphy was gone.

"That's good," said the Exec. "Here's a little thing that you might look into. These men who stand pier watches have to wear a jacket, but the foul weather jacket doesn't look good for a military watch. I'd like to see them wear their pea coats when it's cold." Graven had expected something like this, more of the Exec's picking on him. He responded properly, got up, and left.

Graven told his first lieutenant. "The Exec says the pier head sentries can't wear foul weather jackets anymore. If it's cold they can wear pea coats," he added.

"But the pea coats will get dirty, and then what about personnel inspections?" asked the first lieutenant.

"I don't know," Graven shook his head, "but if the Exec wants pea coats, we give him pea coats!"

"Pea coats!" said the chief boatswain's mate, "Who says so?"

"That's what the Exec wants," said the first lieutenant, "so let's give him pea coats."

"The Exec says pea coats for the pier sentries when it's cold," announced the chief to his boatswain's mates.

A third-class boatswain's mate walked away from the group with a buddy, turned and said, "That Damn Exec. First I got to have all my men polish brightwork on the quarterdeck, now they got to wear pea coats on sentry duty 'stead of foul weather jackets!"

Seaman Kowalski's relief showed up at the sentry booth at 1150. "Roast beef today," constituted the relieving ceremony.

"Good, I like roast beef," was the reply. "Hey, how come the pea coat?"

"Damn Exec's idea," said the relief. "We can't wear foul weather gear no more out here, only pea coats."

"Damn Exec," agreed Kowalski. "Captain didn't say nothin' when he came by."

"The Captain's okay, it's just that Damn Exec. He's the guy who fouls up everything," complained the new sentry.

Seaman Kowalski had just gone aboard the ship when Captain Speaks stepped out on deck to look over his ship. The quarterdeck awning shielded the Captain from the view of those on the quarterdeck, but he could clearly hear the conversation.

"Roast beef today, Ski."

"Yeah, I know, and we wear pea coats from now on."

"Whaddaya mean, pea coats?"

"Yeah, pea coats on the pier, Damn Exec says no more foul weather jackets."

"Well that ain't all, we got to polish this here brightwork 'til it shines every morning before quarters. Damn Exec says that too."

"Damn Exec."

Captain Speaks was shocked. "Why 'Damn Exec' from these seamen?" he thought. It was easy to see that the executive officer had passed the order along in proper military manner. It was easy to see that the junior officers, leading petty officers, and lower petty officers were passing it along saying "The Exec wants. . . ." That's the way orders are passed along. Why? Because "it is easy."

"All ship's officers assemble in the wardroom," the boatswain's mate announced on the loudspeaker system. Lieutenant Commander Lassiter escorted in the Captain. The junior officers took their seats when the Captain was seated. The executive officer remained standing. "Gentlemen, the Captain has a few words to say to us today."

The Captain rose and looked around slowly. "Gentlemen, we are continually exposed to words like administration, leadership, management, capabilities, organization, responsibilities, authority, discipline, and cooperation. You use these words every day. You give lectures to your men and use them, but if I were to ask each of you for a definition of any of these words I would get such a wide variety of answers that an expert couldn't tell what word we were defining. Some we probably couldn't define at all. We still use them, and will continue to use them as they are used in the continually mounting number of articles, instructions, and books we must read.

"If I were to ask any of you how can we improve leadership I would get answers filled with these words—undefined and meaningless.

"If we listed all of the nicely worded theories of leadership, studied them, memorized them, and took a test on them, we would all pass. But this would not improve our ability as leaders one bit. I can tell a story, containing none of these meaningless words, that *will* improve your leadership.

"In 1943, I was secondary battery officer in a cruiser in the South Pacific. In my second battle, gun control was hit and I lost communications with everyone except my 5-inch mounts. I could see that the after main battery turret was badly damaged and two enemy destroyers were closing us from astern. At the time my 5-inch mounts were shooting at airplanes. I ordered my two after 5-inch mounts to use high capacity ammunition and shift targets to the two destroyers closing from astern. 'But Mr. Speaks, we're supposed to handle the air targets; who said to shift targets?' my mount captain asked.

"There were noise and smoke and explosions that day, but the explosion that I heard and felt was not from a shell, but from those words of the mount captain.

"Those attacking destroyers got a few shots in at us before we beat them off. Maybe those shots found a target and some of my shipmates died. I never found out. There was too much other damage.

"I thought over the battle afterward and realized that this entire situation was my fault, not the mount captain's. I may have been responsible for the death of some of my shipmates because up to that day I always gave orders to my subordinates by attaching the originator's name to it.

"What does that mean? It means that it was the easy thing to do, to say, 'the gunnery officer wants us to shift targets.'

"In this peacetime world you may say that we no longer have this struggle on a life or death basis. Quick response does not mean life or death now, but it might tomorrow, or sometime after we've all been transferred elsewhere and this ship is being fought by people we don't know.

"Whether you're cleaning boilers, standing bridge watch, or administering your training program, it's easy to say 'The Exec wants' or 'Mr. Jones says.' It's the easy, lazy way: not the right way. You can sometimes discuss or even argue with an order, but when you give it to a subordinate, make him think it is coming from you.

"Giving orders the lazy way is like a drug. Once you start saying 'The ops officer wants' you will find yourself doing it more and more until you can't get a thing done any other way. Your men will pass along orders that way, too, and it will become a part of your organization right down to the lowest level. When some problem arises and you want action, you'll get 'Who wants this?' or 'Why should we?'

"Each of you ask yourself if you have given an order today or yesterday in the lazy manner. I think almost all of us have. Now ask yourself if that order really originated with the person who gave it to you, or did he receive it from a higher level? We never really know, do we, but why should we even care?

"In almost every unit the 'lazy' ordering starts on a particular level. From personal experience I can tell you that this can be an exact measure of the unit's effectiveness. If it starts at the department head level or higher it's a relatively bad outfit, and if it starts at the chief's level it's a relatively good outfit. You can find the level below which it starts by hearing a new title preceding a primary billet. 'Damn Exec' means that the executive officer is the lowest level giving orders properly. 'Damn division officer' means that the division officers are taking responsibility for the order.

"Here I am using some of those words, responsibility and authority, those undefined terms we want to avoid, but perhaps we have helped define them.

"To be more specific, every officer does some 'lazy' ordering, but we need to do it less and less. We must try to push the 'damn' title down as far as it will go.

"Let's push the 'damn officer' down all the way to the chiefs and below, then we will have a Damn Good Ship."

Ownership

LT Allen Murphy, USN

"Damn Exec" is one of those military parables like the often retold "Message to Garcia" that possesses a great moral for midshipmen and junior officers. The fable-like sea story stresses the importance of ownership for the military leader. Why is ownership so important?

Ownership, like many other attributes of a good leader, is not always easy. Passing down a difficult task or an unpopular order will not help to make any friends among one's subordinates. This is significantly compounded when an individual does not agree with the decision that he or she is passing down. Officers, however, are not in the business of making friends but are instead in the business of supporting the chain of command and enhancing the readiness of their unit at the lowest level. It is easy to "damn" the XO or the Company Officer and pass blame up the chain of command but in time this habit may prove detrimental to one's functionality as a junior officer.

The three most significant problems with the "Damn Exec" approach to leadership are:

1. It demonstrates a lack of ownership or " buy-in" to the organizational goals

A wardroom or company staff must always present a united front to the command. The desires of the Commanding Officer are the desires of the command and must be promoted by every officer in the command down to the most junior Ensign or

Second Lieutenant. If there is grumbling among the officers, the rest of the command will pick up on it and the dissatisfaction and morale will only worsen. Let's think about the following scenario:

Your ship is two weeks away from a major inspection and the Commanding Officer is very concerned with the status of the preparations. On Wednesday, the CO makes the decision that Saturday will be a mandatory workday for the ship in order to continue the final preps. You have tickets to a big football game on Saturday and have some friends coming into town to join you. You are disappointed and not looking forward to working until 1800 on a Saturday but how will you break this news to your division? If you complain to them and "damn the exec" in the process, how will their morale be affected? How much effort and enthusiasm will they display for the rest of the week and on Saturday if they know that you want to be there less than they do?

By claiming ownership of the CO's decision and displaying a high level of command buy-in, you may still get some grumbles among your sailors but your positive attitude and support of the decision will make it easier for them to justify the sacrifice of their Saturday for the needs of the command.

2. Subordinates may begin to view you as merely a puppet of the " Exec"

By consistently pushing the blame of unpopular decisions up the chain of command, an officer is essentially passing off his or her role in any decisions. Sailors and Marines will see this kind of officer as nothing more than a middle manager as opposed to a leader.

3. Subordinates may question the validity of any decisions you make for yourself

This truth was best illustrated in "Damn Exec" when the Mount Captain questioned the decision of the Gunnery Officer at a pivotal moment during combat. By deferring ownership of unpopular decisions to superiors, an officer's credibility is damaged to the point that when he or she does have to make a tough decision, it is second guessed by the subordinates if there is no evidence of validation from above. Let's reexamine the scenario in section one. What if it was you who desired your division to come in on a Saturday because of an unproductive work week or an upcoming assessment? If you were a "Damn Exec" leader, your sailors may seriously question your authority to give that level of order and may even seek verification from another officer.

In closing, be an officer that demonstrates ownership. Although not always easy, it is fundamental to being a commissioned officer. Supporting your chain of command and command level decisions is an important part of being a military officer. If you are constantly damning the exec, your subordinates may begin damning you through a loss of respect and support.

READING 2

"Breaking Ranks: Dissent and the Military Professional" Milburn. Joint Force Quarterly Issue 59 4th Quarter 2010

There are circumstances under which a military officer is not only justified but also obligated to disobey a legal order. In supporting this assertion, I discuss where the tipping point lies between the military officer's customary obligation to obey and his moral obligation to dissent. This topic defies black-and-white specificity but is nevertheless fundamental to an understanding of the military professional's role in the execution of policy. It involves complex issues—among them, the question of balance between strategy and policy, and between military leaders and their civilian masters.

Any member of the military has a commonly understood obligation to disobey an illegal order; such cases are not controversial and therefore do not fall within the purview of this article. Instead, the focus is on orders that present military professionals with moral dilemmas, decisions wherein the needs of the institution appear to weigh on both sides of the equation. Whether the issuer of the order is a superior officer or a civilian leader, the same principles apply. However, because issues at the strategic level of decisionmaking have greater consequences and raise wider issues, I focus on dissent at this level.

In the face of such a dilemma, the military professional must make a decision, which cannot simply owe its justification to the principle of obedience, and must take responsibility for that decision. But when and on what grounds should the officer dissent? And how should he do so? I offer three propositions:

1. The military officer belongs to a profession upon whose members are conferred great responsibility, a code of ethics, and an oath of office. These grant him moral autonomy and obligate him to disobey an order he deems immoral; that is, an order that is likely to harm the *institution writ large*—the Nation, military, and subordinates—in a manner not clearly outweighed by its likely benefits.
2. This obligation is not confined to effects purely military against those related to policy: the complex nature of contemporary operations no longer permits a clear distinction between the two. Indeed, the military professional's obligation to disobey is an important check and balance in the execution of policy.
3. In deciding how to dissent, the military officer must understand that this dilemma demands either acceptance of responsibility or wholehearted disobedience.

Before supporting these propositions, I discuss the "traditional" view of civil-military relations, which owes much to Samuel Huntington and his theory of objective control.

Obedience as Virtue

Samuel Huntington's *The Soldier and the State* remains the touchstone for the study of civil-military relations. However, the book should be viewed in its historical context, written as it was over 50 years ago at the height of the Cold War when the obvious need to centralize decision authority for the use of nuclear weapons lent support to a strict interpretation of civilian control. No doubt also fresh in Huntington's mind was General Douglas MacArthur's narrowly averted threat to cross the Yalu River and thus escalate the Korean War. Huntington's concept of "objective control" delineates clear boundaries between the realm of the soldier and statesman; the former is afforded some functional autonomy within his area of expertise but very little moral autonomy. Huntington argues that the military professional is on thin ice if he dissents on any grounds other than purely military or legal—and that ultimately, his overriding obligation is loyalty to his civilian masters. For Huntington, there is no middle ground: "When the military man receives a legal order from an authorized superior, he does not hesitate, he does not substitute his own views; he obeys instantly."[1]

Huntington's views still have strong influence on U.S civil-military relations today, and this may explain why, despite some ruffled feathers at the nexus between policy and military operations, there have been few recent cases of U.S. military leaders protesting the orders of their civilian masters. As General Richard Myers and Dr. Richard Kohn point out, "There is no tradition of military resignation in the United States, no precedent—and for good reason."[2]

This "good reason" is the principle of civilian control that is embedded in the U.S. Constitution. It gives Congress authority to raise the military, to set the rules for military conduct, and to decide whether to authorize war. It also makes the President the Commander in Chief of the military. Traditionalists argue that this principle is incompatible with any theory of civil-military relations that does not obligate the military professional to absolute obedience. In their view, dissent is justified only under the most exceptional circumstances and must be confined to the purely military aspects of a decision. The Nation's civilian leadership, they argue, has the "right to be wrong."[3]

The comments of General Myers and Dr. Kohn about resignation are quoted from an article entitled "Salute and Disobey?" An impassioned and ostensibly well-reasoned defense of the traditional view of civil-military relations, the article was published in response to accusations of excessive docility among the Nation's military leadership in the conduct of the war in Iraq. The authors object to the idea that a military officer should refuse an order on moral grounds because "one individual's definition of what is moral, ethical, and even professional can differ from someone else's."[4] This claim appears to let the military officer off the hook from making any moral decisions. That argument, by logical extension, would deny the existence of a military profession at all—by relegating its role to the bureaucratic function of executing instructions. It also reflects a weakness in the traditionalist argument by denying moral autonomy to a profession with a clearly defined code of ethics and an oath of allegiance not to any one person, but to the Constitution. I argue that these obligate members of the military profession to exercise moral autonomy beyond its commonly accepted responsibilities to proffer the executive branch candid advice and speak truth to Congress.

The Military Profession

A survey conducted among students at the Marine Corps War College (MCWAR) in January 2010 reveals a view of the military profession that contrasts sharply with the Huntingtonian model espoused in "Salute and Disobey?" The sample is admittedly small; nevertheless, it represents a cross section of 20 senior field-grade officers from all Services and two foreign countries. Without exception, they agreed that there are circumstances under which they would disobey a lawful order. Their criteria vary little, as these excerpts illustrate:

- "If the officer cannot live with obeying the order, then he must disobey and accept the consequences."
- "When I cannot look at myself in the mirror afterwards."
- "When I deem the order to be immoral."
- "When it is going to lead to mission failure."
- "When it will get someone injured or killed needlessly."
- "When it will cause military or institutional disaster."[5]

These comments reflect the view that the military professional has moral obligations more fundamental than obedience and loyalty to their leaders, civilian or military. Myers and Kohn imply that the term *moral* is too subjective to be defendable. However, I argue that the military profession is founded on clearly defined moral principles.

For the purposes of this article, I use the term *military professional* to apply to military officers. I make this distinction based on the nature of the officer's professional military education, which focuses on developing an abstract body of knowledge; his code of ethics, which reflect the "special trust and confidence" conferred on him by the President and Congress in his commission; and his oath of office, which differs in an important aspect from the enlisted oath. These defining characteristics of the military profession impose on him obligations beyond obedience.

Code of Ethics

How a profession views itself does much to shape its identity, and U.S. military officers take pride in belonging to a profession centered on high ethical standards. This belief, inculcated upon entry and constantly reinforced, appears within the profession to be self-evident. Indeed, each Service uses the term *core values* to describe ethical tenets that it regards as fundamental. The emphasis on values reflects an institutional understanding that it is a profession wherein the potential cost of bad decisionmaking is especially high.

The concept of *integrity,* defined as doing what is right both legally and morally, is enshrined in the professional ethics of the Army, Navy, and Marine Corps. The Army lists among its values *Selfless Service,* defined as "Putting the welfare of the nation, the Army, and your subordinates before your own." Although *Loyalty* is also one of the Army values, it is defined as an obligation to safeguard the welfare of subordinates. Obedience is not listed among any Service's core values or code of ethics—nor does it appear as an area of evaluation on fitness reports, although moral courage does.

The Oath of Office

While enlisted Servicemembers take an oath in which they promise to "obey the orders of the officers appointed over me," officers do not undertake any such obligation to obey, but rather to support and defend the Constitution. This difference is significant because it confers on the officer a weighty responsibility to, as Lieutenant General Gregory Newbold put it, "give voice to those who can't—or don't have the opportunity—to speak."[6] The obligation to nation and subordinates cannot conceivably be interpreted as meaning blind obedience to civilian masters. This obligation is given legal codification in the United States Code, Title 10, Armed Forces, which charges commanding officers to "safeguard the morale, the physical well being, and the general welfare of the officers and enlisted persons under their command or charge.[7]

The military professional's core values and oath of office demand the exercise of moral autonomy in carrying out orders. He has sworn to defend the Constitution and safeguard the welfare of his subordinates. Implicit is the obligation to challenge orders whose consequences threaten either without apparent good reason.

Check and Balance

In *Supreme Command,* Elliott Cohen's central theme is one of *unequal dialogue*—a term he uses to describe the method by which civilian leaders must supervise military operations to ensure that force is being used in consonance with policy objectives. I agree with this argument, but not with Cohen's parallel contention that the military officer has no business making decisions in the realm of policy.[8] Significantly, Cohen's discussion focuses on four statesmen renowned for both their strategic acumen and their skill in handling their military commanders. His theory does not recognize the possibility that, at the blurred nexus between strategy and policy, the military professional plays a valuable and constitutionally defendable role as a check on the potentially disastrous decisions of men less capable than Abraham Lincoln or Winston Churchill.

The traditionalist "stay in your lane" argument presupposes a clear distinction between matters of policy and those of military strategy. Even Cohen, who criticizes Huntington for oversimplifying the line between the two, believes that a line has to be drawn somewhere in order to preserve the principle of civilian control. The truth is that the complexity of what military doctrine terms the *Joint Operating Environment* and the nature of roles and missions assigned to top military commanders make any clear distinction impossible.[9]

Clearly, the military professional's realm of decision extends beyond the strict parameters applied by Huntington and even Cohen. I further argue that just as the statesman's involvement in military operations provides a healthy check in the execution of policy, so does the military professional's exercise of moral autonomy. Sound decisionmaking depends on the statesman and soldier sharing alike a responsibility for the execution of both policy and strategy.

The traditionalists, of course, balk at the suggestion that the military professional has an important role to play as a check and balance: "In a democracy, the military is not the one assigned to ensure that civilian politicians are not shirking," commented Peter Feaver, a professor of political science at Duke University.[10] Prima facie, this statement appears true. But when the results of bad decisionmaking are wasted lives and damage to the Nation; when the customary checks laid down in the Constitution—the electoral voice of the people, Congress, or the Supreme Court—are powerless to act in time; and when the military professional alone is in a position to prevent calamity, it makes little sense to argue that he should *not* exercise his discretion.

Take, for instance, the decisions by the Coalition Provisional Authority in May 2003 to disband all Iraqi security institutions and to impose a policy of de-Ba'athification without any corresponding caveats permitting reconciliation. Assume, for the sake of argument, that these were bad policies that fueled the nascent insurgency with thousands of armed, trained, and disgruntled young men with drastic consequences for American forces and U.S. efforts in Iraq. Assume, too, that these consequences can be deemed predictable by the reasonable man. With these assumptions in mind, would not the military chain of command have been justified in refusing the order? The traditional argument would deny military leaders this recourse simply because the orders reflected policy decisions.

Or consider a recent case in which senior military officers complied with an executive decision that violated the Geneva Conventions. In *Hamdan v. Rumsfeld,* June 2006, the Supreme Court ruled that Guantanamo detainees were entitled to the protections provided under Common Article 3 of the Geneva Conventions. This meant that the U.S. Government had violated the Geneva Conventions for over 4 years. It is hard to see this ruling as being anything less than a serious blow to national prestige, undermining U.S. efforts in the all-important arena of strategic communication. But it was more than that—for those who believe that national values are important, it appeared to undermine the very cause that the Nation professed to represent. This point was not lost on the Supreme Court; as Justice Anthony Kennedy observed, "Violations of Common Article 3 are considered war crimes."[11]

The Bush administration's decisions vis-à-vis the Guantanamo detainees also infringed on the Constitution, which military professionals have sworn to support and defend. So decided the Supreme Court in the case of *Boumediene v. Bush,* in which the Justices ruled that the government did not have the constitutional authority to suspend habeas corpus indefinitely.[12] The Constitution declares that "the Privilege of the Writ of Habeas Corpus shall not be suspended, unless when in Cases of Rebellion or Invasion the public Safety may require it." The executive branch had asserted broad authority to detain without trial without claiming either caveat.

My point in discussing the habeas corpus issue is not to debate the rights and wrongs of the case or to argue that the transgression should have been obvious to the military officers involved. Instead, I cite it to exemplify a situation in which an officer would have been justified in refusing an order even though it was a policy decision. In so doing, he would have been upholding his oath by opposing the unconstitutional exercise of executive authority.

There is another facet to this case that emphasizes the military professional's important role as a check and balance. The clause in the Constitution pertaining to the suspension of habeas corpus is under Article I, which deals with Congress, as opposed to Article II, which covers the powers of the President. And yet it was the executive branch that in this case assumed the role granted Congress. Perhaps the most disturbing aspect of this incident was that Congress raised no objection, thus shirking its constitutional role.

In a February 2010 article, Lieutenant Colonel Paul Yingling, USA, accused Congress of "all but abdicating many of its war powers."[13] He is correct. In recent years, Congress has proven less than vigorous in carrying out its constitutional duties pertaining to the military, creating what is essentially a constitutional void. For instance, the function of declaring war is vested in Congress with good reason. It is an expression of public support for the most momentous decision a nation will make; it ensures that the rationale for going to war and the policy goals sought by this decision are clearly defined. And yet not since World War II has Congress exercised its constitutional duty of declaring war.

A congressionally approved declaration of war performs another important function by fulfilling the "public declaration" requirement of the universally accepted theory of just war. The United States and its allies are committed by treaty and policy to conduct military operations within the framework of just war theory.[14] Just war criteria fall into two categories: *jus ad bellum,* the reasons for going to war, and *jus ad bello,* the manner in which war is conducted.[15]

The traditionalist argument holds that military leaders are concerned only with *jus ad bello;* it regards *jus ad bellum* as outside their purview since the decision to go to war is one of policy. However, for reasons already advanced by this article, senior military leaders are obligated to make judgments that fall within the realm of *jus ad bellum,* especially if Congress appears to have neglected its responsibilities in this regard. Of course, this obligation applies only to military officers of the highest rank; subordinate leaders do not have the choice of resigning in preference to going to war. This means, for instance, that a military leader might be justified in insisting that Congress vote to declare war in order to ensure that the decision stems from legitimate authority. He might also be in possession of information not available to the public, indicating that the stated rationale for going to war is invalid, in which case he has an obligation to speak out.

Once war is declared, the power of the purse obligates Congress to oversee its conduct by ensuring that ways and means are matched to the stated ends. With the early years of U.S. involvement in both Afghanistan and Iraq fresh in mind, it is hard to challenge the accusation that congressional oversight has not been zealous. Indeed, the wording of the 2002 authorization for the use of force in Iraq is so open-ended as to abdicate up front all congressional responsibility for subsequent oversight.[16]

The Founding Fathers recognized the need for checks and balances to counteract the frailty of human nature. Yingling concludes his article by saying the only way to ensure that Congress exercises these checks and balances would be to bring back universal military service. Not so, I argue. If the country's military leaders employ moral and intellectual rigor in adhering to their oath of office and professional ethics, there will be no need for so drastic a measure. That is not to say that the resignation of one or more senior leaders would always be enough to awaken the legislature to their constitutional duties, but it might at least gain the attention of the American people.

When the Constitution was written, the army was intended to be only a militia, soon to be disbanded and resurrected only in time of impending crisis. It names the judiciary as a check on both the executive and the legislature. The Supreme Court, however, will only catch those cases that are pushed to its jurisdiction, which may be after much damage has been done, as the Guantanamo cases bear witness. The court is unlikely to be called upon to decide whether a decision to go to war was justified, or whether its subsequent prosecution is in accordance with clearly defined goals, and matched with the necessary resources. In the face of congressional somnolence, the military professional has a duty to speak out in such cases.

The traditionalists need not worry. Recognition of the fact that military commanders have an obligation to make judgments involving policy is not tantamount to permitting politicization of the profession. The military professional cannot pick and choose courses of action that correspond to his political views. He must exercise careful discretion, basing his decision on his oath of office and professional ethics as opposed to a political agenda. The military officer belongs to a profession that demands the highest standards of conduct and that confers great responsibility, to include decisions literally involving life or death. He is entrusted with the Nation's treasure. Surely he can be trusted to handle nuance.

My argument does not challenge civilian control of the military. Civilian leaders retain the authority to direct and fire military leaders who prove inept or disobedient. Nevertheless, the traditionalists appear to assume that allowing military professionals a degree of moral autonomy is a slippery slope culminating in loss of civilian control. To understand this argument, it is necessary to envision their concerns: a military pursuing its own agenda irrespective of civilian direction, and in doing so enacting a de facto coup whereby its leaders call the shots in matters ranging from acquisition programs to foreign policy. But given the highly professional nature of the U.S. military, is this fear realistic? A country's system of government usually evolves with experience. Chile and Argentina now have embedded in their constitutions tight controls on the military—a consequence of recent history in which military juntas seized power in both countries. But the history of the United States is quite different. Not since the Newburgh Conspiracy in 1783 has the military overstepped its bounds by trying to influence Congress, and even then the goal was financial reimbursement rather than political power.[17]

The traditionalists may fear that allowing military leaders moral autonomy will open the floodgates, enabling generals to threaten resignation simply because they do not agree with a particular policy. Human nature, as well as professionalism, provides a bulwark against such an eventuality. It is fair to assume that generals like being generals, and thus would select judiciously those causes for which they were prepared to sacrifice their careers. Greater likelihood and worse consequences attend the other end of the spectrum where senior leaders refuse to make a stand on policy issues—cloaking their reluctance behind a Huntingtonian view of civil-military relations.

The military professional plays a key role as a check and balance at the indistinct juncture between policy and military strategy. He should not try to exclude himself from this role, even on issues that appear to involve policy, any more than the statesman should exclude himself from overseeing the conduct of military operations. He has a moral obligation to dissent rooted in his oath of office and his code of professional ethics. The question remains, how should he do so in a morally defensible manner?

Dissent: What to Do?

If an officer decides that an order is rendered unconscionable by its probable consequences, it follows that he has a moral obligation to dispute the order and, if unsuccessful, to dissent in a manner that has the best chance of averting those consequences, or his dissent is rendered meaningless. Resignation is his ultimate option, but he may choose to take other steps prior to that (for instance, requesting an audience with the President or with the Senate Armed Service Committee). Following resignation, he may decide to "go public" by speaking to the media.

The circumstances surrounding these decisions are seldom clear-cut. The military professional has, as discussed, an obligation to his subordinates. He must consider how his public defiance could affect their morale. It may be that he would cause them to lose confidence at a critical time without changing the course of events. He must also consider what effect his resignation would have. Would it cause a stir sufficient to avert the feared consequences, or is it more likely that he would be replaced by someone who would carry out the order, perhaps in a manner likely to cause even greater harm?

This question raises a difficult issue. Should dissent be founded on the right action or the right effect? A third of the MCWAR officers surveyed argued that in the face of a moral dilemma, the military professional should focus on the effect desired: mitigation of the immoral order, rather than the conscience-salving but possibly ineffectual act of resignation. These officers advocated an indirect approach: addressing higher authority, leaking the story to trusted journalists or politicians, and dragging their feet in execution—"slow rolling" in military parlance. "What else can I do?" asked one officer rhetorically. "My only option is to conduct covert actions to reduce the risks of misfortune and of American casualties."[18] This approach is certainly not without precedent. As one Army colonel commented in response to the survey, "The most (commonly) used form of disobeying an order I've seen is slow-rolling."[19] This option does have some prima facie appeal, combining its own moral logic with a pragmatic focus on effects.

But a profession that values integrity and moral courage cannot at the same time justify a deceptive approach to dissent. By taking an open stand, the military professional displays the courage of his convictions but also implicitly accepts personal consequences, whether he is right or wrong. His stand may persuade the issuer of the order to reconsider or it may draw the attention of the legislature to the issue. On the other hand, it may be purely symbolic—and have no effect on the decision. Regardless, he has exercised his moral autonomy and taken the consequences. He may, after all, have been wrong in his predictions, and this point is key because the military professional, however well placed and intelligent, is *always* fallible. Allowing him moral autonomy to dissent benefits the process of policy execution overall; sanctioning the practice of "slow-rolling" orders deemed to be immoral ultimately sabotages this process. The truth of this statement becomes more apparent when, rather than looking to past examples of bad orders that were slow-rolled to good effect, one looks at a potential policy decision whose consequences could be highly controversial but are by no means predictable.

Suppose the current "Don't Ask, Don't Tell" policy with regard to homosexuals in the military is repealed and that the Service chiefs are ordered to integrate homosexuals in the same manner as were African Americans and women previously. Considering all that I have discussed with reference to the military professional's moral autonomy, could any Service chief—or subordinate unit commander—claim to be justified in dragging his feet in executing the policy? What if one did so, while the others executed the policy wholeheartedly, with consequences that proved that integration was the right thing to do? While open dissent is an act of professionalism, carrying with it an acceptance of personal responsibility, slow-rolling reflects hubris without moral courage. Its practice obfuscates rather than clarifies questions of policy and discredits the military profession.

Lastly, "silent" resignation is likely to accomplish little to divert the decision-maker from his course. Criticism of policy from the haven of retirement lacks the same moral force as public dissent backed by the publicly announced tender of resignation. Moreover, the senior officer must bear in mind that his subordinates do not have the option to resign to avoid, for instance, going to war. This burdens the military professional with the responsibility to use this privilege to accomplish more than the personal, perhaps selfish, goal of conscience appeasement.

The question of how to dissent is not an easy one. Nevertheless, the military professional must exercise his moral autonomy when confronted by a dilemma. He cannot morally justify his subsequent decision on the basis that he was simply obeying orders, that he put up token resistance prior to obeying, or that he dragged his feet in execution.

The topic of military dissent raises issues of fundamental importance to the profession of arms. When faced with a moral dilemma, the military officer not only has grounds for dissent, but also, if his code of ethics and oath of office so guide, has a duty to disobey. He is obligated to exercise moral autonomy, and in so doing must use his professional ethics to guide him down a path that is by no means clearly defined.

Just as civilian leaders have an obligation to challenge military leaders if the latter appear to be pursuing a strategy that undermines policy, military leaders are committed to challenge their civilian masters if the policy appears to be unconstitutional, immoral, or otherwise detrimental to the institution. Civilian control of the military does not obviate this obligation and should not be viewed simply as a unilateral and hierarchical relationship with clear boundaries. This is especially important now in this era of complex operations that blur the boundaries between military strategy and policy.

For the military officer, this underscores the importance of understanding the nature of his profession and its role in executing national policy—both of which appear to have changed markedly since Huntington wrote his famous book a half century ago. **JFQ**

NOTES

1. Samuel P. Huntington, *The Soldier and the State: The Theory and Politics of Civil-Military Relations* (Cambridge: Belknap Press, 1957).
2. Richard B. Myers and Richard H. Kohn, "Salute and Disobey?" *Foreign Affairs,* September–October 2007.
3. Damon Coletta, "Courage in the Service of Virtue: The Case of General Shinseki's Testimony before the Iraq War," *Armed Forces and Society,* October 2007.
4. Myers and Kohn.
5. The author conducted the MCWAR survey at the Marine Corps War College in early January 2010. The subjects were asked: 1) Under what circumstances (short of an illegal order) is a military professional justified in dissenting or disobeying an order; 2) What form should this dissent take?
6. Gregory Newbold, "Why Iraq Was a Mistake," *Time,* April 17, 2006.
7. United States Code, Title 10, Armed Forces (Sections 3583, 85831, 5947).
8. Elliott A. Cohen, *Supreme Command: Soldiers, Statesmen, and Leadership in Wartime* (New York: Anchor Press, 2003).
9. See U.S. Joint Forces Command (USJFCOM), *The Joint Operating Environment 2008: Challenges and Implications for the Future Joint Force* (Norfolk, VA: USJFCOM, 2008): "Above all, joint force commanders, their staffs, and their subordinates must have a clear understanding of the strategic and political goals for which they conduct military operations. In almost every case, they will find themselves working closely with partners, a factor which will demand not only a thorough understanding of U.S. political goals, but coalition goals as well."

10. Peter Feaver, *Armed Servants: Agency, Oversight, and Civil-Military Relations* (Cambridge, MA: Harvard University Press, 2003).

11. Supreme Court of the United States, *Hamdan v. Rumsfeld, Secretary of Defense et al.,* Certiorari to the United States Court of Appeals for the District of Columbia Circuit, No. 05–184. Argued March 28, 2006—decided June 29, 2006, available at <www.law.cornell.edu/supct/html/05-184.ZS.html>.

12. Supreme Court of the United States, *Boumediene et al. v. Bush, President of the United States et al.,* Certiorari to the United States Court of Appeals for the District of Columbia Circuit, No. 06–1195. Argued December 5, 2007—decided June 12, 2008, available at <www.law.cornell.edu/supct/html/06-1195.ZS.html>.

13. Paul Yingling, "How Congress Has Abdicated Its War Powers," *Armed Forces Journal,* February 2010.

14. Just War theory is embodied in the United Nations Charter and the Law of War. Its intent is also reflected by the wording of the National Security Strategy.

15. Michael Walzer, *Just and Unjust Wars* (New York: Basic Books, 1977).

16. "The President is authorized to use the Armed Forces of the United States as he determines to be necessary and appropriate in order to defend the national security of the United States against the continuing threat posed by Iraq." Public Law 107–243, "Authorization for Use of Military Force Against Iraq," Resolution of 2002, October 16, 2002.

17. The officers involved planned to march on Washington to lobby Congress to grant their request for back pay and pension.

18. A MCWAR student with the rank of colonel in response to the survey question, "What form should dissent take?"

19. Ibid.

Lesson

17

Peer Leadership

Paralleling attributes and strategies of ordinary leadership, Peer Leadership changes it's dynamic due to the limitations of how much influence one can effect on their peers while trying to lead them.

- **Reading:** Leading Friends

READING

Leading Friends

by Colonel Arthur J. Athens, USMCR (Retired)
Director, VADM Stockdale Center for Ethical Leadership
United States Naval Academy

So what does it take to lead friends, particularly in an Academy or ROTC setting? Should we love them, direct them, or ignore them? Every midshipman and cadet who has been placed in a leadership position and required to lead friends has struggled with this question. These young leaders wonder whether the basic tenets of leadership apply in this setting or whether there is a different set of personal attributes and strategies required for leading friends.

The theme of this essay is that leading friends in an Academy or ROTC setting requires personal character traits and strategies common to other more traditional leadership situations, but adapted and emphasized for the unique dynamics associated with friend leadership. I will address: (1) a definition of friend leadership, (2) the unique characteristics of friend leadership, (3) the personal attributes required for successful friend leadership, (4) the strategies required for successful friend leadership, and (5) the way ahead to study and address this issue.

A Definition of Friend Leadership

Friend leadership occurs when a peer, within a predominantly homogeneous group, is selected by someone outside the group to oversee, guide, and care for his group and accomplish objectives that are imposed externally, as well as developed internally. This homogeneous group is similar in age, experience, and expertise. Typically, the group has been together for an extended period of time and interacted as peers, without any senior-subordinate relationship. The peer who has been raised to a leadership position also has a number of close personal relationships with individuals within the group. Friend leadership is a distinct subset of peer leadership, differentiated by the group's homogeneity and intimate social ties. When a West Point cadet becomes a Platoon Commander, when an Air Force Academy cadet becomes the Wing Commander, when a Naval ROTC midshipman becomes a Battalion Commander, these individuals will, by definition, be leading friends.

The Unique Characteristics of Friend Leadership

Friend leadership has a unique set of characteristics that cause this type of leadership to be particularly demanding. Though some of these attributes can be found in more traditional leadership settings, they have a tendency to dominate in friend leadership. These characteristics are:

- The friend leader is trying to find the balance between leading and maintaining friendships.
- The friend leader typically has limited leadership experience at the level to which appointed. This results in a crisis of confidence.
- The leader is experiencing loyalty tensions—the tension among loyalty to the organization, loyalty to the group, loyalty to individuals, and loyalty to himself.
- The friend leader has limited authority to punish or reward his subordinates.
- Some members of the group feel jealousy towards the appointed friend leader.
- Some members of the group question the selection process that elevated the peer to a leadership position.
- Conflict resolution between the friend leader and group members is particularly challenging.

Because of these unique attributes, friend leaders need to develop and demonstrate certain personal attributes and implement specific strategies to become successful. These attributes and strategies are outlined in the following sections.

The Personal Attributes Required for Successful Friend Leadership

The attributes presented are not unique to friend leadership, but take on an added importance when leading friends.

Humility: A humble friend leader has a much greater chance of connecting with his group and achieving mission and interpersonal success. Humility tends to diffuse conflict, make the leader approachable, and portray a picture of a peer who is more interested in the group and organization than personal glory or achievement. The description of Level 5 leaders in Jim Collins' book, *Good to Great,* captures the essence of this attribute. Collins describes Level 5 leaders, the ones who successfully transformed their organizations from mediocrity to sustained success, as those characterized by "professional humility and professional will." Collins observes that these leaders "channel their ego needs away from themselves and into the larger goal of building a great company."

The friend leader needs to credit his group for successes and take responsibility for group failures. Assuming responsibility for failure goes a long way in gaining the respect and loyalty of the group. The friend leader also needs to communicate by words and actions that he is not enamored with the trappings associated with the leadership position—whether those trappings are visible rank or special perks.

Moral Courage: A friend leader must be a man or woman of integrity. A breach in this area, even with a seemingly minor compromise, will cause irreparable damage. This moral courage must translate into a willingness to always place others' needs before the leader's own comfort, prestige, or advancement. This moral courage needs to be consistent both downwards and upwards. For example, the friend leader must be equally faithful in confronting his superiors on behalf of the group, relaying an unpopular order or policy from his superior without criticism or complaint, or choosing a particularly close friend for an important job because that friend is best qualified. This takes moral courage and a willingness to "take the heat," either from those above or those below. Ultimately, the friend leader needs to be willing to risk temporary social rejection to retain an unblemished character.

Professionalism and Competency: The friend leader needs to set a professional example in appearance, speech, priorities, and actions. The leader must do this without becoming a "brown nose," "butt shark," or "joe." The motivation for professionalism should not be for show or to impress one's superiors, but instead for the good of the unit. Friends will quickly pick up duplicity or hypocrisy and reject a friend leader who has been "co-opted" by the establishment. Coupled with professionalism must be competency. The friend leader needs to demonstrate the ability to plan, decide, and act. If an important competency is lacking, the friend leader must take the initiative to address the deficiency.

Realistic Mindset: The friend leader must remain cognizant that he must lead by nurturing, supporting, listening, helping, and serving. The friend leader is in a position of authority, but must be ever aware of his roots and the temporary nature of his position. Warren Bennis' image of herding cats is apropos for friend leaders. Bennis, in *Managing People is Like Herding Cats,* writes:

> Cats, of course, won't allow themselves to be herded. They may, however, be coaxed, cajoled, persuaded, adored, and gently led . . . Be humble. Stop trying to "herd cats" and start building trust and mutual respect. Your "cats" will respond. They will sense your purpose, keep your business purring, and even kill your rats.

Friend leaders must be mindful that their role is to build trust, not herd cats.

The Strategies Required for Successful Friend Leadership

Friend leaders must not only demonstrate certain attributes, they must be armed with strategies that can facilitate their work. Like the attributes, these strategies are important in most leadership situations, but they are critical when leading friends.

Develop a compelling vision: People are hungry to become part of a movement larger than themselves. If the friend leader can develop a simple and compelling vision for the group, combined with a few achievable goals, he can gain buy-in from the group on the authority of the mission itself. The leader can continue to return to this vision to unify the group, generate excitement, and address deviations. Max DePree in *Leading Without Power* captures this thought when addressing leadership of volunteers:

> Leadership among volunteers is rather dependent in beautiful ways on shared values and commitment, on understood visions expressed in workable mission statements, and on moral purpose.

Similar comments could be made about the unity found in many athletic teams where the team's goal supplants the individual goals of the athletes.

The vision and goals should be developed with the full participation of the group, though the friend leader will ultimately need to narrow down the possibilities and articulate the direction.

Communicate: A friend leader must constantly communicate with his group. This communication must be less directive and more participative. The friend leader should spend time with people one-on-one and meet with sub-groups. For the friend leader, listening is much more important than talking. The group members want to know that the friend leader has a genuine interest in their lives, hears and understands their problems, and is willing to take action to address these problems. This will only occur through active listening.

Win over the group's informal leaders: There are always members of the group who do not hold an official position, but hold significant sway over others. The friend leader must be aware of these informal leaders, develop rapport with them and creatively win them to his side. The objective is to continue to develop a "critical mass of influence," where the peer pressure presses in a direction that supports the friend leader. Informal leaders are instrumental in achieving this critical mass.

Confront swiftly and with a consistent approach: When a member of the group is out-of-line, the friend leader cannot afford to look the other way. Ignoring a challenge to authority will undermine the leader and permit a rebellious cancer to spread. A method that works in the friend environment is the "4 step confrontation ladder." First, the friend leader approaches the offender one-on-one. The friend leader, in an informal setting, gently, but firmly explains the behavioral or attitudinal problem and asks the individual's support to correct the deficiency. Often, the offender will not realize the offense is a problem and correct it without any further mention. If the behavior or attitude continues, the friend leader should then enlist another member of the group who is well respected to go with him or her to confront the offender. The additional person helps the offender realize that this is not just a conflict between him and the friend leader; the offender now sees that others disapprove of his behavior or attitude. If this method does not work, the friend leader should return with his partner, sit down with the offender in a more formal setting and explain the specific consequences of a failure to conform. The last step is to use formal punishment. Often friend leaders are hesitant to use any type of formal punishment, even when it is warranted. The ladder, however, allows the friend leader to ratchet up the pressure on the group member in a logical and fair manner.

In addition to these four primary strategies, there are a number of other tactical actions that can assist the friend leader in his day-to-day leadership responsibilities:

- Recognize accomplishments in both public and private forums. Making the effort to arrange for a more senior individual to say words of congratulations to your group or present awards has a powerful effect.
- Say thank you to group members. A hand-written note, even to someone you see every day, makes a positive impression.
- Solve a friend's problem.
- Use the unique talents of your friends—give them responsibility and authority.

- Organize team building events like ultimate frisbee games, bowling tournaments, or golf outings.
- Celebrate birthdays and special events as a group.
- Attend events where a member of the group participates. Your presence says a lot and means a lot.

Coupling humility, moral courage, professional competence, and level-headedness with specific strategies and tactics, gives the friend leader a fighting chance to not only survive, but thrive in his position.

The Way Ahead

This essay is only an initial thought piece on friend leadership. The ideas presented are based on years of personal experience and observation. The next step is to develop a sound theoretical foundation derived from experimentation and field study. We should ask questions like:

- What is the relationship between successful friend leadership and personality type?
- What is the relationship between successful friend leadership and emotional intelligence?
- How do various management and leadership theories, such as power-influence, expectancy, and equity, apply to friend leadership?
- Are there other attributes and strategies that facilitate success in the friend leadership environment?
- How can a friend leader's superior best support the friend leader in the execution of his duties?
- How can a friend leader best support his friends in the execution of their duties?
- What is the relationship between successful friend leadership and successful leadership in other settings?
- Is there an optimal methodology to select and prepare friend leaders?

The study of friend leadership is a worthwhile endeavor. It is a dimension of leadership that requires more discussion and debate. Our midshipman and cadet leaders have the potential to influence their peers profoundly and increase the professional excellence of our Brigade, Corp, Wing, Regiments, Squadrons and Battalions; and by extrapolation, our operational units. These midshipman and cadet leaders need and deserve some principles and techniques to help them execute their responsibilities.

Additionally, friend leadership doesn't cease when we trade our academy and college brass for Ensign boards and 2nd Lieutenant bars. As a very junior Marine Corps 1st Lieutenant, my Battalion Commander selected me to command a Firing Battery where a friend of mine, with the same date of rank and career progression, became my Executive Officer. We were friends, but he felt strongly that he should have been the new Battery Commander Officer. The personal attributes that had been honed at the Naval Academy and the strategies I practiced while Brigade Commander provided the tools I needed to make the Battery a success and retain my XO's friendship.

Friend leadership doesn't start and stop with the military either—just ask the Rotary Club President, the Chairman of the Deacon Board, the coordinator for the American Heart Association event, or the captain of the high school football team. Friend leaders have a significant challenge, but also a significant opportunity. We can successfully lead our friends, but only if our attitude is right and our strategies are sound. With those two foundational elements in place, we will find our friends not only following, but following enthusiastically and energetically.

Note: For ease of reading and continuity, he, his, and him have been used throughout the article, but all concepts presented apply equally to men and women.

• • •

Lesson

18 *Leadership Case Study: Interdiction in Afghanistan*

This culminating class uses a fictional case study to identify, review, and analyze major concepts and themes from the semester.

READING

Interdiction in Afghanistan

Written by CAPT Bob Schoultz

The below case study is a fictionalized account based on an incident that actually happened. Some details have been modified, but the key portions of the incident happened as described.

I

It was 2000 hours, March 2002 in the Joint Special Operations Task Force (JSOTF) headquarters in Afghanistan, and LCDR Reynolds had just returned from the chow tent where he had lingered talking with some of the other officers on the JSOTF staff. LCDR Reynolds was a SEAL officer in charge of the SEALs assigned to JSOTF conducting Special Operations during Operation Enduring Freedom. Upon returning to the headquarters building to catch up on paper work and review intelligence reports, he was summoned by the JSOTF Operations Officer, LTC Thompson, who wanted to talk to him about a mission they had just received.

LTC Thompson handed LCDR Reynolds an intelligence report and a copy of an email that had just arrived from the Operations Officer of the Land Forces Component Commander (LFCC). The email directed the JSOTF Commander to provide a concept of operations for interdicting a vehicle convoy of Al Qaeda and Taliban terrorists that was expected to be moving down a road about 70 miles to the south the next morning sometime after 0730, apparently trying to escape Afghanistan into Pakistan. It was believed that the convoy might include some key Taliban or Al Qaeda leadership. The LFCC wanted the mission concept in two hours. This meant essentially that the staff wanted to know if the JSOTF thought they could undertake the mission, what support they would need, and whether their plan could be deconflicted with other ongoing missions. LTC Thompson had already contacted MAJ Mark Wyatt, the XO of the Army H47 Helicopter squadron who would be over momentarily to look at the mission with LCDR Reynolds and his men. The mission was to interdict the convoy, and to capture if possible, kill if necessary, any suspected members of Al Qaeda or Taliban who they might encounter.

II

LCDR Reynolds knew he had limited time to plan, rehearse, and go over contingencies with his team. Tight time-lines had become standard, but they were all fully aware of the increased risk they assumed when they had less time to prepare. A tight time line meant less time to consider and plan for the numerous 'what ifs,' to carefully check the intelligence, and make sure that everyone knew the plan and its various 'branches and sequels.' A recent tragedy could at least in part be attributed to a very abbreviated planning and rehearsal timeline. In a high risk, high stakes operation, a SEAL reconnaissance team had been ambushed on insertion by Al Qaeda forces who had been undetected during the pre-mission reconnaissance. The team had been surprised, and two of their friends and teammates had been killed as well as a number of Rangers, under the relentless fire of the enemy. The deaths of these teammates were fresh in the minds of his men, and had only steeled their resolve to do whatever it took to find and kill these terrorists. But the enemy was not to be underestimated—LCDR Reynolds and his men knew that their planning must be thorough, and in quick reaction, emergent missions, they always had to weigh the trade off between the opportunities presented by late breaking intelligence, and the increased risk of a short planning cycle.

The risks to rapid and short fused planning however had taken an ugly twist two days earlier, when LCDR Reynolds and his team had seen first hand the tragic, but unintended consequences that can come from fast paced operations and decisions made with incomplete or inadequate intelligence. Several days earlier overhead surveillance had seen armed men around a walled compound and corroborating intelligence had indicated that this compound would be used for a meeting of high level Taliban officials. A precision guided missile was launched and struck the main building of the compound during the window when the meeting was scheduled to take place. LCDR Reynolds and his men had been staged to go into the compound minutes after the missile struck to gather any intelligence that remained, capture and treat any wounded, and to determine whether any of the dead or wounded were key Taliban or Al Quada leaders. When they arrived, they found the dead on target had been non-combatants—farmers and their families who were living in the compound. The weapons that were found were personal fire arms that virtually all rural Afghanis possessed and carried for self protection. LCDR Reynolds and his men were shaken by the gruesome results of this miscalculation: elderly people, farmers, women, children, with no apparent connection to the enemy. After determining that there was no exploitable intelligence on the target, he and his men returned to base and reported to his superiors what had happened including his dismay at the mistake. He then refocused his efforts on being ready for his next mission. Part of preparing for the next mission involved dealing with the psychic effects of this one; he contacted the chaplain, told him what had happened, and asked him to talk to the men. Afterward, he knew that having the chaplain meet with them had made a difference, to some of the men more than others, but it felt like the right thing to have done after witnessing, and in a sense participating in the tragic consequences of a mistake in war.

III

After receiving the mission to interdict the convoy from LTC Thompson, LCDR Reynolds knew what to do and started going into his mission planning routine, which had become almost automatic. He was the mission commander, and MAJ Wyatt and the H47s would be under his tactical command. This was just like the seemingly hundreds of exercises he'd conducted, and similar to many of the missions he'd recently conducted during this war. The years of training were paying off. His team was gelling into the type of unit he and every other military officer wants to lead: they only needed to be pointed in the right direction, with a good mission concept and clear commander's intent, and then the plan and preparation just seemed to come together. If everything went as planned and as rehearsed, his role in the execution of the operation would be minimal—communicate with higher headquarters and keep the squad leaders informed about any new developments, and let the squad leaders execute the plan. But of course, nothing ever goes exactly as planned, and it would be his job to make immediate adjustments to whatever unforeseen circumstances they would find, and understand the ripple effect that changes to the plan inevitably caused. That was what he got paid for.

Intelligence indicated that ongoing allied operations were putting significant pressure on Al Qaeda and Taliban forces in Southeast Afghanistan. This increasing pressure was making local Al Qaeda and Taliban movement and operations more and more difficult. Allied forces had received an intelligence tip that some senior leaders, with a group of their armed supporters, would be attempting to escape into Pakistan by vehicle soon after first light the following day. The enemy had already realized that allied aircraft routinely and easily targeted vehicles moving at night; consequently, the terrorists were now seeking to blend in with the normal daylight traffic on the roads. It appeared that Taliban and Al Qaeda were having some success in escaping into Pakistan blending in with the stream of refugees coming out of Afghanistan.

The intelligence indicated that a convoy of three vehicles would be leaving a particular village the next morning and moving toward Pakistan. The vehicles would be SUV's of the Toyota Land Cruiser type and/or compact pick up trucks full of people traveling south on the one road leading to Pakistan. Intelligence sources indicated that normally, the terrorists put their heavily armed men in lead vehicles as an armed reconnaissance element, while the leadership with their personal armed guards would follow some distance behind, maintaining communications with the lead vehicles about any difficulties encountered. Also, and particularly worrisome, were the indicators that the terrorists were probably carrying "Man-portable Air Defense Systems" (MANPADS), specifically, Soviet-era SA-7 shoulder-fired missiles, which are particularly effective against helicopters, especially during daylight when helicopters can easily be seen.

In short order, his men had worked out a plan with MAJ Wyatt and his team. Also the intelligence planners had coordinated with the assigned overhead surveillance; Navy P-3 aircraft would be watching the road and it would be their mission to find and track the targeted vehicles. A very difficult part of the mission was to 'interdict' the convoy in such a way as to achieve complete surprise, while still offering the opportunity for the occupants of the vehicles to surrender without putting his own men at risk. "Capture if possible, kill if necessary" is always tricky, and frequently requires a split second decision, some clear indicator of hostile intent, but also an intuitive sense of threat. But capturing the occupants would be a great coup; he and his men knew that the key to unraveling the terrorist network in Afghanistan was intelligence, and the people in this convoy represented a potential gold mine of intelligence. The SEALs would capture them if they could, but if the terrorists resisted with lethal force, as they usually seemed to do, then the SEALs were to shoot to kill.

IV

LCDR Reynolds went to see COL Smith, the JSOTF commander to discuss his perspective or any limitations he might have for this mission. With the tragedy of the mission a couple of days previously still on his mind, LCDR Reynolds also wanted to know how certain they were of the intelligence, and whether the rules of engagement had changed. The rules of engagement define the circumstances under which lethal force can be used, and what are the restrictions in the use of that force. COL Smith replied that he understood the intelligence to be quite reliable and the rules of engagement hadn't changed. If the vehicles they encounter demonstrate hostile intent, by displaying or firing weapons, they are legitimate targets. COL Smith believed that the reason higher headquarters wanted the JSOTF to send helos and SEALs to do this mission, rather than targeting them from a distance, was because of the desire not to repeat the mistake of two days ago, with which LCDR Reynolds was only too familiar. That said, he reminded LCDR Reynolds that his tactics had to take into account the desire to bring back prisoners if at all possible, while not taking undue risk. In other words, bring back prisoners if you can, but not if it means taking significant risks with the lives of any of your men. COL Smith reiterated to LCDR Reynolds that the rules of engagement gave him all the guidance he needed.

That was what LCDR Reynolds wanted to hear. He felt the rules of engagement as they stood made sense, and gave him and his team the latitude to exercise their professional judgment to complete the mission and stay alive. Rapid assessment of hostile intent in a fast moving tactical environment is a standing requirement, and they had rehearsed and talked through a wide variety of situations many times. He and his men knew the value of prisoners, but they also knew the value of aggressiveness and firepower to staying alive in a gunfight. Their tactics, their survival, and their mission success depended on "Surprise, Speed, and Violence of Action"—there was no room for timidity. Yet they had recently witnessed the tragic results of "Surprise, Speed and Violence of Action" exercised without good judgment—in other words, aggressiveness and firepower misapplied.

V

The plan came together quickly—it had to. MAJ Wyatt would be the lead helo pilot for this mission; LCDR Reynolds would be in his helo. There would be a total of three helos, referred to as Chalk One (with MAJ Wyatt and LCDR Reynolds), and Chalks Two and Three which would carry the rest of the SEALs, led by LCDR Reynolds' Assistant Officer in Charge and Platoon Chief respectively. They talked through the contingencies with the pilots and went over the map, and had the intel guys coordinate with the P3's doing the overhead surveillance.

The plan was submitted and quickly approved. The plan was simple and made sense, and at any rate, there was little time to debate it. Their plan had them taking off at 0645 the next morning and flying to a point near the road where they would loiter at a low altitude, visually and audibly sheltered from the road by the mountains, and wait for a cue from the P3 watching the road. When the P3 saw what appeared to be the convoy, it would notify the helos, and vector them to the vehicles on the road. The helos would then move in under the cover of the mountains and surprise the convoy, quickly determine whether to take the vehicles under fire, or if in doubt, land and put the SEALs on the ground, and let the SEALs make the final determination. The helos would be available to provide cover fire or extraction, as required.

Everyone was very aware of the threat of shoulder fired SA-7's, to which the helos were very vulnerable. An SA-7 missile, in the hands of a reasonably proficient operator, could spell disaster. In daylight however, helos are also easy prey and vulnerable to small arms fire, and bullets from an AK47 can puncture the skin of their aircraft killing and wounding pilots and passengers. A couple of lucky shots from an AK47 can also bring down a helo and kill everyone on board. As the events in Mogadishu and "Black Hawk Down" had made clear, being in a low-flying helo, near the enemy in daylight is very risky business.

VI

Early the next morning, all went as planned. LCDR Reynolds even got a couple of hours of sleep prior to his meeting at 0530 with his squad leaders and the helo pilots, to go over the plan and review details, one final time prior to launch. The SEALs embarked the three H47's, and after all systems checked out and the pilots had established communications with the P3, they took off and headed for the designated loiter point. After about 40 minutes of flight time, they arrived at the loiter point, again checked in with the P3 and began flying in low slow circles, far enough away from the road so as not to be heard, yet close enough to respond quickly when called by the P3.

LCDR Reynolds had been through this drill many times before. Sitting in the helo, with the headset on, partially listening to the relaxed banter of the pilots, he was lost in his own thoughts with the muffled hum and shake of the helo in the background of his awareness. Waiting for the call he mentally walked through the plan for the operation and its various contingencies; how they would make their approach to the convoy, how quickly they would have to determine threat level and response. How far back would the trail vehicle be with the so-called leaders? Would they stumble upon one of the key leaders of the Taliban or Al Qaeda? Did they really have SA-7's?

He pushed from his mind what would happen if the bad guys could get off a shot at the helos with an SA-7 before they could be neutralized. Worrying about it wouldn't do anything. He knew the pilots were very concerned as well; they had discussed it during the planning. But LCDR Reynolds also knew they had a lot going for them on this op—the confidence and skill that comes from extensive training and lots of experience. Surprise, Speed, Violence of Action—their keys to survival, the keys to success.

Approximately 20 minutes after arriving at the loitering point, LCDR Reynolds heard on the head set that the P3 had spotted what appeared to be the target convoy: two pickup trucks traveling together, followed about a mile back by another pick up truck. It would be about 20 minutes before the vehicles reached that section of the road where LCDR Reynolds and the helo pilots had determined that the terrain gave them the greatest advantage for surprise, and the bad guys the least opportunities for escape, on vehicle or on foot. After discussing it briefly with MAJ Wyatt, LCDR Reynolds advised the SEAL Leading Petty Officer (LPO) in his helo what he had just heard, and the LPO alerted the rest of the SEALs. The SEALs then seemed to come alive. Up to that point, they had been sitting in the back with their eyes closed, some probably dozing lightly, some probably rehearsing the mission in their heads, some probably thinking of things completely unrelated to this operation. But now all the men were alert and focused, checking their gear one more time, adjusting their position to be better prepared to exit the helo in a hurry.

MAJ Wyatt continued to get information from the P3. The convoy was continuing down the road toward the interdiction point. After about 10 minutes, the P3 crew advised MAJ Wyatt that it was time to leave the loiter position and begin moving toward the road. LCDR Reynolds advised his LPO and the LPO passed it on to the men in the helo.

As the helos approached the interdiction point, they stayed very low to the ground, flying at about 50 feet, to minimize the chances that the 'wop, wop, wop' of their approach would get over the mountains and alert the convoy. At about 2 minutes out, the P3 passed on some disturbing news. "We've lost the trail vehicle. We haven't seen it for several minutes—last we saw it was about 3 miles back. It might be masked by the mountains between us and them. But two vehicles are on final into your target zone and will be there in a couple of minutes."

"Damn!" LCDR Reynolds thought. Quick decision time. The plan had been for him and MAJ Wyatt to break off from Chalks Two and Three in the last twenty seconds, and to go to the trail vehicle, to permit a simultaneous hit on the lead and trail vehicles. He was going to the trail vehicle, because that was where the real valuable targets would be—the leaders. LCDR Reynolds quickly considered the possibility of his helo flying thru the mountains searching for the trail vehicle while Chalks Two and Three were taking care of the lead vehicles. There was no telling where that vehicle could be or what it could be doing. Even though the primary target was the leadership in the trail vehicle, with this new uncertainty, LCDR Reynolds did not want to take off on a potential wild goose chase, splitting his force, now that the plan may be coming unraveled at the last minute.

He told MAJ Wyatt he wanted to keep all three helos together until they had a better idea what they were up against, or at least until the P3 found the third vehicle. MAJ Wyatt concurred and told the Chalks two and three that the plan had changed and they would stay together and all hit the lead vehicles. They then started their climb up and over the final hill that lay between them and the road, and presumably the two lead vehicles. LCDR Reynolds ensured that the word was passed to the SEALs in Chalks Two and Three. Everyone in the helos was on full alert, the pilots and crew calmly passing information back and forth, the SEALs on their feet, looking out the windows, weapons at the ready, on safe.

VII

As they popped over the summit of the hill, they saw at five hundred feet below them and to the left, two pick up trucks approaching from the north. LCDR Reynolds suddenly experienced that familiar jolt of adrenaline, a combination of stress, excitement, responsibility and complete focus. The helos came over the crest of the hill and headed down low and fast, directly toward the vehicles, approaching at full speed, circling from left to right, counter-clockwise. LCDR Reynolds stared intently at the occupants in the back of the pick up truck, looking for any sign of hostile intent. First the front vehicle, and then the rear vehicle stopped when they saw and heard the helos, and he saw men get out and begin running. Then LCDR Reynolds thought he saw weapons and muzzle flashes. LCDR Reynolds was looking over the shoulder of the left door gunner, who also saw the weapons and muzzle flashes, and immediately opened up on the lead vehicle with his mini gun, shifting to the second vehicle as soon as he could get a good shot at it. At about that time, the second helo picked up the lead vehicle and started cutting it to pieces. LCDR Reynolds saw more muzzle flashes and then saw men fall. No sign of anyone setting up to fire an SA-7. The helos passed the vehicles flying fast and low and putting out a huge volume of fire. The two pick up trucks were being cut to pieces, and men who had not been able to get out of the vehicles in time were being chewed up as well. Those who had left the trucks were scrambling in chaos and disorder, some firing at the helos, several of them falling victim to the withering fire coming from the door gunners. LCDR Reynolds saw that this part was going well. Now, where was the trail vehicle with the leadership?

As his helo was turning to circle the vehicles and make an approach from the other side, LCDR Reynolds felt that Chalks Two and Three could handle this. He said to MAJ Wyatt on the headset, "Mark, I think they've got this under control. Let's go find the trail vehicle. What do you think?" "Roger," he responded. "I'll advise Chalk Two to take control here." (At which point he pulled up out of the pattern and told the pilot of Chalk Two that he and LCDR Reynolds were detaching to go look for the other vehicle.) The P3 had just called to tell them that they still had no sign of the third vehicle. MAJ Wyatt told the P3 what he was doing, and then he turned and headed up the road down which they had seen the two vehicles coming.

VIII

LCDR Reynolds called his LPO up to him, took off his head set, and yelled over noise of the helo to tell him what they were doing. The LPO nodded and then went to the back of the helo to tell the other SEALs who, still very tense and focused, were looking toward him with some anticipation. They knew that something was up. LCDR Reynolds then moved to the door gunner on the right side of the aircraft, since the helo was flying with the road on the right side. The longer it took to find the vehicle, the greater the risk. They had to assume that the trail vehicle had heard the helos and the gunfire, and perhaps even had radio communication from the lead vehicles. That gave the bad guys plenty of time to set up on the helo—they would certainly be expecting them. These were the leaders, and they would have the most devoted soldiers with them as bodyguards, and probably the best weapons, possibly to include SA-7's. Helos are big, easy targets in daylight, especially if you know that they are coming. The right door gunner had not expended any ammunition on the assault on the other two vehicles—he was keyed up, ready, and had a full load of ammo.

As the H47 flew down the narrow valley that hugged the road, there was an intense and anxious silence on the headsets. The pilots, crew and LCDR Reynolds knew that this was where they were most vulnerable. Though they may not achieve complete surprise, they hoped to overwhelm the bad guys by hitting them suddenly and with overwhelming firepower. But they had to be lucky and good.

As the H47 turned a corner in the valley, they looked up a narrow canyon. LCDR Reynolds saw the pick up truck just as he heard MAJ Wyatt calmly say, "There they are." What looked like a truck full of people was stopped on the side of the road about 200 yards ahead to the right. The door gunner had a clear shot, and he quickly swung his mini-gun and took aim.

IX

LCDR Reynolds suddenly sensed something wasn't right. Just as the truck came into view, just as the door gunner swung his weapon in the direction of the truck, just as MAJ Wyatt said, "There they are," LCDR Reynolds in an instant realized that no one was running from the vehicle, and he thought he saw someone in the truck (a woman?) hold something up high as if to display it to the helo. He grabbed the door gunner and yelled "NO!" and held his fist in front of the door gunner's face in the signal for "Stop what you're doing!" The door gunner was confused, but he followed the order and didn't shoot. The helo continued toward the truck, low and fast as LCDR Reynolds looked hard at the truck, looking for signs of hostile intent. In the two long seconds it took to get to and pass the truck, they noticed that this was different from the other vehicles. No one left the truck. No one ran for cover. It was hard to tell whether these people were armed or not, given the speed and approach angle of the helo. The helo sped past the truck so close that the people in the bed of the truck were ducking from the rotor wash, and LCDR Reynolds saw that he had been right—it had been a woman he'd seen, and what she was holding up appeared to be a baby. He didn't see any weapons yet or anyone displaying hostile intent. That didn't mean they weren't bad guys, and that they weren't a threat. LCDR Reynolds told MAJ Wyatt to circle around and land in front of the vehicle, far enough away to be safe, but close enough for the SEALs to quickly envelope the vehicles, clarify the situation, and take appropriate action.

After speeding by the vehicle, MAJ Wyatt exhaled. When he didn't hear the door gunner firing, he thought the weapon had jammed and that they were 'done for'. He flew the H47 at full throttle farther down the road, banked around a bend in the road, and then ascended to fly over a hill to come back to a position several hundred yards in front of the vehicle. He was ever mindful of the possibility that an SA-7 was being prepared for the first clear shot. LCDR Reynolds dashed back to his LPO and told him that the SEALs would debark and move in to observe the vehicle—it wasn't clear if these were hostiles. He then moved back to the front of the helo so that he could get oriented prior to landing.

The helo flared and landed fast. The SEALs quickly debarked out the rear ramp and moved to outside the rotor-wash to set up a hasty perimeter in the nearest cover. The H47 lifted off the ground, turned 180 degrees away from the direction of the vehicle, and took off. The SEALs patrolled to the vicinity of the pick up truck and observed the passengers not moving, sensing their danger. The LCDR Reynolds was able to signal to the passengers to move away from the pick up truck. He then had his team search the pickup truck and its passengers, and determined that they were neither Taliban nor Al Qaeda leadership, nor was there any evidence that they had any connection to them. Either the intel had been wrong about the three-vehicle convoy, or the situation had changed since the source had reported it. It didn't matter. These people did not fit the profile of Taliban or Al Qaeda and happened to be in the wrong place at the wrong time.

LCDR Reynolds realized that he had narrowly avoided making a tragic mistake. He was still worried about a possible trail vehicle, and called MAJ Wyatt to ask him if he had any other information. MAJ Wyatt had been in touch with the P3, and had gone to altitude himself to see if he could see any other vehicles, and there was nothing. LCDR Reynolds then got on the radio with the SEALs who were on the ground at the site of the two lead vehicles. They had already debarked from the helos, taken control of the site with no resistance, and they were inspecting the dead and wounded. All were males and had been carrying arms. Eight were dead, the three wounded were being treated, and they had taken two unscathed prisoners, who had survived the initial assault, and had stood with their hands raised when the SEALs approached. This was all good news.

LCDR Reynolds then had his LPO direct the civilians to sit down and to remain where they were. They were still sitting on the ground away from their pick up truck when the SEALs were picked up by the helo and flown to join their teammates at the site of the two lead vehicles.

X

COL Smith, the JSOTF Commander had heard that his helo pilots believed that LCDR Reynolds had taken undue risk during an operation from which they had just returned, and that this was causing some tension between the SEALs and Army helo crews. COL Smith had heard what had happened and was familiar with the events of the operation, but knew he needed to get the story directly from his two commanders. He called MAJ Wyatt and LCDR Reynolds into his office to get the issues out on the table.

LCDR Reynolds and MAJ Wyatt walked into his office, and after COL Smith indicated that he understood that there was some disagreement about how the operation had been conducted, MAJ Wyatt, clearly emotional, addressed the issue right up front:

"Sir, we could have all been killed, and lost the bird. We were a sitting duck. We're real lucky Tom was right, because if he'd been wrong, we would have a lot of dead Americans and this war would look a lot different right now." MAJ Wyatt stepped back and exhaled slowly.

COL Smith looked at LCDR Reynolds and indicated it was his turn to speak.

"Sir, he's right—we could have all been killed—if I'd been wrong. But I wasn't. I was in charge. And I was right. I made the call based on what I saw, and what I sensed, and I stand by it. It was clearly the right thing to do. We knew we were at risk, but we still have to do the right thing."

MAJ Wyatt jumped on him. "Right Tom, but all the indicators were there that these were bad guys, and you didn't KNOW, and my guys and yours were sitting ducks for several seconds, and that put not only all of us, but potentially the whole focus of everything we're doing here at risk. Can you imagine what this task force would be doing right now if those had been bad guys we had taken an SA-7 right down the throat? I don't want to kill innocent people either, but if you had been wrong, nobody, I mean NOBODY, would forgive you. And we'd all be dead."

"Mark—it just didn't feel right—and, we saw no hostile intent."

"We didn't have time to see hostile intent, Tom! When we took off after that third vehicle, my understanding was that we were going hunting. We knew we had flushed the bad guys, and at that point, we were in a gunfight. When we came around that bend in the road, it was either them, or us. When you stopped my gunner, and I didn't hear the guns, I figured it was us. I expected a flash and woosh and then lights out."

"You two calm down and come back and see me when you get your stuff squared away," interrupted COL Smith. He knew that he was the one who had to take responsibility for risk, and if there was something unclear about risk, he needed to resolve it. "I'm going to have to think about this, and talk to the lawyers. Now get out of here and get some rest. We've got a bunch of other things hopping and we'll need you to be focused."

MAJ Wyatt and LCDR Reynolds left the Colonel's office and agreed to get together in a couple of hours after they had taken care of their men and their gear, and sorted out the other details from their mission. MAJ Wyatt was clearly still upset as he walked away to rejoin the other pilots preparing their reports.

As LCDR Tom Reynolds walked back to where his men were working, he thought about what his friend MAJ Mark Wyatt had said. He had gambled and won, but he had bet the whole farm—not just his farm, but the lives of everyone else in the helo, as well as the future capability of the Special Operations Task Force.